Seagram's

The Spirit of Hospitality

YOUR GUIDE TO SUCCESSFUL ENTERTAINING

Published by Joseph E. Seagram & Sons, Limited
P.O. Box 202, T-D Centre, Toronto, Ontario, Canada M5K 1J3

Seagram's

The Spirit of Hospitality

Joseph E. Seagram & Sons, Limited, Toronto, Canada

Material in this book is prepared from current information available.

PRINTED IN CANADA

FOREWORD

There is probably no greater satisfaction than sitting back after the last guest has left and savouring the knowledge that you have just given a party that has been a happy success. It's what makes the "spirit of hospitality" so rewarding.

And the nice thing about entertaining is that it is a skill which is easily mastered. With a little forethought and some knowledge of the techniques involved, anyone can host the kind of parties everyone enjoys.

That is exactly what this book is all about. It is a practical guide to successful entertaining that covers many aspects of good hostmanship, from the simplest of spur-of-the moment get-togethers, to the formal functions that require the ultimate in etiquette and protocol. And of course, what book of this nature published by Seagram's would be complete without tips on how to become the best mixer in town? We've called this section "So You Want To Be a Bartender!"

So, if improving your techniques as a host or hostess is your aim, we think you'll find "The Spirit of Hospitality" invaluable, and it will no doubt be well-used in the months to come.

Another Entertaining Aid From Seagram's

Perhaps there are some entertaining questions you might have that are not completely answered in this book. For, we've only been able to discuss many topics, that perhaps vary from region to region, on a general basis. This is where Seagram's Reception Service can fill the gap.

Here are some of the areas where we can be of assistance to you.

* Where to get a good, reputable bartender, maid, portable bar, glasses, etc. — in you neighbourhood, and how much each costs.
* Whether or not you can order spirits in quantity and have them delivered. And whether unused, unopened bottles can be returned.
* Specific quantities of spirits required for a given number of people. What wines to serve with meals.
* Provincial and Municipal regulations concerning the sale or use of spirits in public places, permits required, where to obtain them, cost of permits, etc.

If you live in or near Halifax, Quebec City, Trois-Rivières, St. Jean, Montreal, Ottawa, Toronto, Winnipeg, Calgary, Vancouver, or Victoria. This service is as close as your telephone. If it is inconvenient for you to phone Seagram's at one of these locations, your written questions will be answered promptly.

Address correspondence to:

"Seagram's Reception Service"
P.O. Box 202,
T-D Centre,
Toronto, Ontario
M5K 1J3

Happy Hosting!

INTEGRITY - CRAFTSMANSHIP - TRADITION

Seagram was a well-known and respected name in Canada even before Confederation. The original distillery was established in a small grist mill in Waterloo, Ontario, in 1857, and operated by Joseph E. Seagram. Seventy-one years later, Joseph E. Seagram & Sons. Limited formed, with Distillers Corporation Ltd. of Montreal, a Canadian parent company, Distillers Corporation — Seagrams Limited, later to be called The Seagram Company Ltd. Today, its shareholders, who number 20,000, are to be found in every province and territory in Canada.

But while the company has grown from small beginnings in Waterloo to internationalism, and is recognized as the world's largest distilling organization, it is not nearly so concerned with its size as it is with maintaining the high quality of its products. After all, it is only Seagram's dedication to quality that has made its growth possible, and today, with all its vast experience, Seagram knows a great deal about how to maintain quality and ensure that it is there in every bottle.

In Canada, where the popularity and sale of Seagram products far exceeds those of any other distilling company, Seagram operates six plants — Richibucto, N.B.; Beaupré and LaSalle, Que.; Waterloo and Amherstburg, Ont.; and Gimli, Man. From these plants, Seagram not only supplies its loyal Canadian customers, but also exports to some 200 countries such distinguished products as Seagram's Crown Royal — the world's largest selling deluxe whisky — and its premium product, Seagram's V.O. — the world's largest selling Canadian whisky.

Seagram's company people, shareholders and many other Canadians take great and justifiable pride in the fact that throughout the world more V.O. is sold than any other brand of whisky exported from any other country, including Scotland and the U.S. Most Canadians might be surprised to learn that among the many products of every type fully manufactured in Canada, Canadian whisky, as an export product, ranks fourth in importance. This, when coupled with the fact that production of Canadian whisky does not diminish any of Canada's natural resources, points up the tremendous importance and value to Canada of this unique Canadian product.

Another statistic worth noting is that 93% of Seagram's business is done outside Canada, and this is not due entirely to exporting. Seagram has developed businesses in foreign countries, producing other types of distilled products and wines. In addition to selling these locally, it ships them to almost every civilized country on earth.

Seagram's products are among the most popular in the world, attributable to the dedication to quality that is an integral part of the Seagram tradition. Perhaps the most accurate way to describe them is to cite the company motto, because the quality in each brand produced by Seagram is a reflection of these three words — "Integrity, Carftsmanship, Tradition".

CONTENTS

PART I

"LET'S HAVE A PARTY!"

To most of us, this sounds like a great idea. It's fun to entertain good friends in your own home — to create an attractive, relaxed atmosphere and provide something extra-special in the way of food, drink and entertainment.

If you are a person who likes going to parties, whether they be gala affairs or casual get-togethers, but never seem to get around to hosting yourself, then this section of the book is for you. Home entertaining is such an enjoyable way of being with friends that you shouldn't miss out on the pleasures of hosting.

Of course, if you're an old hand at entertaining, you already know how much fun it can be, and we think you'll enjoy this section as well. It's full of helpful hints on the fine points of hospitality that perhaps you would like to read over to enhance your reputation as the perfect host.

If your hosting is confined to "non-organized" parties — having the gang over for drinks, or entertaining unexpected relatives or friends — that type of thing, you'll find lots of ideas that come in handy for these last-minute affairs as well.

But even the most casual party involves some planning, or at least forethought, so that you are prepared for the unexpected. The following pages are devoted to **all** of the details involved in planning even the most elaborate affair. But you will realize as you read through them that the basic rules of preparation, etiquette and planning are always the same, regardless of the number of people you invite or the type of party you are hosting.

Before You Take The Plunge...

Think About Space

Take a good look at the size of your home and decide just how many people you can entertain comfortably. How many people could you seat if you could get your hands on some more chairs? How many people could you accommodate if they were standing around talking, with drinks in their hands, leaving enough space to manoeuvre?

If yours is a bachelor apartment or studio pad, you could probably invite as many as 25 congenial people for an informal "drinks-in-the-hand" get-together, where they could mill about and perch on furniture or sit on the floor to eat.

With that amount of space, however, you probably won't have enough kitchen or dining area to stage a sit-down dinner for more than two (three at the most) couples.

But keep cool. Once you know what you're doing, it's just as easy to give two parties as it is to give one. And if you plan properly, it won't cost any more.

At the other end of the scale, if you have a large house with a family room or basement for the occasion, you could invite the entire neighbourhood for an informal affair.

Think About The Cost

Available space is only one primary consideration. There's also the question of money.

Even though you might be planning a relatively small party, it's still going to cost a penny or two. Which is another good reason for planning ahead. Apart from food and liquor, there are some other party incidentals which, though not individually costly in themselves, can mount up and will need to be taken into account when you're budgeting.

Invitations and postage, for instance. Perhaps flowers, special decorations (if your party has a theme), party napkins and coasters — maybe some extra glasses, spare light bulbs, guest soaps, etc. We'll go into these details later.

If this is your first party (and even if you're a seasoned party-giver) it's a good idea to keep careful track of how much it costs you. Then, next time you get the entertaining urge — and it could easily become a habit! — you can budget even better.

Think About The Reasons Behind Giving The Party

This is another factor that will govern the size of your party — after available space and money considerations.

Probably the most common reason is the simple fact that it's your turn to repay other people's hospitality. Or perhaps there's a special occasion coming up.

Stop to think about it. There's a reason behind every party that's ever been staged.

As an extreme example: Perle Mesta, the original Hostess with the Mostes', made a complete and spectacular career out of her talent for party-giving. Novelist Truman Capote is almost as famous for his parties as he is for his books. That's a little out of our league. But don't forget that many people who are good at entertaining often use their talent for other reasons. To raise funds or promote causes, to help themselves in business, just to name a few. Of course, a great many parties are given to celebrate festivals — Christmas, Thanksgiving, New Year, etc. — or a special occasion, whether it's personal (an engagement, anniversary, Bar Mitzvah, birthday) or national (Grey Cup, Canada Day, Election Night).

But, when you come right down to it, the biggest reason for party-giving is simply — people. The sheer pleasure of gathering friends around you, of getting to know the new ones better and spending more time with those you like best. On the other side of the coin, there is always the very real pleasure of giving others an enjoyable time.

So you've got the reason and now you've decided to give a party. You know the maximum number of people you can invite without having the walls bulge, if it's an indoor party — or before the neighbours complain, if it's to be outdoors. And you've got a rough idea of how much money you can spend.

Now, let's get the show on the road.

1 "WHAT KIND OF PARTY?"

The choice is almost limitless, as you'll see on pages 58 to 78.

Choosing the type of party you'll have is almost a chicken-and-egg situation. It depends on who you're going to invite. Which, in turn, depends on your reason for the party in the first place. And you're the only one who knows that reason.

So we'll go back to our original assumption that you're a beginner in the party-giving business. In which case, your reason could very well be one of simple social obligation.

Suppose that, upon browsing through your diary, you find you owe hospitality to 20 people. You now have a choice.

Should you host a series of small, easily manageable gatherings? Perhaps elegant little dinner parties, evenings of bridge or informal patio brunches — if the weather is reliable and you have the facilities?

Or would it be better to dive right off the deep end and host one large party?

Let's take a look at these two alternatives.

In Praise of Small Parties

There's a lot to be said in favour of entertaining in small groups.

On the face of it, you might think there is much more work involved in giving, say, four parties instead of one. But there really isn't. Especially if you enjoy cooking, or can afford to spend some of your party budget hiring professional help.

Dinner for six or eight people is an intimate affair — pleasant, relaxed, friendly. But choose your guests with care. Make sure you don't invite people who dislike each other, or who have little in common.

Small parties allow you to pay much more attention to your guests. You can get to know each better. It's a chance, too, for good conversation, something that is difficult in the hurly-burly of a large gathering.

As for the work involved, pre-party preparations are quite simple. There is no necessity to rack your brains and scour the stores looking for way-out party decorations. An attractive table-setting and perhaps flowers in the living room are all you need.

It's easier, too, to provide coat-and-boot space (if it's a winter party) for six people, rather than twenty.

The key to your small party, of course, is the menu. You've probably got a special main dish up your sleeve — something you can cook with confidence and serve with pride. This is the time to produce it with a flourish.

This is *not* the time to try your hand at the Pain de Boeuf Tourangelle that looked so great in the weekend paper. For one thing, it might not turn out. For another, and more important, you'll waste too much nervous energy over it.

Having planned a good menu for your first party, could you repeat it for the other three? Why not, if it makes you happier? It will cut down the work, especially if you include one course — say, a frozen dessert — that can be prepared well ahead of time and kept in the freezer.

Don't worry about all 20 guests getting together later and comparing notes about the food you served. They're not likely to. And even if they do, it doesn't matter. The best restaurant in town has a specialty, so why shouldn't you?

If, as they say, "practice makes perfect," it's not a bad idea to start your party-giving career by entertaining small groups. By the time you have discharged all your outstanding social obligations, you should be an accomplished host. What's more, if you look back over your parties, you will realize that everybody — including yourself — had a fine time.

And that's what entertaining is all about.

In Praise of Big Parties

There's a lot to be said in favour of these, too. Even for the novice.

If the key to a small party is the menu, the key to a large one is atmosphere. Which is why so many non-seasonal parties have some sort of theme.

For you, having a theme is simply an aid to atmosphere-creating. For your guests, it's a chance to enter more fully into the spirit of the occasion and to prepare themselves for an evening's fun before the party starts.

If you're invited to an unadorned cocktail party, you know more or less what to expect. You turn up, in your best clothes, all set to stand around for two or three hours with a glass in your hand, making small talk with people you hope will turn out to be old friends or congenial strangers.

But, if you receive an invitation to a Luau, doesn't it immediately conjure up pleasant visions in your mind? Even though you know perfectly well it's only a reasonable facsimile being held in a basement playroom.

Chances are, you'll be offered something really exotic in the way of rum-and-fruit punches. There'll be Hawaiian music on the stereo and maybe you've been asked to wear a grass skirt or similar tropical attire. It sounds like a lot more fun than your average run-of-the-mill cocktail party, and you start off all ready to enjoy yourself.

Which is a great help to the host.

With a large party, of course, you don't have to consider seating guests at tables to feed them. An indoor buffet or outdoor barbecue is the answer. Naturally, the food and drink you offer should be the best you can manage on your budget and in keeping with the theme. But that doesn't mean it has to be extravagant.

For some parties, only the simplest menu is required. For a Barn Dance, you wouldn't even consider pretty jellied salads and miniscule hors d'oeuvres, for example. Pork and beans, fried chicken, a tossed green salad and mugs (not dainty cups) of steaming coffee are much more to the point.

Atmosphere for a large "theme" party depends to a large extent on how you decorate your party room. If your guests arrive, expecting to spend an evening in Hawaii or at a Spanish Fiesta, the spell would be broken by an unadorned room, or by the Rolling Stones on hi-fi, instead of the Hawaiian War Chant or Flamenco guitar music.

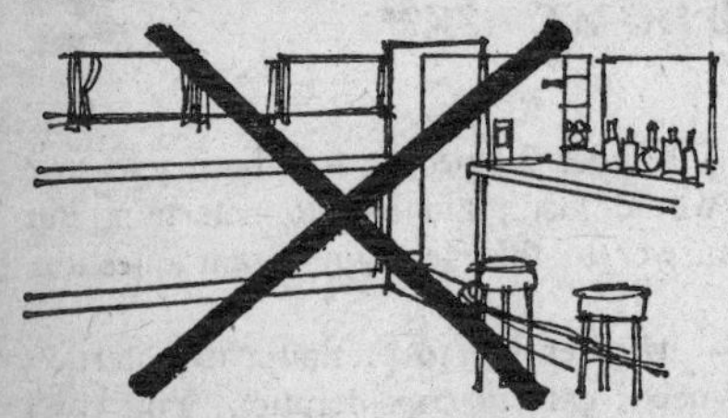

You'll have to put more thought and imagination and a bit more work into a large party. And it will be more difficult for you, the host, to settle down to a lengthy chat with any one person.

Once the party gets under way, your job is to keep it moving; to stop it from disintegrating. (Remember the last party you went to, where the men drifted off into one corner or the kitchen and talked about cars, while the women sat huddled in another and discussed children and diapers? Pretty dull, wasn't it?)

Later on, we'll mention several proven anti-disintegration techniques, as well as some foolproof ways to help make your party — even your very first party — go the way you want it to.

At this point however, you've still got those 20 people you are going to entertain; either in four small groups or one large bunch. Let's have another, more careful look at them.

2 "WHO DO WE ASK?"

In your case, of course, it's those 20 people to whom you owe hospitality, or whom you would just plain like to entertain. But they're not the complete answer to this very important question. Not by a long shot.

Any kind of guest list — whether you're planning to entertain a crowd or two couples — needs careful consideration. You can't just gather together a group of people with divergent interests and expect them to have a good time. They probably won't — no matter how hard you work to make it a success.

You can reproduce a Hawaiian island in glorious living colour, work yourself to a frazzle getting people to circulate as you dash around with hors d'oeuvres, but if too many of your guests have too little in common, your party may well go over like the proverbial lead balloon.

Look At The People You Know

They're a mixed bunch, aren't they? Everything from relatives and old school friends, to that nice-looking couple who live at No. 485 and keep making vague "We must get together" noises. Then there are your neighbours, your friends from work, from the church, the sports club and the "Home and School" — people you see now and then at community functions and at other people's parties.

Right there, you probably have a few dozen people whose only obvious common denominator is the fact that they know you.

This, in itself, is no guarantee they're going to get along together and enjoy each other's company. Think carefully about each prospective guest and how he or she will fit in with others before you put names on your list. And, more than that, consider each one in the light of the reason for your party.

Obviously, if you are planning a Grey Cup party, you will only invite known or suspected football enthusiasts. This might not be the time to invite your new, somewhat shy neighbours.

Football fans tend to lose their inhibitions on such occasions.

If you are planning the party to introduce those newcomers to the neighbourhood, then you will presumably not invite friends from other parts of town. Unless they have something special in common with the new neighbours, or particularly asked to meet them.

The Party Mix

While there are no definite rules for inviting people to a social (as opposed to family) party, there are some useful guidelines for beginners. Remember, you're aiming for harmony. So . . .

- Choose people who, to the best of your knowledge, will enjoy each other's company. The smaller the gathering, the more important this is.
- Try to keep guests within a 10-year age span. Even so, you probably know some people who are virtually ageless and fit comfortably into any age group.
- Don't, if you can help it, invite more women than men to a large, mixed party. Extra men, on the other hand, are usually an asset.
- If it's a round-the-table dinner party, numbers should be equal.
- Watch out for the overly-opinionated conversation-hoggers. If you are obliged to include one of these, try to find another. Then, hopefully, they can slug it out together.
- Add some listeners to your party mix; introverts as well as extroverts.
- Try to mix the people who all know each other with some who don't know each other. That way, everyone has a chance to enlarge his or her circle of friends. (But this doesn't mean one or two "outside" couples who end up clinging together in self-defence. Try to make the mix 50-50 or at least 60-40.)
- Don't invite too many people in the same line of business to a purely social get-together, unless you really want them to spend most of the evening in a huddle, talking shop.
- On the other hand, if you have a group of friends with one common enthusiasm (sailing, skeet-shooting, old movies or whatever) get them all together — without any non-enthusiasts.
- If you're planning party games, make reasonably sure you're inviting only those people who genuinely enjoy such games. Some people don't.

- Got a friend with a talent — musician, magician, impersonator? He or she could be another party asset. But make sure you don't pressure them into entertaining by asking them to perform while people are standing nearby. It can be embarrassing to have to refuse in front of others. And be absolutely sure, before you ask, that their talents will be genuinely appreciated by your other guests.

The more you know about people you know, the more adventurous you can be about mixing them up together. It's the unknown quantity that creates the potential problem.

Some experienced party-givers seem to mix ages, personalities and life-styles without a qualm. Their parties are usually the most interesting, as well as fun, to attend. That's because they are pros at party-giving and know their ingredients, something which comes only through practice.

By the way, if you're hosting a party for somebody special — to introduce them, or wave them off on a trip or business move to another city — it's only sensible to discuss your list with the guest of honour.

But don't allow yourself to be brow-beaten. Though somebody else is the star of the show, it's still *your* party, held in *your* home. It's up to you to set the limit on the size of your guest list, and make the final decisions as to who comes.

Now, What About YOUR Party?

If You Decide On Several Small Affairs...

...take your list and match the people up into groups, considering their individual interests and personalities.

See who goes well with whom. You might decide on two parties to entertain two couples, then two more with three couples. Or five parties, asking two couples to each. Try juggling them around and see which combination is the most comfortable.

Entertain the easiest-going first and keep any problem-people for last. By that time, you'll be an old hand at entertaining, with all the confidence in the world.

If you're going to invite them all at once...

...try to be sure these 20 people make a good party mix.

Your guests will then enjoy each other's company and your party will be well on the way to being a great success.

3

"BE OUR GUEST!"

In the spirit of today's informality, it's a great temptation just to pick up the phone and invite friends to a party. Which is certainly fine for those last-minute get-togethers, and for the very casual type of entertaining.

However, even though it costs a little in time, effort and cash, a written invitation is generally a better idea for the fairly formal affair.

For one thing, a written invitation shows that you care enough, which gives a guest a nice, warm, wanted feeling.

Another thing; it ensures that your guests have all the information they need — the day, time and place of your party, any special parking arrangements, how to get there, as well as the kind of occasion it will be.

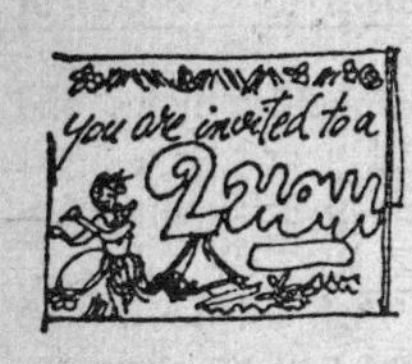

If special dress (formal, costume, come-as-you-were) is required, or you want people to bring skates or swimsuits, it's all there on the invitation, which sets the tone of your party. Invitations, if properly used, can generate excitement and anticipation, and start putting people in the party mood. And an out-of-the-ordinary affair gives you a chance to be creative about your invitations, which can be fun in itself.

Then too, a written invitation can be much easier on your guests, especially guests who are not close friends, than an out-of-the-blue phone call.

It can be difficult without having an engagement book or calendar handy, to remember off the top of your head what (if anything) is already booked for two or three weeks from now.

And it's often quite difficult to refuse a telephoned invitation gracefully.

Let's face it, there is always the chance that you have guessed wrong about somebody's idea of fun. The last thing in the world that some people want to do — at any time — is turn out for a costume party or a treasure hunt. If you catch them unawares with a phone call, it could cause embarrassment and you could wind up with badly fractured feelings.

Finally, though you yourself might be organized, there are plenty of people with short memories about. A written invitation is a reasonable guarantee that these delightful people won't turn up on the wrong day, or in the wrong clothes, or forget your party entirely.

At least it won't be your fault if they do.

How To Invite Them

The physical form of your invitation depends on the kind of occasion it will be.

For a formal wedding reception, you would order — as soon as the date has been set — custom-printed or engraved invitations, complete with acceptance cards, from a printer or stationery store that takes printing orders. Most printers and stationers have a large sample book showing all the suitable formats and styles of invitations. In the front of these books are ideas for the correct wording to be used on each occasion.

For a fun party, you can buy, make or embellish notes and cards to carry your invitation and the theme of your party. Most gift stores sell very attractive party invitations that require only the filling in of particulars.

There are some social niceties, however, that should always be observed, no matter what style of invitation you are sending.

- Always write in ink, never type, both the note or card, and the envelope it goes into.
- No abbreviations and no initials for formal invitations (weddings etc.) — everything down to the province or state is written out in full. Always include postal code.
- Rather than address an envelope "and Family," send the younger guests their own invitations.
- Always stamp the envelope, rather than have it meter-cancelled.
- Mail invitations well in advance of the party. Two weeks at the minimum for most occasions, and even more for formal affairs and those with out-of-town guests.

What's In A Name?

In every family, it is usually the wife who issues and accepts invitations on behalf of herself and her husband. The only exception to this rule is the strictly formal wedding, debut, banquet, etc., when they are co-hosts.

If you are at all confused about the correct way to address people, it goes like this:

Married couples: Mr. and Mrs. Edward Guest
Unmarried teenagers: Mr. David Guest
Miss (or Ms.) Elizabeth Guest
Two or more unmarried sisters:
Misses (or The Misses) Jane, Joan and Janet Guest
A single woman: Miss (or Ms.) Jane Guest
A married woman: Mrs. (or Ms.) Henry (or Jane) Guest
A married or single man: Mr. Charles Guest

Strictly speaking, a divorcée should be addressed using both her maiden name and the name of her ex-husband (Mrs. Thompson Guest). Which is all very well, providing you know her maiden name. In many cases you won't, and you're probably safe in addressing her simply as Mrs. (or Ms.) Jane Guest.

When To Be Casual

You can, of course, send a written invitation to come for a cup of coffee. But unless it's to a new acquaintance, this is a little pretentious.

Spur-of-the-moment hospitality, such as "Come and have a potluck super tomorrow" or "Let's get together over the weekend" is usually initiated among good friends by phone or simply by word of mouth.

However, if you have arranged a casual get-together by phone for quite a few days hence, it's a good idea to send a short note — just as a reminder.

How To Tell Who's Coming

"R.S.V.P.
789-9476"

This, as you know, is the beautifully-mannered French way of indicating at the bottom of an invitation that you'd like to know, as soon as possible, whether it has been accepted or not. This abbreviated style is used all over the world.

Today though, there is a new twist being used in the more informal style of invitations. You can ask people to let you know only if they're *not* coming. Like this:

"Regrets Only
789-9476"

If it's more convenient, you can put your address rather than your phone number, but of course this means people will have to send a written reply.

How Many Will Show Up

In spite of all this, and even if you R.S.V.P. all your invitations, you can't assume everyone is going to reply.

Human nature being what it is, you probably won't have heard from 10-20% of them by the time your party is five days away — sometimes for perfectly valid reasons, like being away when the invitation arrived.

Sometimes, alas, through sheer neglect.

What you do about this depends on how well you know the delinquents, and how vital it is to know precise numbers. With close friends, you'll have no real problem about phoning to find out if they are coming or not. A good approach is: "I really hope you can make it on Friday — there are some people coming we'd especially like you to meet."

This doesn't sound as though you're needling them, and will most likely produce a sincere apology for a lapse of memory — or manners.

If you haven't got the nerve to phone and check, play it safe and assume that everyone invited who didn't reply is going to attend. The worst that can happen with a buffet-type party is that you'll have to feed the family leftovers for a few more meals.

For some occasions, you don't really need to know numbers down to the last guest. At a cocktail party, for instance, where you'll only be serving drinks and canapés. You may not even need to ask people to reply. In which case, take it for granted 75% will appear.

With Pleasure, or Regret!

All formal invitations should be accepted with pleasure or refused with regret, in just the same literary style and lay-out as the original invitation.

"There's This Friend..."

Be prepared! How were you expected to know that the Harrisons had house-guests? If you're unlucky, they may come right out and ask if their guest can come along too. It isn't the best of manners, but it happens. If you're already catering for a crowd, one or two more people shouldn't make any difference to your arrangements.

But if this is to be a sit-down dinner around a beautifully decorated table, then you're on the spot.

You might have to rearrange your seating plan, and, if it's a single uninvited guest, invite someone at the last moment to balance your table — or find a tactful way to say no. Which isn't easy.

If you're lucky, though, the original guest will have the sense to refuse your invitation on the grounds that an old college friend is visiting that week. Then it's up to you to say, "By all means, bring him/her along." Or, "What a pity — maybe we can make it another time."

No-Shows

There are always the people who accept your invitation and never turn up.

Nobody is likely to do this if they know you're slaving away over a six-course dinner for them. But it does happen with the informal, buffet-style parties and there's nothing much you can do about it, except hope they have the courtesy to phone the next day, with a good excuse.

It's All Off!

You know what Robert Burns had to say about the best-laid plans of mice and men?

It just might happen that, after all your planning and hard work, something unforeseen occurs and your party has to be cancelled or, at best, postponed.

What do you do?

You keep your head, find your guest list and get out your pen — unless your party was the casual kind, in which case, you get on the phone.

Here's The Procedure

- Naturally, you let all your guests know immediately that plans have been changed.
- If it's a formal party, and there is time, write, following the style of the original invitation.
- If it's at the last minute, use the phone or send a telegram.
- If the whole thing has to be cancelled, tell everyone the reason.
- If it is being postponed to a later date, you don't have to give the reason if you don't want to.
- If the party is postponed, you are obliged to reinvite *all* the original guests. You can't leave anyone out. Of course, you can always add a few more.

4 THE SECRET IS ORGANIZATION

"In all things, success depends upon previous preparation, and without such preparation there is sure to be failure." — *(Confucius)*

The first unbreakable rule for party-givers is: Think Positive.

The second is: Plan.

Preferably with the help of a timetable. (You can revise it to suit each occasion.)

Planning Saves

By organizing your efforts well, you can save time, money and your own energy.

By listing and then doing a few of the necessary things each day, you'll do them better with less effort, and be relaxed when party-time comes.

By allowing yourself plenty of time to shop, you'll save money. You won't have to make any last-minute trips to the delicatessen for things you forgot. You can make, instead of buy, your own invitations, if you like doing that sort of thing.

By organizing everything in easy stages, you will create a relaxed atmosphere. Guests will immediately feel that it's a pleasure for you to entertain them. And if you're relaxed, you'll easily cope with any minor problems that might occur along the way.

Easy Paperwork

Although on the surface it **may** sound like a needless waste of time, experienced hosts agree some simple paperwork goes a long way toward easier entertaining.

You've probably already got an address book. A Party Book is equally valuable. Any size will do, so long as there is plenty of room to enter vital statistics each time you entertain.

If you've got a shutterbug in the family, you might even think of turning this Party Book into a photo album as well. You'll have a ball looking over it a few years from now.

Why are you going to all this trouble?

That's easy. So that future parties will provide the maximum pleasure for your guests with a minimum of fuss for you. And so that budgeting and planning for each occasion will become easier and more accurate.

Vital Statistics

These are the facts you will want to record for your future reference.

- *Date, place, kind of party, reason* for giving it and perhaps the name of the guest of honour.
- *The guests.* You won't always want to entertain the same group, talking about the same things. This way, you can vary the mix next time. Or repeat it, if it proved successful the first time.
- *The menu.* No matter how great your gourmet specialty is, there's nothing worse than being remembered by some of your more frequent guests as Mr. and Mrs. Chicken Tetrazzini. By keeping notes, you can check to make sure you haven't been overdoing your "pièce de résistance" with the same people. For buffet-style menus, make a note if one particular dish disappears fast. Then you can produce a larger quantity next time. On the other hand, if nobody braved the braised squid . . .
  If you keep accurate track of the cost of your party food (dish by dish, if you can) it will be a guideline for future budgeting.
- *Drinks served.* Before, during and after your party. With costs. For the same reasons as above.
- *Decorations.* Table centerpieces, party room decor.
- *Special notes.* This section is especially valuable. And often not for publication. Here's where you make notes to yourself like: "Don't ever invite the Jacksons with the Stewarts again — they can't even agree on the time of day." "Ann is allergic to eggs." "Repeat curried shrimp. It was great."
- *Total cost of party and comments.* (Financial, that is.) Note what proved to be good deals, a less expensive place to rent glassware, a wonderful barman or maid, etc.

Your Party Timetable

For a very formal or large party, your timetable should go something like this:

One Month Before

- Decide on the type of party.
- Decide where you are going to hold it and make arrangements for space, if it's not in your home. If you are going to hold it at home, now is the time to make those last-minute repairs, or undertake the new paint job you've been planning.
- Make up your guest list.
- Engage extra help, if needed.
- If you are hiring entertainment, book it now.

Three Weeks Before

- Send out invitations.
- Plan menu on work sheet.
- Plan flowers, decor, etc.
- Check linen supply, arrange laundering if required.
- Order rental of furniture, equipment (see page 22).

One Week Before

- Make a grocery list.
- Shop for staples.
- Check liquor, mixers; order if necessary.
- List on work sheet, the tableware, dishes, etc. needed.
- Wash china, glassware that hasn't been used recently.

Four Days Before

- Polish silver, copper, brass and wrap in plastic sheeting.
- Check on guests who haven't R.S.V.P.-ed.
- Work out seating, write place cards, if any.
  (At this stage of the game, you should have completed everything that does not have to be done in the remaining three days.)

Three Days Before

- Clean house or apartment thoroughly.

Two Days Before

- Buy fresh food.
- Decorate party room (non-perishable decorations).
- Prepare party dishes and hors d'oeuvres that can be frozen.

One Day Before

- Check party clothes; be sure they're pressed.
- Assemble all equipment so that it is right where it is to be used.
- Finish decorating.
- Do quick vacuum and dusting.
- Arrange space for coat and boot storage.
- Set table(s).
- Do some preliminary preparation of perishable foods.
- Stock up on extra ice, if you have a large enough freezer, or if the weather's cold enough.

Party Day

- Remove frozen foods for defrosting.
- Hair-do, manicure.
- Prepare food as early in the day as possible.
- Set up bar — liquor, mixers and beer cooling, garnishes cut and ready, equipment at hand, etc.
- Ice is delivered, (if you have no storage facilities).
- Flowers delivered from florist.
- Freshen and check bathroom. Put out clean towels, fresh soap, tissues.
- Put out clean ashtrays, coasters, matches, etc.
- Take a good nap before dressing to receive first guest.

Note: For a smaller party, your timetable need not start so early. Simply combine the first two sets of items under the heading "Two Weeks Before." Some of them will in all probability not apply, such as hiring entertainment, renting furniture, etc. Otherwise, the rest of the timetable applies.

5 HELP IS AT HAND

If you're planning a large gathering, you'll be glad of any help you can get. After all, there's no law that says you have to do all the work on your own. Even if you happen to live alone. (Come to think of it, particularly if you happen to live alone.) A quick look in the Yellow Pages will show you it's possible to rent just about anything that isn't nailed down, from party furniture, glassware and decorations, to an experienced dishwasher or butler.

The only consideration is your budget.

The Pros and Cons of Catering

These are quite straightforward. The basic pro is that a good catering service can take over completely, if that's what you want.

If you approach a reputable firm of caterers or rental agencies in a big city, you'll probably find they can supply any or all of the items or services listed below.

- Prepared food (hot or cold)
- Flowers, centerpieces
- Glassware
- Chairs
- Coffee makers
- Kitchen and dishwashing help
- Bartenders
- Beverages
- Linens
- Silver flatware
- Tables
- Garden furniture
- Waiters, maids
- Butlers
- Ice
- China
- Serving dishes, cutlery
- Portable bars
- Coat and hat racks
- Coat checkers

The con, of course, is that you'll have to pay for whatever service you need.

How much? That depends on the going rates in your area, how elaborate the food and drink is to be, and how many people are to be served.

You may decide to let the caterer provide the food, while you buy your own liquor. That's usually more economical.

Or you may want them to produce the hot dishes, while you make the cold hors d'oeuvres and desserts.

If you plan on using a caterer in any capacity, this is how to go about it.

- Get a recommendation from someone who has used a reliable outfit. Make sure this recommendation is for a similar type of party.
- If you can't find someone through these sources, check through "Caterers" in the Yellow Pages.
- Compare prices; give at least three companies the basic data (number of guests, type of food and drink, time and probable duration of party, etc.) before making a final choice.
- Ask the companies you call to give you names of a couple of their customers; then call them to check the caterer out.
- Discuss your party thoroughly with the company's representative: he should be an expert.
- Save money by using as much of your own equipment as possible. Remember, you pay for each item rented.
- Always examine rental equipment before committing yourself, to ensure that glasses aren't scratched, china isn't chipped, silver is in good condition, etc. Both the quality and condition of all equipment is your responsibility, so make sure you're satisfied before signing.
- Be sure the staff coming to work in your home is bonded and has the necessary qualifications.
- Be sure you get a detailed written list of your requirements along with the price quoted by the company. Check everything carefully, because mistakes can happen.
- Also, on the day of the party, check to be sure you get everything ordered.
- You may be asked to sign a contract. That's simply standard practice.
- If you're ordering food, you'll probably be asked to put down a deposit. Perhaps 50% of the total cost.
- Be sure to straighten out the question of tips — whether you hand them out, or whether they're included in the bill.
- When returning items to the caterer, make sure there is not going to be any future conflict over breakages etc. Get whoever picks the material up to sign a slip that indicates "Equipment returned in good condition" or "Broken or missing items are as follows."

Partially Catered

Don't overlook local restaurants when planning food for your party. Maybe you can come to some arrangement with the owner, the manager or chef — even though the establishment is not normally in the catering business.

If the local hotel is famous for its Brome Duck — and this is just what you need to highlight your dinner — it might be more than happy to prepare your entrée in the hotel kitchens and rush it over at party time.

If the local bakery specializes in mouth-watering rolls or crispy croissants, it might agree to deliver hot from the oven, in time for your brunch.

One inexperienced hostess, presented with a huge, freshly-caught salmon just before her party, dragged it into a restaurant on her way to work . . . collected it on her way home, beautifully cooked and garnished. Since she'd never been known to offer anything more adventurous than spaghetti-and-meatballs before, her guests were all pleasantly surprised, and they never did discover her secret.

Don't forget to consider the possibility of using the services of the local "takeout" restaurant either.

But there is one important fact to remember. Food that is fresh from the oven will always taste better than that which is delivered to your home. It suffers in delivery, whether it comes from the best restaurant in town, or is brought by that little man in the Honda with the sign on top. This, of course, often does not apply to food which will be served cold.

Rent — Don't Buy

Are you short of chairs or glasses for your party? Do you wish you had a better colour TV Set on Grey Cup day? Or an awning, to give some shade for your Patio Brunch?

Back to the Yellow Pages. They're full of places that provide everything you can think of in the way of party supplies.

Renting makes good sense if you don't plan to use these items often. A jumbo punch bowl and cups can occupy most of a cupboard. And if it's only used once a year, why spend all that money? It's easier, less expensive, and more convenient to rent.

Charges are based on the individual items and how long you keep them. Some firms make a minimum charge. Check this out. A rental price rule of thumb is that you will probably have to pay 1/5 of the cost of the item itself, plus the price of installation and delivery.

A word of caution: generally speaking, you are responsible for wear and tear of rented goods while they are on your premises. If anything gets lost or broken, you'll get a bill.

Helping Hands

Where do you look for people to lend a hand?. That is, after you've eliminated the possibility of using the family, who are obviously the first to be pressed into service.

Teenagers

This is where the local young people can come into their own. A reliable boy or girl can be a blessing in the kitchen — at the stove or sink, depending on talent.

You can even consider using them waiting at table, circulating hors d'oeuvres, removing dishes during a buffet, etc., but they will probably need a little coaching beforehand.

If you have a very young family, hire your teenage baby-sitter to come in and take charge of the children, while you prepare for the party, and while it is in progress. She can feed the little ones, entertain them and put them to bed.

When negotiating teenage help for your party, add 15% to the going hourly rate they charge for baby-sitting services. And don't forget to arrange transportation home for the girls.

Cleaning Ladies

Another source of help is your own cleaning lady. She has the advantage of knowing your home, and is likely to be glad to come in and help with the cooking, serving and cleaning up. Or, she might know of someone who does this sort of work. If you want her to wait at table, suggest she wear a plain black dress with a white apron.

Hourly pay for this sort of service is usually a little higher than the normal daily rate. If you pay \$20 a day for house-cleaning, \$25 for an evening's party work is probably about right.

University Students

Some universities and colleges have student employment agencies that provide party help.

Professionals

There are always the part-time professionals — maids, butlers, bartenders, waiters — who work on a free-lance basis, or through agencies.

If you engage a free-lancer, be sure to ask for, and thoroughly check references.

Agency personnel are usually bonded. This means you don't have to worry about the possibility of petty theft. They're covered by the agency's insurance.

Wages are either paid directly to the agency, or to the help at the end of the party. As with caterers, if you're dealing through an agency, find out beforehand whether tips are added to the bill or paid at the end of the party — and if so, how much is expected.

In most of these areas we've discussed, you'll find that the Seagram's Reception Service can be a real boon. More detailed information on the services it offers and how to contact your representative can be found in the foreword to this book.

A Short Course In Employee Relations

A word to the wise. Very often, people who do not have paid help in their homes regularly, do not know how to react, or how to treat them. The answer is — as capable, competent people who are there to do a job, they are not guests, nor are they slaves. Be pleasant but firm with them. Tell them exactly what you want them to do, make sure they do it, and tell them when they do not. Don't encourage or allow them to carry on small talk with your guests; or to indulge in a little extra-curricular nibbling or imbibing. And whatever you do, don't apologize to them for anything or let them make you feel embarrassed. It's your house and your party, and things will be run the way you want them to be run, not the other way round. Remember, you don't have to account to them in any way.

On the other hand, don't treat them like the domestics of Dickens' day either. Treat them with respect and dignity, and chances are they will respond in kind.

The Entertainers

As we've already mentioned, though you may have some talented guests at your party, don't assume they want to perform. They came to enjoy themselves, not necessarily to work.

But some parties simply cry out for live entertainment. And with all the local talent around today, this shouldn't be difficult to arrange.

Musically speaking, you don't necessarily have to go to the pros. What has your town got in the way of amateur talent? If your mind is a blank, the local weekly newspaper should give you some leads.

High school dance band? Barber shop quartet? Glee club? Church soloist or organist? Give them enough warning and you'll find they'll be pleased to perform at your party.

Apart from musicians (solo or by the brunch), other entertainers to bear in mind are magicians, fortunetellers, quick-sketch artists, handwriting experts.

If you plan to hire professional musicians, today's rates in the larger cities are about $75 for 4 hours per musician on a group basis. Double this for a soloist. You might also consider the travelling deejays who bring in their own stereo equipment, turntables, records, etc., and provide a constant flow of music to suit the mood of the party, and the ever-changing temperament of the guests.

Let Your Fingers Do The Walking

Even your best friends will sometimes be most secretive about passing on party-giving information. If they pride themselves on their entertaining ability, they are often reluctant about divulging their sources of supply.

But there's nothing secretive about the Yellow Pages — if you know where to look. These are some headings taken directly from the Montreal and Toronto directories that might help you.

- Amusement Devices (Jukeboxes, Pinball Machines etc.)
- Artificial Flowers and Plants
- Automobile Rentals
- Awnings and Canopies
- Boat Rental and Charter
- Caterers
- Caterers — Equipment and Supplies
- Decoration Contractors, Party, Convention etc.
- Electrical Contractors
- Employment Agencies
- Employment Contractors — Temporary Help
- Entertainers
- Favours
- Flameproofing
- Formal Wear — Rental
- Fur Rental
- Furniture Rental
- Limousine Service
- Motion Picture Equipment and Supplies — Rental
- Musical Instruments — Dealers, Rental
- Orchestras and Bands
- Party Decorations
- Party Equipment and Supplies
- Party Floral Arrangements
- Party Planning Service
- Party Supplies — Retail and Rental
- Photographers — Commercial
- Recorders — Sound — Equipment and Supplies
- Sound Systems and Equipment
- Television Rental

If you live in a smaller town, your listing may not be as extensive, but look in the book anyway — you might be pleasantly surprised.

6

BON APPETIT!

Now, for the heart of the matter — your menu.

Food can be one of the biggest contributing factors to the success of your party. A delicious dinner can mean the difference between a "pleasant evening" and a "smashing success." This is not to imply that you have to suddenly become a gourmet chef in order to impress. Simple, well chosen, well-cooked and attractively-served food is all that's required — whether you're doing a dinner for eight or a buffet for eighty.

The only real problem is that of timing. This too can be easily solved, if you take the whole exercise step-by-step and remember to:

- Keep it simple.
- Plan well ahead.
- Allow yourself plenty of time, and
- Keep cool.

Presumably, you can cook. Hopefully, you enjoy cooking. In which case, you've probably got several favourite recipes which can be produced or adapted for your party.

There are recipes in this book too, but before you look at those, or reach for your own cookbooks . . .

Know Your Kitchen

What you choose to serve will depend a great deal on your kitchen equipment and facilities. Hot food *must* be kept hot, and cold dishes must be really cold when they come to the table. So, if either your facilities or space is limited, you'll have to use some initiative.

A freezer is a real boon, because it means you can do some cooking ahead of time. If you don't own one and there's no room in your refrigerator freezing compartment, see if you can arrange to borrow some sub-zero space from a neighbour.

Short of chilling and crisping space? An insulated picnic cooler can help here. With a couple of plastic bags of ice cubes and the lid firmly shut, greens will keep just as fresh for as long as they would in the fridge.

If you have a double-oven stove, you'll have no trouble keeping things warm. If not, try borrowing or renting a portable electric oven to warm bread, baked potatoes, etc. An open waffle iron or griddle can also be pressed into service — temper the heat with a crumpled sheet of heavy-duty foil.

While you're at it, check that you have all the necessary tools to cut, mash, stir, whip, grate, bake, roast, cool, chop, blend, scrape and strain.

Now, Start Planning Your Menu

And plan, at the same time, to spend as little party-time as possible in the kitchen.

If you're cooking dinner for eight people, remember...

Don't Over-Reach Yourself

There's no need to produce more than three courses, and two are perfectly acceptable. Plus, of course, coffee served in the living room afterwards.

1. Soup or hors d'oeuvres
2. Main meat or fish course
3. Dessert

That's plenty. You might want to substitute a salad for the first course. Or, if you're short of kitchen space, you could serve appetizers with the pre-dinner drinks and make the cocktail hour an integral part of the dinner.

Keep It Simple

This cannot be over-emphasized. Both for your sake and the sake of your guests.

Unless you really *are* a gourmet cook, this is *not* the time to experiment. Cook only what you cook best.

If you absolutely have to include something new to you in the menu, rehearse it beforehand. Several times, if necessary. Then you'll be completely confident that it will turn out right, and that your timing in co-ordinating the whole meal will be right on.

Balance The Taste

...of each course, and of the complete meal. Some foods are delicious on their own, but they can taste like nothing on earth when combined inappropriately.

Candied sweet potatoes and fruit salads go well with poultry, ham or pork. But they don't do a thing for beef, which needs starch and green vegetables.

If you've used ginger butter on your carrots in the main course, you won't want a gingery topping on the dessert. You wouldn't serve a cheese soufflé followed by cheesecake.

Always follow a rich dish (Lobster Thermidor or Lasagna, for example) with a simple, refreshing dessert (fresh fruit or sherbet). A plain first course paves the way for something sweet and creamy, like a sherry-laden Bagatelle.

Balance The Colour, Too

A pale meal may taste great — but only if you eat it with your eyes shut, because appearance is almost as important as flavour.

A white fish, in a white sauce, served with white boiled potatoes and cauliflower isn't likely to set the mouth watering in anticipation. Peas and beans are almost identical greens, so don't serve them on the same plate.

Make sure that the dessert is a good colour contrast to the first course.

Contrasts Are Important

Incorporate something soft and something crunchy into your menu. Something sweet and something sour, something hot and something cold.

This last point is as much for your benefit as anyone else's. If you try to dish up hot hors d'oeuvres, a hot main course with hot vegetables, plus a steaming hot dessert, and then coffee, you'll never get out of the kitchen. Besides, your guests will find the meal somewhat monotonous.

Even if this is to be a cold summer luncheon, add variety by starting off with a cup of hot bouillon.

Another thing — there are some menus that are definitely more suitable for ladies' luncheons than mixed dinner parties. For example, the ladies really go for sweet moulded salads, aspics and the like, while most men prefer hearty, green no-nonsense salads and chunks of crusty bread.

Consider The Season

There's no real reason why you shouldn't serve Christmas Pudding or pumpkin pie in the middle of summer. But somehow, it just doesn't seem right. Unless you're having a Christmas-in-July or Hot-Weather-Hallowe'en Party.

And, of course, each season brings with it certain food items that are plentiful, less expensive, and usually at their best. So why buck the tide?

In summer, you're far better to take advantage of the too-short berry season. Consider fresh strawberries, raspberries, or blueberries, served with powdered sugar and cream. Leave the pumpkin pie to the nippy days of October.

Now For The Hors d'Oeuvres

If you're going to offer anything more elaborate than salted peanuts and potato chips with pre-dinner drinks, the hors d'oeuvres should complement the menu — not overload it.

Also, they're supposed to stimulate appetites, not fill people so full they can't do justice to your cooking.

If you're serving something in tomato sauce for dinner, then don't serve tomato canapés before. The same goes for cheese, seafood, etc.

Easiest for the unassisted cook are the many different cold canapés that can be prepared in advance — and can be relied on not to lose their looks or flavour in the interim.

Some hors d'oeuvres can be prepared ahead and frozen. They can be heated at the last minute and served in chafing dishes or on warming trays.

When it comes to quantity, you're wiser to prepare a small, tasty selection of hors d'oeuvres than to be too lavish in this department. Allow five or six per person.

Talking Of Quantities

This is the other big difference between cooking for the family and cooking for a party. Don't take anything for granted. Not even your favourite cookbook.

If the recipe says it will serve eight people, and you have never proved to yourself that it does, increase the quantities. It's always better to have too much on hand than too little.

If you're used to cooking one specific recipe for four and you want to adapt it for eight, double all ingredients — except the salt. Taste and add extra salt at the last moment, if it's needed.

Remember too, if you increase the quantity, you also have to allow more cooking time. The four-serving soufflé that normally takes an hour to bake is likely to take an hour and a half, if quantities have been doubled to feed eight.

Don't trust your memory about anything. Write it all down. If you've altered a recipe or a cooking temperature or added something extra in the way of seasoning, make a note of it.

Once more — it is always better to serve too much, rather than too little. There are few things more embarrassing than running out of food.

Tips For Timing

When it comes to working out your food-preparation schedule, it's all up to you. Everything depends on your choice of menu.

Work it out on paper. If you're not sure, do a dummy run with the family a week or so beforehand, and make the necessary adjustments to your timetable.

Suppose you have asked your guests to come at 6:30.

Allow another half-hour for latecomers. There's always someone whose car wouldn't start, who lost their way, or who had to wait for the baby-sitter.

That means your actual timetable for the cocktail hour will run from 7:00 to 8:00. Ample time for a couple of drinks and some hors d'oeuvres.

Dinner's at 8:00. Work your cooking and defrosting schedule backwards from there. If the success of your main dish depends on precision timing, allow enough time for guests to have finished their soup or hors d'oeuvres — and for the dishes to be cleared into the kitchen. Then you can appear with your Shish Kebab crackling hot on skewers.

Getting Ahead Of The Game

- Peel potatoes a day in advance, if necessary. Cover them with water, add a drop or two of vinegar and refrigerate till cooking time.
- Washed, torn, cut or shredded green salad ingredients can be kept fresh and crisp by putting them in a paper-lined bowl. Put more paper napkins or towels on top and refrigerate. But don't mix your salad until the last moment. Sitting around in salad dressing causes green leaves to wilt.
- A moulded salad can be turned out onto its dish early in the day, and returned to the refrigerator to reset.

- And while we're on the subject of jellied things: to avoid this kind of dish going soft around the sides, strengthen the gelatin action when you prepare it. If you're using flavoured gelatin, reduce the liquid called for in the recipe by about 10% or 15%. For unflavoured gelatin, add an extra 1/2 envelope for every one called for in the recipe.
- You can buy celery and lettuce earlier than you think. They'll keep for a long time in the refrigerator if stored in paper bags. Leave the outer leaves on till it's time for washing.
- Buy fresh parsley beforehand. Wash, trim the stems, dry in a towel. Then roll in foil and freeze. When you need it, grate what you need and refreeze the rest. (This saves chopping and snipping.)

A Bountiful Buffet

Planning a buffet for a few dozen is easier, oddly enough, than arranging a sit-down dinner for a just few.

For one thing, timing isn't so crucial. In fact, there need hardly be any timing at all, if you serve a completely cold buffet, with hot coffee to follow. Just take things out of the refrigerator when you need them, or out of the freezer in time for them to defrost.

If you're worried about a mixed salad going soggy after sitting on a buffet table for an hour or so, simply offer a plain, undressed bowl of mixed greens, several dishes of other ingredients (cucumber, hard-cooked eggs, anchovies, etc.), plus a selection of different dressings and mayonnaise, and let people build their own.

The other thing you won't need to worry about is the balancing of colour, texture and taste.

Just set out enough colourful foods in their separate containers to make the whole buffet attractive. Offer different textures and a variety of tastes. Then if your guests choose to heap their plates with roast beef and fruit salad, that's their business.

There's only one rule to remember when planning a buffet menu. Unless there's room for everyone to sit, make sure that the food can be eaten comfortably with a fork alone.

You'll probably want one hot dish, particularly if it's a winter party. Casseroles, curries, spaghetti, etc. will keep hot perched on a table heater. (Remember to switch it on five minutes before you bring the dishes in, if it's electric; or light the fuel so that the chafing dish itself will get hot.)

Colourful mugs of hot soup or bowls of jellied consommé can be served just as your guests are finishing cocktails, and before you formally declare the buffet open. This saves buffet space and leaves more room for food.

Always make your buffets as colourful and as lavish as possible. Not in terms of extravagantly prepared dishes — but in sheer quantity. Calculate how much of each dish your guests can eat, and then add a bit more. Maybe it's all that exercise — walking around the table and helping themselves — that stimulates appetites. Whatever the reason, people seem to eat more when they get to a buffet table. Do you recall the time you went to a buffet and were the last to get into the line-up? By the time you got to the Boeuf Bourguignon, all that was left was gravy. Kind of disappointing wasn't it? Don't let that happen at your party.

Some Tricks Of The Trade

If your menu is basically plain, there are all kinds of party touches you can add to give dishes colour, excitement and a new subtle flavour.

Try these variations:

- Sour cream and black caviar on baked potatoes.
- Wrap meat loaf in smoked bacon strips.
- Add toasted slivered almonds, sliced water chestnuts or mushrooms to buttered grean beans.
- Beat butter with a favourite herb, chill it and serve on asparagus or broccoli.
- Cook frozen green peas without water — still frozen, with 1 tbsp. butter, 2 fresh sprigs or 1 tsp. dried mint, ½ tsp. sugar, ½ tsp. salt. Cover and cook over medium heat, shaking often, for 5 mins., or until peas wrinkle when the lid is removed.
- Sprinkle nutmeg on cooked, buttered Brussels sprouts.
- Add 1 tsp. caraway seeds to cooking spinach, or a sprinkle of celery seed when it's ready to serve.

- Surround ham with whole spiced apricots, crab apples or sliced peaches, as a change from pineapple.
- Serve buttered asparagus, beans or Brussels sprouts with a topping of seasoned breadcrumbs.
- Mix, marinate and serve wax, green and lima beans along with bits of pimento.
- Grate cooked egg yolks over potato, chicken or green salads.
- Combine grapefruit or orange sections in green salads.
  green seedless grapes with chicken salad.
  ham or chicken slivers with fruit salad.
  avocados with any salad.
- Add dark green, raw spinach leaves to a green salad; or dandelion leaves to a summer salad.
- Top a mashed sweet potato casserole with chopped pecans and a sprinkle of cinnamon. If you're doing the Southern Belle bit, add marshmallows on top and brown in oven.
- Add cocoa and sugar, or 1 tsp. instant coffee to whipped cream.
- Add chopped or frozen chives to buttered carrots, peas, beans, bean sprouts.
- Colour a white sauce with a dash of paprika.
- Shake cinnamon or nutmeg over whipped cream.
- Boil potatoes and carrots in one pan, then whip them together for a colourful, delicately-flavoured, new vegetable dish.
- Use wine, liquor and liqueurs in your cooking.

Be A Spirited Cook

This does not mean standing at the stove with a drink in one hand and a wooden spoon in the other. It means adding a small quantity of carefully-chosen spirit or wine to a dish, to give it a new and intriguing flavour and aroma.

Let's get one thing clear, right now.

The "vin" in your Coq au Vin is no longer "vin" by the time it gets to the table. The alcohol has been cooked away and all that remains is the flavour and that delicious aroma.

Obviously, this does not apply if you pour a liqueur straight from the bottle over ice cream, or ladle sherry into a trifle.

As usual, there are some guidelines.

- Take it easy. The addition of wine or spirits is supposed to highlight the flavour, not dominate it. Better to add too little than too much.

- **Robust, full-bodied spirits are best in hearty, well-seasoned dishes; lighter spirits in delicate ones.**
- Use white wine for chicken, fish, veal, cheese, creamed dishes; red wine for red meat. Use dry wines only — unless the recipe specifically calls for something semi-dry or sweet.

What quality wine should you use for cooking? There are two schools of thought about this. Some people insist that it should be the best you can afford. Others say it couldn't matter less. Make up your own mind about this.

What Goes Well In What?

You'll probably create your own specialties. But here are some ideas to start you off on a spirited cooking career.

Chemineaud Brandy

Has a natural affinity for coffee, chocolate, fruit and just about anything sweet.

- Add Chemineaud Brandy to pancake syrup for a glamorous brunch dish.

- Add Chemineaud to a blue cheese dressing.

- Soak a Camembert cheese in Chemineaud Brandy, then sprinkle with chopped walnuts.

- After sautéing meat in a pan, use Chemineaud Brandy as you would water to make a gravy in the pan. Stir in all the small, flavourful bits, heat and serve with the meat.

- And of course, Chemineaud Brandy is the perfect spirit to use when you want to prepare flaming dishes. See the section on flambé-ing, "The Burning Question," a little further on in this chapter, for details.

For a dramatic Shish Kebab: pour an ounce of warmed brandy on a heatproof platter. Lay the skewered Shish Kebab across it and ignite. When the flame dies, slide meat off the skewer onto individual plates.

To be sure your Christmas Pudding bursts into festive flames, light warmed brandy in the ladle and pour it over, while flaming.

Rum

(Captain Morgan Black Label, Gold Label, Morgan White, or Trelawny White)

- Add a small amount to sautéed mushrooms, or canned cream of mushroom soup.
- Marinate pineapple slices in Gold Label Rum; dip in batter and deep-fry for a sensational dessert.
- Add Morgan White Rum to Coquille St. Jacques.
- Add 3 tbsc. Black Label to Boeuf Bourguignon (as well as the dry red wine the recipe calls for).
- Add Black Label to chocolate pudding, top with whipped cream flavoured with Leroux Crème de Café.
- Use Morgan Gold Label with chocolate, coffee, pineapple, lemon, lime, with cake fillings and icings.

Scotch

(Seagram's 100 Pipers or Black Watch)

- Adds a delicious smoky flavour to fish sauces.
- Baste it over a roasting loin of pork.
- Add 2 tbsp. of 100 Pipers to sautéed chicken livers, or to braised onion slices and sautéed shrimps.

Gin

(Boodles British Gin, Seagram's King Arthur or Seagram's Extra Dry)

- Adds personality to a clam dip. The subtle botanicals and aromatics in gin combine nicely with the seafood and cream. It also adds a tang.
- Combine it with parsley and butter, on sole.
- Complements cranberries by adding a zesty taste that is more refreshing than the cranberries alone.
- Combine it with soy sauce and ginger, in Steak Mandarin.

Bolshoi Vodka

Because it's essentially flavourless, it should only be used in uncooked foods where the nip of the alcohol is the flavour that counts.

- Try cold Bloody Mary Soup. (See recipe section page 97.)

- Delicious with scallops, in Ceviche Mary. (See recipe section page 105.)
- Bloody Mary Aspic (see recipe section page 100) goes well with cold seafood.
- As a Martini French Dressing. (See recipe section page 104.)

Canadian Whisky

(Seagram's V.O., Seagram's 83, or Seagram's Five Star)

- Stir a little into bean soup, barbecue sauce, hamburger mix.
- Add a touch to salted, unsweetened whipped cream, and drop a spoonful into each serving of tomato soup.
- Sprinkle peach halves with brown sugar and V.O.; dab with butter and broil.
- Fine chefs know that there is a natural marriage of tastes between good Canadian whisky & beef. Try adding a little to your brown beef gravies, pot roast, beef meat balls etc.

Liqueurs

(Leroux offers a choice of seven fine liqueurs that can add to your flair as a spirited cook — Green and White Crème de Menthe, Cherry Whisky and Brandy, Apricot Brandy, Triple Sec, Crème de Café.)

- Use any of the above straight, as a sauce over sherbets, ice cream.
- Layer with ice cream in a tall parfait glass, or spoon over fruit.
- Pour a little Leroux Crème de Menthe over ice-cold pineapple slices or chunks. after the liquid has been almost all drained off.
- Mix in Leroux Triple Sec or Leroux Cherry Brandy with fruit cocktail.
- Add just a little Leroux Triple Sec to Chicken à la King.
- Marinate pear halves in Leroux Green Crème de Menthe. Serve with lamb instead of mint jelly.
- Add Leroux Triple Sec to dessert omelettes, soufflés, crêpes, carrots, sherbets, pork, duck, chicken. (Remember, you are using it as a sweetener: 1 tsp. = 1 tsp. sugar.)
- Add Leroux Apricot Brandy and ginger to canned pears, duck, pork.

Generally Speaking...

- Always allow enough cooking time for the alcohol to evaporate, usually about ten minutes. A tablespoon of neat spirit in a pan over a hot burner will only need a moment or two.
- Always add as one of the last ingredients.
- To repeat: Go easy! Especially when *adding* liquor or liqueurs, as opposed to *cooking* them. You want to make your food more flavourful, not drown it.
- Too much liquor in a frozen dessert or ice cream will slow up — even prevent — the freezing process.
- When blending spirits with eggs (whole or separated), do it slowly. If you pour it in too fast, the eggs will curdle.
- When using liqueurs with meat, poultry or fish, you can cut the sweetness to taste by adding a spot of lemon juice, brandy or whisky.

The Burning Question

To flambé or not to flambé? One definite rule. Don't take your first stab at it at the party itself. Good liquor is volatile and you should know exactly what it will do when you touch a match to it. This is something that definitely needs rehearsing.

But it's not too difficult. And it certainly is a dramatic way to improve the flavour of your dish and whet your guests' appetites. These are the points to remember.

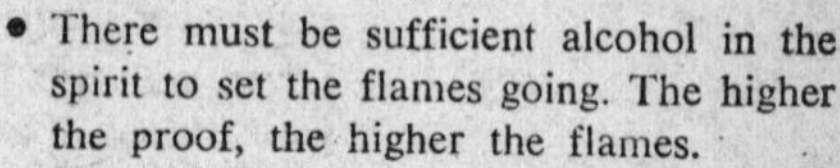

- There must be sufficient alcohol in the spirit to set the flames going. The higher the proof, the higher the flames.
- If you're using a low-proof liquor, add brandy or vodka, so that it will burn more readily. Or sprinkle the food lightly with sugar to increase the blaze, but this will add a caramel taste.
- The spirit should first be lightly warmed in a spoon or ladle held over a chafing dish warmer or candle. The warmed spoon makes the spirit light readily.
- Don't overheat or it may burst into flames before you're ready for it.
- You can either light the spirit in the warmed ladle and pour it flaming over the food, or light it after it has been poured on.

- If you're using a chafing dish or shallow cook-and-serve pan, add warmed spirit to the dish or pan and then ignite.
- If you've transferred the food to a serving platter, light the warmed spirit in a long-handled ladle and pour on while it is flaming.
- Never lean over the platter or chafing dish when igniting, always avert your face, and use a long match — otherwise you could lose your eyebrows.
- Never pour additional spirit straight from the bottle onto the flaming dish.
- Allow the flames to die out naturally. If you are using a chafing dish, simmer the food for a few more moments.

What Went Wrong?

If, having followed all those instructions, the flames could only be described as unenthusiastic, check that:

- The dish you were trying to flambé was not too moist. (With syrupy desserts, drain well before flambé-ing and serve syrup separately.)
- The spirit was of high enough proof.

Don't Forget The Fondues . . .

. . . when you're planning hors d'oeuvres, snacks, buffets or informal dinner parties. Fondues are one of today's most popular entertaining dishes. Originally, a fondue was a simple Swiss way of serving bread and cheese. Today, people are happily fondue-ing everything from seafood to strawberries.

If this is something new to you, and you'd like to try it, get one of the many books devoted to the fun of fondues. Having tried it, you may never want to serve your guests regular meals again!

Basically, a fondue is a cross between the time-honoured dunking (shrimps into spicey sauce) and Chinese wok-cooking (quickly cooking small morsels of food in hot oil).

You'll need a fondue pot that can be kept heated (not just warm) with an open flame or electric element, and enough long-handled, small-tined forks so that there are one or two for each guest. Into the pot goes something hot and tasty (such as the traditional wine-cheese seasoning mix). The contents are heated until they are piping hot and then maintained at this temperature.

Guests dunk bits of crusty bread on the ends of their forks into the pot and then into their mouths. Or you can fill your fondue pot with a flavoured liquid (hot fish bouillon), and allow guests to boil fork-skewered, bite-sized bits of seafood in it. You can also use the pot as a mini deep-fryer filled with oil — to cook speared steak pieces.

Important: Both hot oil and hot broths will heat the immersed fork to the point where it can cause a nasty burn if it comes in contact with the lips. So if you are fondue-ing this way, give your guests a plate and extra fork so they can transfer the hot tidbit from one fork to the other before they pop it into their mouths. Be sure, if they are fondue-ing neophytes, to warn them about this.

For dessert: fondue pots of hot melted chocolate, caramel, peppermint sauce — an endless variety of sweet liquids can be used. Into these sweet cauldrons dunk fruit, cake, cookies, marshmallows — use your imagination.

In the recipe and entertaining ideas sections, you'll find many more details under the headings "Fondues and Fondue Sauces" (page 92) and "Fondue Fun" (page 65) respectively.

But if you want to know more about equipment — the advantages of different types of burners, how much you have to pay for this equipment, some of the really amazing things that can be fondued and how, be sure to get a good book on the subject. It makes fascinating reading.

The Finishing Touch

Naturally, you'll plan to end your beautifully-cooked meal with tea or coffee.

Ignore the fact that some people habitually drink coffee with their dessert. Or even all through the meal. Serving coffee at the table means extra work for you, and that's not the object of this exercise.

Move everyone firmly out of the dining room and into the living room at the end of the meal. Then you can either turn your back on the table debris, or signal the kitchen-help that it's all theirs.

By arranging a tray beforehand with cups or demitasses, coffee spoons, cream, sugar etc., you can serve coffee quickly and efficiently, without dashing to and fro.

Let's not get into a hassle about the best way to make coffee. Everyone has their own idea, including you. And the only generally agreed points are that you need a clean pot and plenty of fresh coffee of the right grind.

After all your hard work in the kitchen, don't use instant coffee. To most coffee-lovers it would be a let-down, rather than a finishing touch.

After-luncheon and after-dinner coffee is always served black, with sugar and cream offered separately. You could also offer guests a cinnamon-stick stirrer. It adds a delicious flavor to black coffee.

Or, try adding Leroux Crème de Café or Chemineaud Brandy to coffee for added zest. For that matter, any Leroux liqueur served with coffee (separately) is a great way to end a meal — and easy.

How about coffee that's different? It can be that added extra that will have your guests going home thinking you really know what entertaining is all about. Buy a can of the dark-roasted finely-ground Italian espresso coffee. Brew according to the directions and serve in demitasses with sugar and a twist of lemon. No cream.

Use espresso also for:

- **Caffe Cappuccino** — equal parts of espresso and hot milk, sprinkled lightly with cinnamon and nutmeg. Serve in a demitasse, with sugar.
- **Roman Espresso** — espresso coffee served in small wine-glasses, with a twist of lemon peel.
- **Caffe Borgia** — equal amounts of espresso and hot chocolate, served in demitasses with whipped cream topping and grated orange peel.
- **Caffe Cioccolata** — half espresso, half hot chocolate, served in tall cups and topped with shavings of dark chocolate.

Then, of course, there's always **Irish Coffee.** (See Recipe No. 43 in the "So You Want To Be A Bartender!" section.)

For an afternoon party: try **Viennese Coffee** (regular blend) served black, in demitasses, with a dollop of sweetened whipped cream on top.

7 SERVICE WITH A SMILE

It goes without saying, you'll produce your best china and all your sparkling silver and glassware when you entertain. A beautifully-set table — formal or informal — is half the party battle. It can help transform the simplest casserole into a repast fit for a king.

It's also a chance to display all your fine table linens that you probably get too few chances to use in day-do-day living. Or, for those of you who'd rather forego ironing that huge damask tablecloth, today you have an option. A popular trend now (even for formal dinners) is to use place mats to protect the table surface and add colour to the setting. Whatever your table, remember that silverware should always be arranged in the order in which it is used — working from the outside in, towards the plate. With knife blades facing the plate. For strictly formal occasions, no more than three knives and three forks are supposed to appear on the table at once. Dessert plates and silver are presented together later on at the appropriate time.

Glassware too, goes by the rules. Wineglasses to the right of the water glass. For formal dinners, reading from left to right, they are: water, red wine and white wine. On informal tables, where only one wine is served, the glass still goes to the right of the water goblet.

There are four conventional ways to set a table: (1) for a breakfast or brunch; (2) for lunch or an informal dinner; (3) for a formal dinner; (4) for a buffet. This is how each looks.

Note: in all these illustrations, the table is set for a cold main course. Obviously, if the entrée is to be hot, the plates will also be hot. In which case, they would more than likely be brought in warm from the kitchen after the first course, or kept warm on a table heater.

Breakfast Or Brunch

Served on the patio or in the dining room, with a gaily-coloured cloth and matching napkins. An 8½" breakfast plate goes under the cereal dish. Cereal spoon to the right of the knife; the fork to the left of the plate. The coffee spoon may be set in the saucer, or at the right of the cereal spoon. Bread-and-butter plate just

above the fork; salt and pepper shakers above the plate; juice glass above the knife.

Lunch Or Informal Supper

No tablecloth is necessary, but use place mats and napkins (paper, if you like) folded any way you please. An 8½″ plate; meat fork on the outside left, salad fork next. (If salad is served first, the forks would be reversed.) To the right of the plate, from the outside in: teaspoon for fruit cocktail, soup spoon, knife. Dessert spoon and fork can be placed, as illustrated, above the plate, or brought in later on the dessert plate. Water glass above the knife, bread-and-butter plate and knife above forks. Coffee spoon is placed on demitasse saucer, when coffee is served.

Formal Dinner

Larger 10″ or 10½″ plate. Fork and salad fork on the left; cocktail or oyster fork, soup spoon and knife to the right. (If a fish course is added to this setting, the fork should go on the outside left, the fish knife between the knife and soup spoon on the right.) Water goblet and wineglass(es) above the knife. White cloth napkin (never paper), folded oblong or square, to the left of the fork. Or, if you're using one, on the side plate.

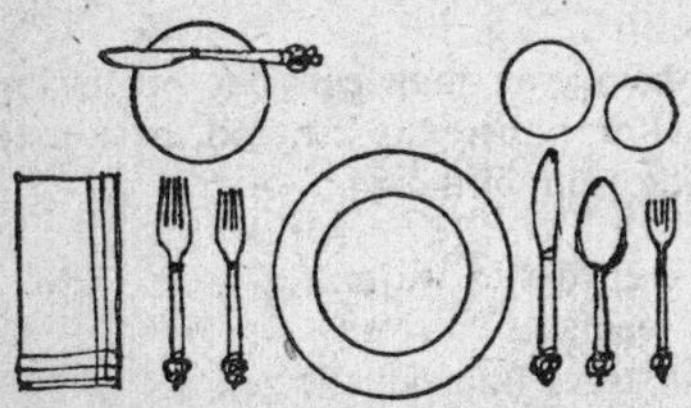

The Buffet

Since the serve-yourself guest-line moves traditionally from left to right around a buffet table, it makes sense to have the plates piled at the far left of the table. Place silverware at the other end, to be picked up last.

Stack plates interleaved with paper napkins. It makes them easier to pick up and saves table space.

Other than that, there are no hard-and-fast rules, though you would be wise to:

- Put a serving spoon by each dish.
- Place complementary dishes in groups. Entrée with nearby sauces, vegetables, relishes, etc. Dressings close to salad bowl. Bread and rolls next to butter (in convenient pats) and cheese board.
- If you're feeding a real crowd, think about duplicating dishes — two salads, two entrées, etc. — on separate tables. Or on both sides of a long table. It'll keep the line moving faster.
- Serve clear soups in a pitcher, with a stack of mugs. Chunky soups should be served from a tureen with a ladle.
- If possible, set out desserts and coffee on a separate table. Even in another room.
- Have someone on hand to remove used plates, replenish empty dishes and take immediate care of spills.
- Always use a tablecloth on your buffet serving table because it is going to need all the protection it can get. Especially from spills. Use white or coloured cloth, just so long as it's washable. To help soak up liquid spills before they reach the table, use a felt undercloth if you have one. If not, a folded sheet.

Useful Extras For Easier Entertaining

If you don't already own them, you may consider borrowing some of these for your party. Remember this list, too, next time anyone asks what you want for your birthday!

- Electric table heater, to keep dishes warm.
- Electric 12 to 36-cup coffeemaker.
- A set of small nesting ash trays (individual size).
- Individual salt and pepper containers.
- Giant pepper mills.
- Decorative trays.
- Coasters (you can't have too many).
- Trivets (brass, iron, silver, tile, possibly electrically heated) to go under hot dishes.
- Wooden or wicker bun servers.
- Wooden boards for cheese, coffee cake, special breads.
- Large, unusual serving plates.
- Coffee mugs (use them also for nose-warmers such as hot bouillon, madrilene).
- Salad bowls.
- Wooden scissor-type salad servers — one-handed gadgets, useful for buffets.

- Chafing dishes, fondue pots and burners.
- Serving stands with warming candles or Sterno.
- Serving cart — invaluable for round-the-fire entertaining and all types of parties.

The Center of Attraction

Focal point of your dinner, lunch or brunch table will be the centerpiece. For a buffet though, a lavish and colourful array of food may be all the decoration you need.

What you use for table decoration, of course, depends on your budget, the season, your imagination, talent and taste. But whatever you order from the florist or create yourself, do take the scale of the centerpiece into account — as well as the colour scheme.

A high-rise arrangement of gladioli and greenery will look glorious — in the hallway. Your guests won't be able to see each other across the table if you use it as a centerpiece. By the same token, dainty thimble-sized flower arrangements may be perfect for trays or card tables. Put them on the average dining table and they'll be swamped by the salt and pepper shakers.

If you've got party-going candlesticks, maybe they're all the decoration you need. If you feel they could be more festive, festoon them with ivy. (Let cut ivy stand for several hours in water before using it.)

For a brunch or patio luncheon, use a pot of growing plants for a change. Different coloured African violets, geraniums, a small azalea bush will look charming with informal cottage-style table linen — in their (well-scrubbed) red clay pots, set on colourful saucers.

Don't be afraid to combine artificial flowers with live greenery. And vice versa. Those first, so very welcome spring daffodils look even better arranged with fat, glossy green artificial leaves. A shallow basket of wintergreen becomes quite summery with a few well-chosen, good quality artificial blooms. A word of caution. There are very good and very bad artificial flowers and leaves. Use only the best and most realistic you can find.

Utilize your house-plants, if you don't want to spend too much on table decorations. A small, healthy pot of heart-leafed philodendron — one that trails attractively — can be set in a pottery or silver bowl in the center of your table. Add some tiny artificial flowers, put a candestick at each side and you have something quite original.

English ivy is just as co-operative. Any old ivy, come to that.

Cut some at the last minute and use it to garnish a bowlful of fresh, washed and highly-polished fruit. A pineapple, bananas, red apples, lemons, limes, plums — whatever is available. Arranged in a bowl, you have a colourful centrepiece. And an extra course.

Have you ever thought of making an informal party decoration from fresh vegetables? Not onions, of course. But red and green peppers, tomatoes, squash, corn cobs, artichoke all look beautiful arranged on wood, a cheese board or in a wicker basket.

Please Be Seated

Formal or informal, one thing never changes when you are entertaining around a table. The host always sits at the head of the table, and the hostess at the foot. Or opposite each other, if it's a round table.

You've got a guest of honour? Male VIP's sit to the left of the hostess, females to the right of the host.

As for the rest of the guests: separate the married couples and arrange the seating so the sexes alternate around the table.

How About Place Cards?

They're optional. And like so many other aspects of party-giving, they depend on the kind and size of your party and the people who are coming.

If you're giving a dinner for eight people or more that you don't know too well, perhaps you might consider it.

- Use plain, unadorned white board cards. Fold them neatly in half.
- On one half write the guest's name and title (Mr. Guest), or
- If you've got two Mr. Guests at the table, his title, given name and surname (Mr. Simon Guest).
- Place each folded card above the center plate in the place setting.

At informal parties, place cards are mostly for fun, for extra decoration, and to carry through the theme of the party. In that case, you can let your imagination take over — and you don't have to be at all formal about writing in the names.

Some Thoughts On Serving

One very good reason for the popularity of buffet-style entertaining is that it does away with all the worry about getting the food from serving platter to plate, without breaking a lot of unwritten rules. Actually, serving at the table can be done easily and efficiently, with a minimum of fuss. So let's see how you fill plates and get rid of them — gracefully. Starting with the easiest kind of party.

For informal service, you have two options.

1. Platters and plates are put in front of the host or hostess, who fills each plate and passes it to the guest. Vegetable dishes are circulated around the table. Salad, mixed by the server (preferably a moment before guests are called to the table) can be passed before, during or after the entrée, depending on the menu. When the course is finished, the hostess (if there's no help around) quickly and quietly removes the plates and dishes to the kitchen and produces necessary dishes for the next course.
2. If you have a buffet or sideboard, use it to keep the entrée and all the trimmings (including plates) hot, while the first course is under way. When the soup plates have been cleared, invite guests — starting with the female guest of honour and other ladies — to step up and help themselves. The hostess still has the job of getting the used paraphernalia unobtrusively into the kitchen.

Whether food is served at the table or at the sideboard, it's always Ladies First. Then the male guests, the hostess and finally the host.

So far, so good. Now, what about the kind of dinner party where the service must be immaculate? And where there are too many people for the hostess to cope on her own. (The general rule is that for six or more guests, it's better to have some help.)

We've discussed all this earlier on. Your only real problem, if you've hired non-professional waiting help, is to make sure they put on a reasonably professional show.

Explain that:

- The idea, in theory, is never to allow a place setting to be without a plate. As a used one is removed with the right hand, the plate for the next course is put down with the left.
- Food is offered to each guest from his or her left side. For the simple reason that most people, being right-handed, find it easier to help themselves from this side.
- The woman on the host's right is served first.
- After that, service continues counter-clockwise around the table, till the host is served last.
- Serving dishes are never placed on the table.
- The table is cleared of all plates before dessert is served.

Having told your waiter/waitress all that, put them through their paces, until the service goes smoothly and confidently.

A willing but inexperienced waiter might well find the first point (removing a used plate and replacing it with a clean one) a little too much to handle. In which case, it is perfectly proper to have all the used plates removed — taking one in the left hand and one in the right — before placing clean ones.

Can You Carve?

This is often a worrying area. And, just like the art of flambé-ing, carving should be practised in private before being performed in public.

The tools: a very sharp, very sturdy carving knife; a sharpening steel, to keep it that way; a two-tined carving fork, with guard. And some self-confidence.

The secret is to know your meat. Know where the bones are, so you can avoid them. Know which way the grain goes. If you slice across the fibres, you will increase the tenderness.

And here's a word to the wise. All meat is much easier to carve if it's cool. So let a roast or a bird stand for about ten minutes before getting at it. Serve it on hot plates, with piping hot sauce or gravy and nobody will know the difference.

HOW TO ENJOY YOUR OWN PARTY 8

This is it! All the hard work has been done and everything is ready right down to the coat-and-overshoe-leaving arrangements and the supply of fancy guest towels in your fresh, shining bathroom.

The bar is set out. Kitchen activities are under control. The puppy has gone to spend the evening with friends. And you've spotted and hastily removed the candy dishes that somehow got into the party room. (Candy before dinner? What a horrible thought!)

It's now two hours to party-time. So will you please go and take a nap? If you won't do that, at least stretch out and relax for an hour. Then you can dress at leisure, make a last-minute kitchen check, and be relaxed and ready for action when the door bell rings.

Greeting Your Guests

If you can, appoint an official door-opener. Someone to take and dispose of coats and boots. To show ladies where they can freshen up before making their appearance in the party room.

As guests arrive, greet them warmly, make the introductions, then offer them a drink.

If there is a guest of honour, other guests must all meet him or her, since this is the point of the whole party. If you are entertaining a dozen or so, make sure everyone meets everyone else. If it's a large crowd, take each newly-arrived guest to the nearest conversational group — or to a group that you are sure he'd enjoy.

"I'd Like You to Meet . . ."

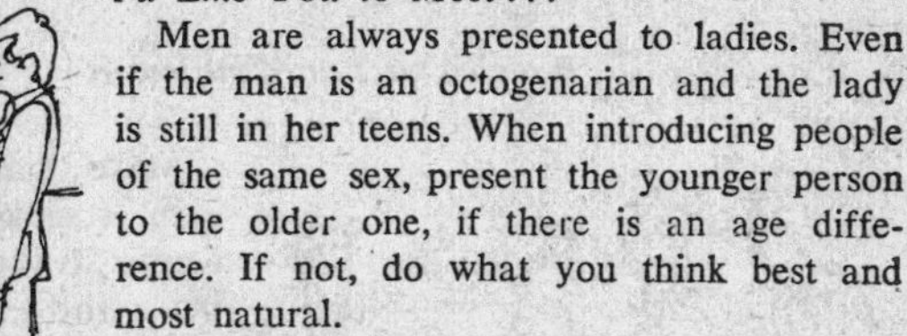

Men are always presented to ladies. Even if the man is an octogenarian and the lady is still in her teens. When introducing people of the same sex, present the younger person to the older one, if there is an age difference. If not, do what you think best and most natural.

Wherever possible, don't just introduce one person to another. Add a few pertinent words to start them off on a conversation. If you know they have something in common, mention it —

without launching into biographies. If you're introducing one person to a group, don't rattle names off and confuse the newcomer completely. Take it slowly, so the names sink in. Some people have great difficulty in remembering names at the best of times.

The Party Structure

Almost all parties fall quite neatly into three sections.

1. The pre-dinner (lunch/supper) drinks or cocktail hour. Which, as far as you're concerned, is an hour and a half, because you've allowed for late arrivals.
2. The dinner/luncheon/supper — which should not be hurried. Nobody has a train to catch, so relax and allow everyone to enjoy your good food.
3. The post-dinner activities. Which, in the case of a small group, could be something as pleasantly simple as sitting around the fire enjoying good conversation with coffee and liqueurs. With larger parties, this may mean planned activities such as dancing or games, depending on the type, theme and purpose.

The host or hostess's job, from start to finish, is to keep everything going smoothly and make sure everyone enjoys themselves.

Keep People Circulating

Not at breakneck speed, of course. But watch out for self-contained groups and mix them up, after a decent interval, by introducing some new people. Or by marching one or two members off to meet other guests.

Watch Out For Wallflowers

Make sure nobody is ever standing or sitting alone. If you're introducing a shy guest to an individual or group, don't leave until he or she is properly included in the conversation.

Keep An Eye On Extroverts

Some of one's best friends can come on quite strong, given the chance. If you notice a glazed look come over a group, remove the offender to the other end of the room.

Be Brave About Accidents

Occasionally, a drink may be spilled. People may drop ash on your precious Persian rug. Fix that smile firmly on your face and say, convincingly, that it couldn't matter less. If you wring your hands or dash around with mops, you'll make everyone uncomfortable. Anyway, which is more important — people or things?

Listen

As well as talk. It's your responsibility to see that the conversation never gets too heated or too boring. That your guests' feelings are not hurt.

- Unless you're very sure of everyone's opinions and reactions, steer away from political or religious arguments.
- Try to discourage talk about mutual friends, who are not present. It tends to get "catty."
- Spread yourself. Take care not to spend too long with any one guest or group of guests.
- Don't indulge in "in" conversations with some of the guests. The others will feel very left out.
- Go easy on "I" and "we." Concentrate on the subject of "you."
- Your children, pets and ailments may fascinate you, but others may not be so interested.
- Have some stand-by topics at the back of your mind — a new book, some current news item — to produce when the conversation obviously needs changing.
- Try to avoid the party breaking up into male and female groups.

Be Alert

Keep your antennae in good working order, so you can pick up warning signals.

As we've mentioned before, in spite of your homework, there is always the chance that you have guessed wrong about the people you're entertaining. The two couples you were so sure would get along beautifully may turn out to have only one thing in common: mutual dislike.

This is awkward. But if you sense it before everyone else does, you can rescue your party from potential disaster.

First Aid For Flagging Parties

If you have no planned activities or entertainment, something as simple as a change in the background music might do the trick. Perhaps you can roll back the carpet and dance.

Then, of course, there are games — such as charades — which have made quite a comeback on the party scene recently, particularly at small gatherings.

Jig Saws . . .

are a current craze. If you have a really challenging one — like the new reversible circular or modern art varieties — this might be the moment to produce it. But insist on a time limit. Otherwise you could wind up cooking breakfast for everybody.

Card Games . . .

It's always wise to keep some fresh decks on hand, for just this kind of emergency. Consider bridge, poker (for chips only), gin rummy, cribbage.

Board Games . . .

if you have them around. The old favourites like Scrabble, Monopoly (the short version) or one of the new and popular Battle games. Think twice before producing a roulette board or portable crap table. Are there any high-rollers present? Gambling for fun is one thing. But you don't want anyone to take this too seriously — or any of your guests to go home with empty pockets.

Pencil-and-Paper Games...

Anagram, Categories, Alphabet.

Word Games...

Like Charades, Twenty-Questions and Rigamarole.

You might, of course, have a basement already equipped with party-savers such as table-tennis, darts or billiards.

In which case, move everyone down there.

It's Been Fun

When the first guests start to make homeward-going signs, by all means express your regret. But don't press them to stay, even if they seem to be leaving early. It doesn't mean they haven't enjoyed your party. They've got their own reasons for leaving.

Tell them how much you have enjoyed their company, help them with coats and see them to the front door. If your home is an apartment, it is mannerly to escort guests to the elevator. If it's a house, remain by the door until they are off the premises.

Sometimes the first departure will start a general exodus. If you feel the affair has gone on long enough, just let it happen.

Sometimes, however, people won't budge, even though you are out on your feet and stifling yawns. One host swears that when this happens, he suggests showing home movies. "Clears the house in no time," he says. Another makes a point of offering final nightcaps, with polite emphasis on the final. Another couple have a good working arrangement with their dog, who miraculously appears demanding walks, just when everyone seems to have settled down for the night.

Short of announcing that you're going to bed, probably the most graceful way to handle this situation is to have a quick, confidential word with the guest you know best, and beg him or her to make a conspicuous exit. Hopefully, the others will get the message.

Another word of warning. When you've heaved a sigh of relief — don't crawl straight to bed.

Sit for a few minutes, relax and reflect on the evening. On the fun your party has given your guests and yourself. Everything went well, didn't it? Then take a little time to congratulate yourself.

Besides, guests have been known to reappear to collect something they've left behind — and you wouldn't want to greet them in night-gear!

Dealing With The Debris

Faced with that mountain of dishes, glasses, silverware, dirty ashtrays and half-nibbled canapés, you probably wish you'd allocated some of the party budget to hiring kitchen help. Or making the down-payment on an automatic dishwasher.

Never mind, you'll know better next time.

Now for the all-important question. Is it better to get it all cleaned up now, while every bone in your body is aching for bed — or leave the whole mess till the morning? It's up to you.

However, there are three things that you must do, right now.

Make sure that:

- All perishable foods are safely placed in the refrigerator.
- Liquor bottles are properly stoppered, to prevent evaporation.
- Nobody has left a burning cigarette in an ashtray or anywhere else. Check this carefully, for obvious reasons.

While you're checking these points, light two or three fresh candles in each party room, to clear the air of stale smoke. Open a few windows, weather permitting, to freshen the place.

If you have the energy, it really is better to do as much clearing up as possible before you turn in for what's left of the night. The morning will be more pleasant that way.

Glasses should be rinsed now. The sticky residue will be much harder to remove tomorrow. The same applies to silverware. China? You could stretch a point and leave that in a sinkful of soapy water. But having got this far, you might just as well finish the job.

Sling all soiled linen in the laundry hamper and think about that later. But if one of your precious items — tablecloths, napkins, etc., has been stained, now is the time to soak it in clear, cold water until you are ready for the wash. Move any floral arrangements into a cool spot, to let them recover from the warm, smoky atmosphere. Tomorrow, you can snip the stems of cut flowers, change the water, add a pinch of sugar to it — and enjoy your party flowers for days.

9 DROP-OF-THE-HAT HOSTING

Some of the very best parties are not planned at all. They just happen.

People drop in. Or don't go home. Or phone to say they're passing through town. How do you handle this kind of impromptu entertaining — say, on a Sunday, when there's not one store open?

Easily.

The secret is to have squirrelled away some basic supplies for just such a spur-of-the-moment occasion. With emergency food, drink and accessories on hand, you can entertain instantly. Replenish your stocks as soon as possible after one party, and you're all set for the next.

There is usually a seven-day store open somewhere reasonably close. Memorize its location. But keep in mind that these stores frequently do not have as wide a selection of grocery items as does your regular store.

Instant Party Props

Keep one corner of a cupboard for these, so you can set an attractive and informal table at a moment's notice. (If you unearth the best china and start polishing the sterling, your drop-of-the-hat guests will get the uncomfortable feeling that you're going to too much trouble.)

Useful accessories might include:

- A large paper tablecloth, with matching napkins.
- Place mats, coasters — also of paper.
- Attractive, inexpensive glasses.
- Plastic flowers, kept clean in plastic bags.
- Two or three colourful flower containers.
- Pottery candlesticks.
- Coloured candles.
- Baskets for hot bread or biscuits.
- Plain white paper napkins, to line baskets.
- Salad bowl, with servers.
- Supply of large plastic-coated paper plates, for instant patio parties.

Use these with everyday china and flatware, and you can produce a festive table in minutes. What you serve on it, of course, will depend on what you have tucked away in your emergency stores.

Instant Party Fare

(See the recipe section under the heading "Brunch Dishes" for many of the dishes listed below.)

There's no way of knowing what you consider to be a well-stocked store cupboard, freezer or refrigerator. Everyone has their own idea about that.

But it's a good idea to keep the ingredients for at least one main party dish and one party dessert on hand at all times. Enough, maybe, to serve six extra people. Plus canapés or canapé ingredients, and a supply of serving-stretchers such as noodles, biscuit mix, rice and ready-to-heat rolls.

Anyone with a freezer or ample freezing space in a refrigerator has no real problem in producing a meal in short order. If you have to rely mainly on dry stores and canned goods, Paella makes a good party dish. For an impromptu brunch, how about Clam Cakes and Bacon? With fresh eggs and a package of English muffins in the refrigerator, Eggs Benedict Arnold makes a great supper.

Quick Tricks

- A can of cream of chicken soup mixed with a can of pea soup, a can of milk and a dash of curry powder. Very tasty, topped with a dollop of whipped cream.
- Instant bouillabaisse: one can of crab soup, plus a can of Shrimp Creole (shrimp in rich tomato sauce). Serve with sliced garlic-buttered French bread, warmed in foil.
- Stretch a salad by adding canned or cooked vegetables (peas, beans, carrots, beets) drained and marinated in a mixture of oil, vinegar, seasoning and onion slices.
- If all you have on hand are eggs and some Camembert, Eggs Normandie are something special. See page 89.
- For dessert: soften vanilla ice cream, sprinkle lavishly with powdered cinnamon, whip and refreeze.
- Jamaican Orange: peel seedless oranges, separate into sections. Sprinkle with brown sugar, light rum and a dash of cinnamon. Chill before serving.
- Raspberry Freeze: blend a package of frozen raspberries with a small can of evaporated milk and 1 thin lemon slice. When smooth, pour into tray and freeze.

- Fresh blueberries served in half a cantaloupe, sprinkled with 2 tbsp. Grenadine and chilled — delicious!

If You're Really Caught Short...

with only a clutch of eggs in the fridge and some oddments in the cupboard, you can still put on a good drop-of-the-hat show. Provided, of course, that your oddments include staples like bread, butter, milk, cheese and bacon as well as salad ingredients, mushrooms and so on.

With six eggs and some left-over mashed potato, you can serve Eggs Parmentier. See page 90.

With three large potatoes, some grated cheese and a little cream, you can turn those six eggs into Eggs Boulangère (page 89). Add a salad and you're in business.

Or you can whip up a Spanish Omelette if you can rustle up onions, red and green peppers, tomatoes or tomato paste, mushrooms and parsley.

However, if you're seriously trying to feed six people on only three eggs, then you're in a certain amount of trouble.

If nobody suggests sending out for pizza, then your best bet is probably to scramble them (using as much cream or milk as you can decently incorporate) and add whatever you can find in the way of cubed ham, crumbled bacon, grated cheese, etc. Serve defiantly on buttered toast or muffin halves, garnish with parsley — and promise yourself you'll never be caught quite so short again!

PART II

ENTERTAINING IDEAS

How about making your next party a little different? It takes a little more thought in planning and preparation, but after all, isn't that half the fun? It gives you a chance to be a little creative and gives your guests an added feeling of anticipation.

On the following pages, you'll find some thoughts on 27 different kinds of parties:

Après-Ski Party
Autumn Picnic
Barn Dance
Before-and-After Party
Caribbean Caper
Cocktail Party
Costume Party
Dinner for the Boss
Fondue Fun
Grey Cup Brunch
Happy Anniversary
Happy Birthday
Hawaiian Luau
Housewarming Luncheon
Italian Carnival
La Vie Parisienne
Mardi Gras
Mexican Fiesta
Patio Supper
Round-the-World Party
Scavenger Hunt
Showers
Stag Night
Surprise Party
Treasure Hunt
TV Night
Wine-and-Cheese Party

You'll find detailed recipes for food and drinks discussed in Parts III and IV.

Of course, no one is expected to serve all the dishes and drinks mentioned with each party. They are simply shown as suggestions.

APRES-SKI

Whether it's held in your own home or the winter chalet, a quiet, cosy après-ski party is the perfect finale to an energetic day on the slopes or, for that matter, to any kind of outdoor winter activity. It's an early affair. Ask guests for 6 p.m. and they'll probably start drifting home by 10:30.

Basic essentials: a roaring fire and someone to provide sing-along music on the guitar, piano or harmonica.

Hearty food, simply served, is what is called for, and if most of it can be prepared the day before, so much the better. (See also "Before-and-After" party suggestions.)

Suggested dishes: Beef with Dumplings, Belgian Salad, cheese, crackers, fresh fruit and coffee.

To drink: Café Royale, Gluehwein, Hot Buttered Rum, Toddy, Tom & Jerry.

AUTUMN PICNIC

Do you live among, or within driving distance of the annual spectacular of the changing leaves? Gather some friends and camera equipment, pack up a picnic and take off for the day. Or invite people to your summer cottage just before closing it for the winter.

Weather could be nippy, so a hot casserole might be considered. Wrap it in several layers of newspaper and carry in an insulated bag. Take a ready-dressed salad in screw-top jar or covered plastic box; relishes in the same kind of container. A homemade cake travels well if it's left in the baking pan. Hot and cold liquids stay that way in thermos flasks — and the whole meal can easily be prepared at home and packed in a minute.

Suggested dishes: Ice-cold Borscht, Chicken Tang or Chile Con Carne with Tomato and Onion Salad, Poppy Seed Rolls, cake and coffee.

To drink: Collins, Gluehwein, King's Apple, Sour, Tom & Jerry.

BARN DANCE

For the basement only, unless you have a real barn. Remove everything moveable, except the bar. Dress the room with pumpkins, gourds, automn leaves, rakes and brooms — anything remotely rustic. Decorate walls with (homemade, if necessary) auction, plowing match, cattle sale posters. Create an illusion of timbered beams by stretching crêpe paper across the ceiling; or from ceiling center, to form and archway. Light with old-fashioned lanterns hung high. (Inexpensive reproductions of the old originals can now be found in hardwares). Better still, modern replicas with light bulbs are also available.

Have guests come in denims and peasant skirts and blouses. Provide straw hats as party favours. Try to include a caller (professional or amateur) on your guest list. Otherwise, learn to do it yourself. If all else fails, there are barn dance records available, complete with instructions. Invite a fiddler, if you can.

Check radio stations for country-and-western programs for ready-made background music. Tapes or records fill in the gaps. You could also provide song sheets, so the party can switch from dancing to a sing-along.

Use sturdy trestle or picnic tables covered with checked gingham to serve plenty of rib-sticking country-style food.

Suggested dishes: Baked ham, cold fried chicken with homemade relishes, hot buttered corn muffins, coleslaw, Kidney Bear. Salad, fruit pies, cakes of all kinds.

To drink: Screwdriver, Collins, Salty Dog, Clover Club and Clover Leaf, Orange Blossom.

BEFORE-AND-AFTER

Before and after what? It depends on the time of year. But a real fun party is the one which includes an outside activity. Like going to the ball game, out bicycling, for a hay ride, or horseback riding. Everyone congregates at your place for drinks and a snack before setting off. Then again later, for a relaxed informal supper.

Though this sounds like a lot of work, it's easy enough if you plan a menu that only keeps you in the kitchen for 15-20 minutes on your return.

Serve quite substantial hors d'oeuvres with your initial drinks. It'll be several hours to supper. Have a buffet table all prepared; cold food all arranged on platters and waiting in the refrigerator. Maybe a pan of soup ready for final heating.

After all that fresh air (particularly if the weather's nippy), you'll probably be in the mood for something hot and tasty. Steaming bowls of Senegal Soup can be served in a moment. While that is going on, heat up an apple pie and whip up some Amber Cream for dessert. The decision as to what to drink is entirely up to you — it depends on the season, and what the party is before or after. But pre-mixed Collins, Gimlets and Screwdrivers never go wrong.

CARIBBEAN CAPER

Just the thing for a cold Canadian winter! After an interlude of rum punches and Calypso music, spring will seem just around the corner.

Basic decorations are very much like those for a Luau, except for the long, low, green-strewn table, which is strictly Polynesian. Arrange food on a regular table, with flowers and fruit for added colour. Use yellow light bulbs to give a sunny effect.

Music is a big part of the fun. Steel band records (have mercy on the neighbours and play them early in the evening), calypsos,

Belafonte, the Merrymen — the selection is great. Be sure to include some limbo music and provide a length of rope or bamboo pole, so everyone can try this musical contortion.

Suggested dishes: If you want to include some genuine Caribbean recipes, there's Cayman Lobster and Chicken Cashew, which are hot. Banana Meringue is a favourite island dessert.

To drink: Collins, Mariner's Grog, Morgan Punch, Mai Tai, Daiquiri.

COCKTAIL PARTY

Invitations for a straightforward cocktail party (no theme, no special decorations, no entertainment or activities other than drinking, nibbling and being sociable) should go out at least two weeks in advance. If you want the party to finish by a certain time, say so: "Cocktails 6-8 p.m."

Depending on the size of the party and your room, either remove all extra furniture so there is space to move about, or add more, so that everyone can sit. You'll need plenty of ashtrays, unspoilable surfaces for drinks, small cocktail serviettes, books of matches or table lighters. Be sure that flowers are placed where they won't get knocked over. Background music, if any, should be low enough not to drown out the conversation.

For helpers, you'll need someone to greet guests at the door, deal with their coats, show them into the party room. Helpers to remove empty glasses, have them washed in the kitchen and returned to circulation. Someone to serve drinks, of course. Plus people to pass canapés.

As for the smooth running of your party, most of the remarks under the heading "How to Enjoy Your Own Party," Part I, Chapter Eight, apply here.

COSTUME PARTY

If you thought only kids enjoyed dressing up, organize a costume party and prove yourself wrong! Some ideas to work on: Historical Characters, Famous Movie Stars, Fathers (and Mothers) of Confederation, Literary Characters, Book Titles, That Wonderful Year, Colourful Canadians . . .

A party ice-breaker, along with the drinks, is guessing who or what guests represent — award prizes for the best score.

This would be the evening for dancing or games, since everyone is in a frivolous frame of mind.

Suggested dishes: Set up a Scandinavian Smorgasbord in a separate room. Dishes could include herring (smoked, pickled or marinated, in sour cream or in tomato, wine or dill sauce); potato salad; cold cuts or sliced rare roast beef, tongue, chicken, ham, salami; thinly sliced smoked salmon with lemon slices; sardines; shrimp (small ones); anchovies with capers; coleslaw; pickled beets; a hot casserole of Swedish Meatballs; rye, pumpernickel bread; Norwegian crispbreads; sweet butter and a selection of cheese and fresh fruit.

To drink: Sour, Old Fashioned, Ward "8", On the Rocks, or something to suit the occasion such as a Habitant, Mariner's Grog, etc.

For a more elegant costume party, make it a . . .

MARDI GRAS

Staged traditionally on Shrove Tuesday (Pancake Day) and featuring famous Creole cooking. Guests should wear masks, as well as the most fanciful costumes they can devise.

For decoration: balloons everywhere, even as a buffet centerpiece. Colourful paper streamers too — as much glitter and sparkle as possible.

If you wish, you could take liberties with the calendar and hold this type of party on New Year's Eve.

For a beautiful table, cover it with two contrasting layers of pastel theatrical gauze: green over blue, or mauve over pink. Pick one of the two colours for napkins. Have a silver bowl as centerpiece, fill it with silvery baubles and noisemakers.

Among Mardi Gras supper dishes, you could include Shrimp Creole and Champagne Carnival Cups, Finish with an exotic coffee. And for such a festive occasion, festive drinks are in order: Champagne Punch, French "75", French Rose, Alexander, Fizz, Stinger.

DINNER FOR THE BOSS

The secret of a successful evening is to plan a menu that leaves you free to spend as much pre-dinner time as possible with your guests. If you're constantly making forays into the kitchen, it will make you appear nervous.

How about a cold soup? Say, chilled Salmon Bisque. Followed by Highland Chicken with frozen puff potatoes and Peas in Lettuce. A Mimosa Salad and Frozen Lime Foam will create a beautiful impression on your guests. Soup and dessert can be prepared earlier in the day. The chicken only needs last-minute attention, as does the salad. It's an elegant meal and easy to coordinate. As for drinks, stay simple and elegant, and make sure you know the boss's favourite. It will probably be a Boodles British Gin Dry Martini, Black Watch Scotch or Seagram's Crown Royal. And don't forget a bottle of B&G Wine with the meal. May we suggest B&G Medoc (red); or B&G Chablis or B&G Graves (white).

FONDUE FUN

If there are a dozen of you, set up three separate tables, each with a washable or expendable cloth; the fondue pot in the middle, with a tray underneath to catch dribbles and spills, and a communal breadbasket for cheese fondues; a platter of beef cubes, seafood etc., and an easy-to-reach selection of sauces and condiments for bourguignons. Give each person a plate and a long wooden-handled fondue fork. Remember the danger of burning (see page 40) and set an extra fork for each guest. Provide the largest paper or linen napkins you can find.

Check that you have enough fuel, if you're not using electric pots. Keep a spare fuel container on hand. Be sure the flames are out of drafts or direct breezes. You can only depend on candlepower for the dessert dips that can be maintained at low heat. Cooking oil or bouillon must be kept piping hot in their pots.

You could serve a cheesy Fondue Neuchateloise at one table, Fondue Boeuf Bourguignon at another and Deep Sea Fondue at the third. Let guests pick their own menu. Or table-hop.

With Fondue Neuchateloise serve: crusty French bread, cooked cocktail franks, tiny meat balls for dunking.

Boeuf Bourguignon: ¾" to 1" cubes of steak (trimmed, patted dry with paper towels) are cooked in hot peanut oil, to which a teaspoon of salt has been added to prevent splattering. Allow ½ lb. prepared meat per person. Alternative or additional dunkers: pork, lamb, ham, veal, chicken pieces, frankfurter chunks, meat balls. Serve with sauces (see recipe section), relishes, pickled mushrooms, onion rings, etc.

Deep Sea Fondue: a tangy fish bouillon in which is cooked individual portions of scallops (cut into thirds), lobster chunks, shrimps, small strips of fillet of sole. Offer a batter, lemon wedges, seafood sauces.

It takes practice and a heap of equipment to serve a complete fondue meal from appetizers to dessert. If this is your first effort, you'd probably be wise to follow it with a simple dessert from the refrigerator. Again, the choice of pre-dinner drinks is yours, but they should be simple and not too sweet — Highballs, Sours, Fizzes, Martinis, Manhattans — and of course a good dry red (beef) or white (cheese, seafood) wine with the fondue. Chemineaud Brandy and coffee go particularly well after this enjoyable meal.

GREY CUP BRUNCH

If you have the kind of kitchen that can take a crowd, a come-and-get-it brunch is the best way to feed Grey Cup guests. Alternatively, round up all the hot plates you can find and serve food within easy reach of the TV set.

Keep it as informal as you can. With plenty of your best breakfast coffee, a selection of interesting hot breads (muffins, scones, brioches, croissants), crocks of sweet butter and preserves.

Fruit juice, Screwdrivers and Bloody Marys all look more exciting served from a big pitcher nestling in an ice-bucket. If omelettes are your specialty, prepare a selection of fillings (bacon and mushroom, grated cheddar cheese, western mix, chopped ham, tomatoes, jelly, chicken livers, etc.) and cook them up to order.

For those who like their fruit with a kick to it, prepare Cantaloupe King Arthur. Main dishes might include: Kedgeree, Corned Beef Hash, Orange French Toast with maple syrup — as large and hearty a menu as you can manage.

Incidentally, a brunch is a great way to say **Bon Voyage** to a vacationing friend. Decorations to suit his or her destination. Pack tiny, inexpensive gifts (address book, travelling clothes line with pegs, tissues, road maps, aspirins, first aid kit) into a toy trunk covered with hotel and airline stickers.

For brunch drinks: Fizz, Bloody Mary, Salty Dog, Screwdriver, Bull Shooter, Red Snapper, Rickey.

HAPPY ANNIVERSARY

Your parents are celebrating their wedding anniversary? If you're planning an intimate family dinner, you could invite friends and well-wishers afterwards for Dessert-and-Coffee. Say around 8:00 p.m.

Decorations, colour scheme and trimmings will naturally tie in with the anniversary symbol. Make the party as pretty as possible; with flowers, candlelight, ribbons and bells. Before sending invitations (two to three weeks ahead of time) you would, of course, discuss the guest list with the guests of honour.

Extra touches: have a guest book, which everyone signs. And a roving photographer (amateur or professional) taking candid shots. When it's all over, paste in the pictures and present the book as a memento. Arrange for live or recorded music for the evening from the year the couple were married.

Highlight will obviously be the Anniversary Cake and the Toast. Unless the cake is to be homemade, order it well in advance of the party. Among your selection of desserts, you might include ice cream in a meringue shell topped with Crème de Menthe or crème de Café, Chocolate Mousse Supreme and fresh fruit salad.

To drink: Mumm Extra Dry Champagne, of course.

HAPPY BIRTHDAY

Why should children have all the fun? Arrange a birthday party for an adult and take as the theme the appropriate sign of the zodiac. It's much more tactful than mentioning age!

Brief the guests about the guest of honour's tastes, hobbies, interests. Insist that nobody spends more than a small set amount on the gift. Or you could make it "gag-gifts" only. Put all the packages in a presentation container: a big bowl, basket, or even a decorated waste paper basket.

As for the menu, this would certainly be made up of the guest of honour's favourite dishes. And the evening's activities, too, will be his or her choice. Maybe bridge. That big game on TV. Or just sitting around with a drink or two and chatting.

For the birthday boy or girl who has outgrown the taste for iced cake, offer decorated Cheescake de Luxe, or a Birthday Baked Alaska.

To drink: Champagne for the toast, and perhaps a festive Champagne Punch along with the guest of honour's favourite.

To Organize A Surprise Party

Keep the guest list to special friends (this is not the time to repay any social obligations) and telephone the invitations.

If the party is for a member of the family, you'll have to devise some way of keeping him or her out of the house until everyone is assembled. If it's for a neighbour or friend, issue his or her invitation for a good half-hour after everyone else.

HAWAIIAN LUAU

Fun for the beach, backyard or basement. Polynesian props include: paper "grass" mats, candles burning in hollowed-out pineapples or in those bamboo-and-glass hanging patio holders that are available everywhere. Decorated fish nets, shells, crêpe paper palm fronds, glass fishing balls, beachcomber hats, grass skirts, all the flowers and big green leaves you can raise. Plus, or course, paper leis for your muumuu-ed and tropical-shirted guests.

Spread a long, low table (boards over a stack of blankets or newspapers) with green crêpe paper or burlap. Cover with shiny green leaves, fruit and flowers, candles. Background music can be genuine island hula and folk songs or the more commercial kind. Have a hula record: "Do the Hula" (Waikiki label). Don Ho is also popular.

Suggested dishes: Almond Chicken; Hawaiian Rice; green salad with avocado chunks; relishes in little dishes: chutneys, chopped egg and chive, sliced tomatoes with basil, sliced cucumber in yoghourt and dill, sliced bananas sprinkled with lime juice and brown sugar. For dessert: fresh fruit salad served in scooped-out pineapple shells. This is also a great time to use the mini-hibachis that are available. Soak the charcoal in wood alcohol (not mineral spirits or barbecue fuel), light, and while flame is burning, have guests cook such tempting tidbits as water chestnuts and chicken livers wrapped in bacon; miniature egg rolls; bits of marinated steak; fried won ton; finger-long strips of toast spread with ham and cheese and then dipped in an egg and bread-crumb mix; cocktail wieners and sausages, etc.

To drink: Collins, Morgan Punch, Mai Tai, Mariner's Grog, Daiquiri.

HOUSE-WARMING

An old-fashioned Open House Luncheon is one of the most convenient ways to warm your new home and show it off to friends. With a buffet spread and food that requires no knives or forks, you can cut work to a minimum and spend more time with your guests.

Add to your list of buffet dishes: Virginia Baked Ham, Puffed Chicken Salad, Cheese Biscuits and Coconut Pralines.

If you're wondering how to eat ham without a fork, this is the way it goes. Have one person carve paper-thin slices of ham and pass them along to a helper who cuts the slices into manageable bits and places them on split hot Cheese Biscuits. Guests then help themselves.

To drink: Highballs, Screwdriver, Martini, Manhattan.

ITALIAN CARNIVAL

This is an easy atmosphere to create, whether you're having an evening of opera-on-records or just a festive get-together.

For a true Italian colour scheme, pick red-white-and-green. Set small tables with the European-style checkered cloths, a wax-dripped straw-covered wine bottle holding a candle, a glassful of bread sticks. Arrange your supper on a buffet or sideboard and let guests help themselves. If it's to be a spaghetti supper, large bibs would be appreciated.

Start with Antipasto: small individual dishes of anchovies, sardines, pickled beets, eggplant, pimento, olives, sliced tomatoes, celery, sliced hard-cooked eggs, marinated artichoke hearts and lentils. Guests pick what they want and season with red wine vinegar and olive oil.

Other suggested dishes: Veal Scaloppine with green salad and that luscious Italian dessert — Zabaglione.

To drink: What Italian evening would be complete without Brolio Chianti Classico? Also perhaps Noilly Pratt Italian Vermouth Cocktails, and any of the drinks shown in Part IV with the sunny flavours of Leroux Apricot or Cherry Brandy.

LA VIE PARISIENNE

Invite your friends — en Français, s'il vous plait — to spend an evening in the Latin Quarter. Or at a sidewalk café. Or both.

If you keep your bar in the basement, it's easy enough to transform it into a Left Bank nightclub. Turn the lights down low, arrange check-clothed tables around a small dancing area. Decorate the bar with a striped red-white-and-blue canopy, the walls with posters of Paris landmarks or Toulouse-Lautrec illustrations. Build a typical Paris kiosk around a small round table using 1″ x 2″ pine struts wrapped with crêpe paper. If the table is small enough, the round top of one of those collapsible garden tables or an open umbrella can serve as the roof. Stick magazine covers in random fashion all round the crêpe paper walls.

If the party is outside, the small check-clothed tables, striped garden umbrellas and baskets of flowers will add atmosphere. A wandering accordionist is an extra attraction. As guests arrive (dressed the way they think Left Bankers look) hand each a sketch pad and crayons. Offers prizes for the best artistic efforts, the best Apache dancers, the best (or worst) dressed Parisians. Have plenty of French and Quebec music on discs or tapes.

Suggested dishes: French Onion Soup, Coq au Vin with parsley potatoes and tossed green salad, French bread, a fresh fruit sherbet.

To drink: French "75", Champagne Punch, Alexander, Débutante, and after the meal, Café Royale.

MEXICAN FIESTA

On the patio or indoors, depending on the season, a Mexican party is always in style. And with loads of that lilting Mexican music, it will be an evening to remember.

Red, orange and yellow are the dominant Mexican colours. If you can find a real sarape, or Mexican blanket, use it on your table. Look for tall wrought-iron candlesticks and red candles; big floppy Mexican paper flowers (These can be made from crêpe paper, or facial tissues); a sombrero, to turn upside-down and fill with polished fruit or red and green peppers; pottery dishes; big earthenware serving bowls. For some extra fun, try and get some of the many different types of Mexican rhythm instruments (maracas, castinets, etc.). Use them as part of your table decor and then later put on some Mexican music with a beat and let those guests so inspired add to the rhythm section.

Suggested dishes: Guacamole Salad. Chili con Carne with Tortillas (to sop up the juice) and a Caramel Flan (to put out the flames!).

To drink: Salty Dog, Fizz, Villeneuve Special, Gin and Tonic, Banana Daiquiri, Marguarita, and Tequila Sunrise.

PATIO SUPPER

Or a balcony supper, if you live in an apartment. The sort of elegant little meal that you cook in the kitchen and either wheel or carry outside. It may be eaten around a table, or in comfortable chairs from individual TV-tables. Coloured citronella candles add an attractive glow and keep marauding bugs away. Gentle background music and good conversation make for a delightful warm-weather occasion.

Suggested dishes: Gazpacho, Coquille St. Jacques, and Maple Mousse.

To drink: Collins, Rickey, Gin and Tonic, Martini, Rob Roy, Manhattan (all on the rocks), Highballs, Screwdriver, Stinger.

ROUND-THE-WORLD

Give your guests the best of all possible worlds — and an invitation in the form of a fake airline ticket to as many faraway places as you can stage in your party room.

Pick an exciting, easy-to-decorate, easy-to-cater itinerary. Set up your stopovers around the room, each with its characteristic decoration, food and drink. For background music, ring in the changes on a stack of records. Consult the current Schwann listing (under International Pop & Folk Music) or your local record library.

If you are serving a meal, you might want to spread it out among the various countries. Appetizers in one, entrée in another, and so on. Or offer one national meal, from soup to nuts, and just serve snacks at the other locations.

Here are some ideas to get you started.

Japan: Decorate with bamboo mats, crêpe paper cherry blossoms, low tables with single-flower arrangements. Make guests discard shoes, provide paper slippers. Cushions to sit on. Serve Tempura; Sukiyaki in bowls, with chopsticks; Mustard and Sweet-and-Sour sauce; Jasmine tea.

Arabia: Brass bowls, cushions to sit on, an Oriental rug tacked to the wall. Drape crêpe paper to create a tentlike effect. Serve Shish-Kebab with Pilaf, Marinated Eggplant, Cucumber in Yoghourt, dates, Turkish Coffee.

India: Copper or brass bowl of red, orange or yellow flowers. Indian print shawl or bedspread as a tablecloth. Leather hassocks, strings of brass bells, carved ivory elephants. Serve Curried Chicken with plain boiled rice; chutneys and dishes of grated coconut, chopped egg, crumbled crisp bacon, chopped green onions, banana slices, peanuts.

Scandinavia: Bright bold colours, sleek-lined furniture and tableware. Travel posters, Danish-style mobiles. Wooden or ironwork candlesticks on the table. Serve Smorrebrod sandwiches and a fresh fruit salad.

And so on, for all the countries that appeal to you.

SHOWERS

Though they are usually Bridal or Baby, a Shower may actually be given for any reason: going away, coming home, housewarming, birthday. This is almost always a strictly feminine affair. And since guests are required to bring a gift here are a few suggestions.

- Showers are always arranged by and for close friends, not members of the family.

- Whatever the theme, it should not oblige guests to bring expensive presents. You would not, for instance, arrange a Jewellery Shower.

- Guests can be asked to club together to buy one costly gift or a group of related gifts (kitchen, bathroom, etc.).

Provide an attractive and appropriate container for the gifts (a crib for a Baby Shower, a clothes hamper for a Bathroom Shower). Place the traditional and well-decorated open umbrella over the top. Have enough seats so all guests can sit for the gift-opening ceremony.

Whether it is a lunch or a supper, the meal and the decor should be appropriately feminine.

Suggested dishes: Shrimp Cocktail Dip, Jellied Chicken Salad, Herb Biscuits and a favourite dessert.

To drink: Sours; Gimlets; Leroux Crème de Menthe, Cherry Brandy or Triple Sec Frappés; Old Fashioneds.

STAG NIGHT

Mixed parties are fine, but now and then it is good to "get away from it all." This applies to the ladies as well as the men, and it is our observation that the fairer sex take more advantage of the opportunity than do their male counterparts (bridge marathons, bingo, good works activities, etc.).

Of course, many men do curl, play golf, bowl, etc. But if you are not inclined, or simply would enjoy a night of good fellowship with "the boys," why not consider planning a stag night? The evening's activities can revolve around poker, bridge, cribbage or just plain good conversation. It's also an ideal way to plan a hunting or fishing trip, or look at movies and slides of past adventures.

If this is a night for "men only" it is suggested the lady of the house hang around just long enough to dish up the main course — then make plans to get out and perhaps catch up on the current top-run movie.

For pre-party arrangements: forget anything fanciful in the way of decorations. Provide plenty of large ashtrays and coasters. Make the seating comfortable, the food and drink plentiful. Set out large bowls of potato chips, pretzels, peanuts and the like, and don't forget to have an ample store of ice on hand. Check your supply of mixers and make sure they are well chilled in advance. You'll probably want more club soda and ginger ale than usual. It's a good idea to put a couple of pitchers of water in the fridge as well.

You'll find additional suggestions that could also be used on a stag night in this section of the book, under the headings, "Grey Cup Brunch" and "TV Night."

Suggested dishes: Swiss Mozzarella Steak with French fries, a green salad with Mustard French Dressing, followed by Nesselrode Bavarian and coffee.

To drink: Make them men's drinks — simple and to the point. Martinis, On-the-Rocks, Highballs, Rickeys, Mists.

TREASURE HUNT

It takes some preparation and friends who are "young at heart," but the fun of a Treasure Hunt makes it well worth the effort. Arrange one for a fall weekend at the cottage, or for a long summer evening at home.

Hide "treasures" — small inexpensive gifts — at the end of a trail of clues. Then bend your brain to create tricky clues to lead (or mislead) the treasure-hunters. Rhyming couplets, if you can be that creative, and as many as you can manage. There may be a dozen clues, each carefully hidden, before the treasure is turned up. If you are playing this game in the house or in an area where teams can see what the others are doing, you'd best provide separate clues, hiding places and "treasures" for each team so that they each go their own separate ways. Pair everyone off, set a time limit and award an extra prize for the couple who brings the booty home first.

Another Fun variation Is a . . . Scavenger Hunt

Which doesn't require nearly so much hard work or brain power, and is the sort of game that can be played all around the neighbourhood, providing you know your neighbours, otherwise they might not appreciate it.

Hand your guests the list of things they must find — somehow, somewhere and without breaking the law. Make them as difficult as you can, but not impossible. A 1924 penny, one red shoe, and an old 78-rpm record. The trick is to list things which are out of date, unusual or hard to find.

The hunters will come back hungry after all that activity.

Suggested dishes: Old Thyme Pork Chops with baked potatoes and a mixed green salad and Fresh Lime Cream, which can be prepared in advance.

To drink: Something tall and easy — Screwdriver, Villeneuve Special, Collins, so everyone can help themselves whenever they are near "action central."

TV NIGHT

It's the day of the big game or perhaps it's election night and the gang's invited. Perhaps you'll want to rent that extra-large colour TV. Maybe a couple of them, if you have a large room and a crowd of guests. Don't bother with decorations — the action on the set's the thing! Arrange seating so everyone has an uninterrupted view. Make sure ashtrays are large and difficult to knock over, that there is plenty of space to put glasses, snacks within easy reach. Make a pool on the time and scorer of the winning point, or the total points, or the margin your new representative will win by, etc. and have an appropriate prize.

So that nobody has to tear themselves away from the screen, set food out on a buffet table. Provide trays, so guests can serve themselves and return to the action. Set out a stack of trays and have knives and forks rolled into colourful paper napkins, so no time is wasted picking out cutlery.

Suggested dishes: Ham Rolls au Gratin with buttered broccoli, Brandy Flan. Crab Soup can be easily made in less than five minutes. Serve it in mugs, with a spoon to catch the crabmeat. As for sandwiches, make them earlier in the day and keep them under waxed paper in the refrigerator. A bowl of fresh fruit could complete your menu.

To drink: Keep it simple (you want to watch the TV too). Highballs, Screwdrivers, etc. You pour the first drink, show people where the bar is, and then let them help themselves.

WINE-AND-CHEESE PARTY

A wonderfully easy way to entertain — particularly if you're working during the day. All it takes is trays of as many different cheeses as you can collect. Label each and serve with an assortment of crackers, biscuits, French and Italian bread, etc., and a large crock of butter. Fresh pears, apples and grapes are all you need for dessert. Plus coffee, of course.

Look for these cheeses:

Bel Paese — semi-soft, mild. Italian.
Brick — semi-soft, sweet. American.
Brie — mild, salted, white, soft. French.
Camembert — mellow, soft, creamy, white crust. French.
Cheddar — hard, smooth, white or yellow, sharp, medium or mild taste. Canadian. Also **Port Wine** or **Smoked Cheddar.**
Cheshire — hard, yellow, orange or white, cheddar-like. English.
Danish Blue — rich, blue-veined, sharp, pungent, crumbly. Danish.
Edam — mild, hard, yellow, coated with red wax. Dutch.
Gorgonzola — strong flavour and odour, veined. Italian.
Gouda — mild, semi-hard, usually coated with red wax. Dutch
Gruyère — firm. pale, yellow, mild, small holes. Swiss or French.
Limburger — soft; strong odour and flavour. German.
Monterey Jack — mild, moist cheddar. American.
Muenster — white, semi-soft, mild. German.
Neufchâtel — soft, white, similar to cream cheese. French.
Oka — mild, strong odour, semi-soft to soft. Canadian.
Pont L'Evêque — mild, pungent, yellow, soft center. French.
Port Salut — yellow, mild, semi-soft, made in a French monastery.
Roquefort — sheep's milk cheese, strong flavour, veined with mould, crumbly. French.
Stilton — rich, waxy, white, veined with mould. English.
Swiss or Emmenthaler — firm, pale yellow, large holes. Swiss.
Tilsit — semi-hard, light yellow, like Limburger. German.

To help you with your selection of wines, see the Wine Selection Chart starting on page 180.

PART III

NOW FOR SOME RECIPES

Just a few — because it's all too easy to get carried away in this department and try to include everyone's favourite dishes. Which is not the idea at all. This is a book about the art of entertaining and it never set out to be a complete cookbook.

Coming up, therefore, is a limited collection of unusual and interesting recipes, all of which tie in directly with the party ideas we've discussed. So please don't take it amiss if your favourite dish doesn't even get a mention. The recipes include hors d'oeuvres; canapés and dips; sandwiches; brunch dishes; fondues; soups; salads and dressings; seafood dishes; entrées; vegetables; biscuits etc., and to top it all off — desserts.

And don't forget the other hints on cooking to be found throughout the book, such as "Some Tricks of the Trade" (vegetables) page 33, "Instant Party Fare" page 56; "Be A Spirited Cook" (all about cooking with liquor) page 34; "What Goes Well In What?" (again cooking with liquor) page 35; "The Burning Question" (about flambéed dishes) page 38; "Don't Forget The Fondues" page 39, and "The Finishing Touch" (ideas with coffee) page 40. If you'd like to know more about various cheeses, they are discussed under "Wine-and-Cheese Parties" on page 78.

HORS D'OEUVRES, CANAPÉS AND DIPS 1

HORS D'OEUVRES

What is an hors d'oeuvre?

Literally translated, it is a little something delicious that is served "outside the meal." To quote food expert James Beard, it is: "A rite rather than a course, and its duty is to enchant the eye, please the palate and excite the flow of gastric juices."

An hors d'oeuvre is a hot or cold self-contained appetizer — no toast or crackers — a bite-sized morsel of fish, meat, vegetable, cheese, egg, etc., that can be eaten in the fingers, off a toothpick or with a fork.

Bajan Bangers (4 servings)

½ lb. pork cocktail sausages
¼ cup soy sauce
¼ cup brown sugar
2 tbsp. ketchup
¼ cup Captain Morgan Gold Label Rum

Brown sausages over medium heat. Pour off fat. Add soy sauce, brown sugar, ketchup. Cover pan and cook about 10 mins. Ignite rum, pour over sauce in pan. Spoon sauce over sausages until flames die out. Serve on cocktail picks.

Nuts 'n Bolts (8 cups)

8 cups assorted small, unsugared breakfast cereals (such as Cheerios, spoon-sized Shredded Wheat, etc.), pretzel sticks and peanuts
Garlic powder
Chili powder
Salt
Butter

Combine cereal, pretzel sticks and peanuts. Add generous sprinkling of garlic and chili powder. Salt to taste. Dot with butter and bake at 250°F for 45-60 mins. Salt again before serving, hot or cold. Can be stored in airtight tins.

Curried Nuts (2 cups)

¼ cup olive oil
1 tbsp. curry powder
1 tbsp. Worcestershire sauce
⅛ tsp. cayenne
2 cups assorted, shelled nuts

Combine oil, curry powder, Worcestershire sauce and cayenne in pan and heat till very hot. Stir in nuts and keep stirring until they are well coated. Pour into baking pan lined with brown paper. Bake at 300°F about 10 mins., or until crisp.

Seagram's V.O. Beef Balls (8 servings)

1 lb. ground beef
1 tbsp. vegetable oil
7½-oz. can tomato sauce
½ bay leaf, crumbled
Salt, pepper to taste
¼ cup V.O. Whisky

Shape beef into small balls. Heat oil, add beef balls and cook over low heat till brown on all sides. Drain off drippings. Pour tomato sauce over beef balls; stir in bay leaf, salt and pepper and V.O. Cover and cook over low heat 5 more mins. Serve on cocktail picks.

CANAPÉS

If you look up the word canapé in a French-English dictionary, you'll find it translates as "sofa." Which is fair enough. A canapé sits on a piece of toast, biscuit or pastry. And to prevent that "sofa" from becoming soggy, it always requires some kind of insulating butter — preferably savoury — between the base and the topping.

Butters

Here are eight ways to make this most essential part of your canapé more interesting. Take ¼ lb. of butter and . . .

- Blend with 12 chopped or pounded anchovy fillets, a few drops of lemon juice; sieve finely.
- Add 2 tbsp. finely chopped chutney with a pinch of curry powder.
- Add one mashed lobster claw, ½ tsp. salt and a little fresh dill; sieve finely.

- Cream with ¼ lb. chopped, cooked lobster, ½ tsp. salt, ½ tsp. ground pepper, pinch of paprika; sieve finely.
- Cream with 1 cup cooked chopped shrimp, ½ tsp. salt, a few drops lemon juice, ground pepper.
- Cream with ½ lb. chopped or pounded smoked salmon, ½ tsp. ground pepper.
- Cream with several crushed cloves of garlic, ½ tsp. salt.
- Cream with 1 tbsp. capers, 1 tbsp. chives, 2 small sweet gherkins, 1 anchovy fillet, 3 pickled onions, a few tarragon leaves — all chopped. Force through fine sieve.

Canapé Toppings

To complement the plain or fancy butter, top with:

- 2 small or 1 large shrimp, nesting on a dab of thick mayonnaise, sprinkled with a little very hard, finely chopped egg, chopped chives.
- Creamed Roquefort, sprinkled with chopped walnuts.
- Creamed Roquefort, topped with drained lichee nut and decorated with speck of pimento.
- Strips of cold chicken alternated with chopped blanched almonds; decorate with strips of green pepper.
- 1 skinless, boneless sardine per canapé; cover with onion rings, decorate with finely chopped egg and chives.
- Square of smoked salmon topped with 3 or 4 beads of salmon roe caviar.
- Slice of whole, hard-cooked egg topped with 3 or 4 beads of black caviar.

SIX DIFFERENT DIPS

Dips, dunks — whatever you call them, no party is complete without them. There are several old stand-bys that you are probably already familiar with. (See the recipes on almost any package of dried onion soup mix, if you're new at the game.) Here are six additional suggestions that will put your dips in a class by themselves.

If you have simply used potato chips or crackers as "dippers" in the past, try such variations as tortillas, corn sticks, corn chips, celery and carrot sticks, cucumber slices, cauliflower pieces, whole shrimps, or even small cherry tomatoes.

Chili Dip (2¾ cups)

12 oz. cream cheese
½ cup mayonnaise
½ cup chili sauce
3 tbsp. prepared horseradish
2 tbsp. sweet pickle relish, drained

Soften cheese. Combine with mayonnaise. Add chili sauce, horseradish, relish and mix well.

Clam Dip (2 cups)

8 oz. cream cheese
2 tbsp. King Arthur Gin
2 tbsp. sour cream
7 oz. drained, minced clams
1 tsp. fresh dill (or ¼ tsp. of dried)
1 tbsp. chopped pimento
¼ cup chopped celery
½ tsp. prepared horseradish
1 tsp. grated onion
¼ tsp. salt
Paprika for garnish

Soften cheese and beat with gin and sour cream until well mixed. Add other ingredients and blend well. Turn into serving bowl, garnish with paprika.

Provençale Dip (blender recipe, 3 cups)

7-oz. can tuna with oil
2-oz. can anchovy fillets
3¾-oz. can sardines, with oil
¼ cup capers
2 large cloves garlic, chopped
20 pitted olives
⅓ cup olive oil
¼ tsp. pepper
⅛ tsp. dry mustard
1 tbsp. lemon juice
¼ cup Chemineaud Brandy

Combine tuna, anchovies, sardines, capers, garlic, olives in bowl. Transfer this mixture (about one-third at a time) to the blender glass and blend until just smooth. Also gradually add oil (one-third the amount with each batch being blended). Turn into bowl. Stir in pepper, mustard, lemon juice and brandy. Serve with dippers. Or spoon over hard-cooked eggs and serve with French bread. Or use as open sandwich spread and top with hard-cooked egg slices.

Shrimp Cocktail Dip (1 cup)

½ cup chili sauce
½ cup ketchup
½ tsp. dry mustard
½ tsp. salt
1 tbsp. horseradish
¼ tsp. black pepper
1 tbsp. Seagram's V.O. Whisky

Mix first 6 ingredients well. Stir in V.O. Chill before serving as dip for shrimps; or in lobster, crab, oyster or clam cocktails.

Jamaican Dip (1 cup)

1 cup mayonnaise
1 large clove garlic, pressed
½ tsp. salt
½ tsp. ground pepper
2 tsp. Captain Morgan Gold Label Rum
1 tsp. chili sauce

Blend all ingredients together until well mixed.

Tomato-Avocado Dip (3 cups)

2 ripe avocados, peeled and pitted
2 tbsp. lemon juice
2 tbsp. wine vinegar
1 medium tomato, peeled, chopped, drained
¼ cup finely chopped onion
4 dashes Tabasco sauce
2½ tsp. salt
1 tsp. Worcestershire sauce
⅛ tsp. pepper
½ tsp. sugar

Press avocados through coarse sieve. Add lemon juice, vinegar (at once, to preserve colour). Add tomato and blend. Add remaining ingredients and mix well. Cover tightly and chill. Serve with vegetable sticks (raw carrots, celery, turnip, cucumber, etc.).

SANDWICH FILLINGS AND DANISH SMORREBROD

2

Sandwich Fillings

White Meat of Chicken and Turkey with:

— chutney or curry butter
— chopped almond or Brazil nuts
— sweet gherkin slices

Thin Slices of Baked Ham with:

— mustard butter on nut bread
— tomato butter on white
— chutney on pumpernickel
— sweet butter and smoked salmon, on black bread
— slivers of white chicken meat on white or brown

Chopped Ham with:

— English mustard
— fresh horseradish and cream
— sweet gherkin
— chopped pineapple
— chopped olive and grated cheese
— equal amounts of chopped chicken and chopped toasted Brazil nuts, seasoned with horseradish

Thinly Sliced Tongue with:

— French mustard, chopped chives

— Roquefort butter
— grated fresh horseradish and cream
— sweet gherkins and chopped Gruyère cheese with mayonnaise

Rare Roast Beef, Thinly Sliced with:

— English mustard
— horseradish and cream

Thinly Sliced Avocado with:

— garlic butter

Chopped Lamb with:

— curry butter and chutney

Thin Slices of Roast Lamb with:

— garlic butter
— rosemary butter

Smoked Salmon with:

— horseradish
— cream cheese (not sweet)

Hard-Cooked Eggs, Mixed as a Paste with:

— sour cream, chopped chives, salt, paprika and lemon juice
— chopped pecan meats
— chopped stuffed olives, mayonnaise
— minced anchovies, minced celery, mayonnaise
— liver pâté
— shrimp or crabmeat marinated in French dressing, or in mayonnaise and a dash of Worcestershire sauce

Danish Smorrebrod (Glazed Sandwiches)

Open-faced sandwiches, with a variety of ingredients piled on thinnest possible whole bread slices, then glazed. (See next page.)

Egg and Shrimp: Use buttered whole wheat or white bread.

Top each slice with 3 hard-cooked egg slices, 5 cooked jumbo shrimps; garnish with sliced stuffed olives.

Ham and Asparagus: On buttered rye. Top with 2 tomato wedges, 2 slices of ham, rolled around 2 to 4 asparagus spears; garnish with sliced olives.

Blue Cheese and Chicken: Buttered whole wheat or white bread, topped with 2 tbsp. blue cheese, 1 strip crisp bacon, 2 to 4 slices chicken; garnish with cucumber slices.

Tongue and Swiss Cheese: Buttered whole wheat bread, topped with 2 slices Swiss cheese, 2 slices tongue, slivered gherkins and radishes.

Also Build Smorrebrod with: Sardines, smoked mussels or oysters, anchovies; garnish with pimento strips, green pepper rings, onion rings, thin lemon slices, paprika, chopped parsley.

Smorrebrod Glaze (2 cups, enough for 8 open-faced sandwiches)

1 cup tomato juice
⅛ tsp. peppercorns
½ bay leaf
¾ tsp. salt
⅛ tsp. whole cloves
1 tbsp. chopped onion
¼ cup chopped celery
3-oz. package lemon gelatin
2 tbsp. vinegar
½ cup cold water

Combine tomato juice, peppercorns, bay leaf, salt, cloves, onion, celery. Cover and simmer for 10 mins. Strain. Dissolve gelatin in hot liquid. Add vinegar and cold water. Chill until slightly thickened. Place sandwiches on rack, pour slightly thickened glaze over filling, allowing ¼ cup of glaze for each. Chill until firm.

3 BRUNCH DISHES

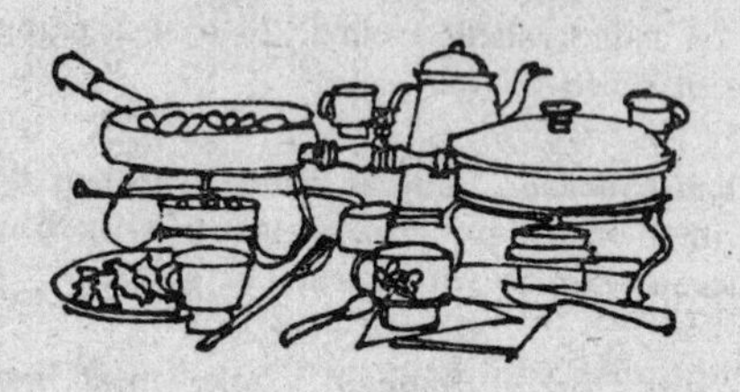

Clam Cakes

5-oz. can clams
Extra clam juice (if required)
Pancake Mix

Follow usual pancake mix package directions as to amount you want to make, substituting clam juice for indicated liquid. Use slightly more than called for in recipe. Chop clams. Add to pancake batter and fry. Serve with strips of bacon. Also delicious served with broiled lamb kidneys.

Corned Beef Hash (4 servings)

2 cups cubed cooked corned beef (tinned or fresh)
3 medium potatoes, cooked, cubed
2 tbsp. melted butter
¾ cup heavy (35%) cream
1 tsp. Worcestershire sauce
3 tbsp. chopped parsley
1 tbsp. chopped chives
4 poached eggs

Combine corned beef and potatoes, and toss lightly. Combine butter, cream, Worcestershire sauce, parsley, chives. Pour this combination over beef and potatoes. Press mixture into 4 large patties. Brown in butter and cook until thoroughly heated. Make an indentation in each patty, fill with poached egg. (Trim poached egg and drain on paper towel first.)

Eggs Benedict Arnold (4 servings)

4-oz. package cream cheese
1 tbsp. butter
1 cup light (15%) cream
½ tsp. salt
½ tsp. pepper
¼ tsp. garlic powder
6 eggs
2 tbsp. sherry
4 English muffins
Parsley
Chives

Melt cheese and butter in top half of double boiler. In another pan, scald cream, stir in cheese-and-butter mixture. Add salt, pepper, garlic powder. Break eggs into sauce. Before whites are completely firm, stir; add sherry and continue stirring until thick. Serve on toasted split English muffins. Garnish with chopped parsley and chives.

Eggs Normandie (4 servings)

4 oz. Camembert cheese
9 eggs
1 tsp. ground pepper
½ tsp. tarragon
1 tsp. salt
½ tsp. garlic powder
½ tsp. curry powder
½ cup white wine
¼ cup butter
Buttered toast or English muffins

Dice cheese, rind and all. Stir with eggs, pepper, tarragon, salt, garlic powder, curry powder and wine. Melt butter. Add egg mixture and cook over very low heat until fluffy — stirring slowly. Serve on buttered toast or English muffins.

Eggs Boulangère (6 servings)

3 large potatoes
Salt, pepper
Dash of nutmeg
4 tbsp. butter
⅓ cup grated Swiss, Parmesan, or Cheddar cheese
6 eggs
½ cup cream

Slice potatoes thinly. Sprinkle with salt, pepper, nutmeg. Sauté in almost all the butter (reserve enough to butter baking dish) until tender and brown on both sides. Stir constantly, to prevent burning. Spread cooked potatoes in buttered baking dish. Sprinkle with cheese. Carefully break eggs on top of cheese, so they are separated from each other. Add salt and pepper; cover with cream. Bake for 10 mins. at 350°F.

Quiche Lorraine (6 servings)

9″ unbaked pie shell
12 slices Swiss or Gruyère cheese
6 slices bacon
4 eggs
1 tbsp. flour
Sprinkle of nutmeg
½ tsp. salt
Cayenne pepper
2 cups cream (15%)
1½ tbsp. melted butter

Line pie crust with overlapping layers of cheese and broiled, drained bacon slices. Beat eggs with flour, nutmeg, salt and cayenne. Add cream and stir in melted butter. Pour this custard over bacon and cheese. Bake at 375°F for about 40 mins., or until custard is set and top is brown.

Eggs Parmentier (6 servings)

1 tsp. grated onion
3 cups hot, well-seasoned mashed potato
3 tbsp. butter
6 eggs
Salt, paprika
⅓ cup grated cheese
Watercress or parsley

Beat onion into mashed potato, so it is all smooth and creamy. Divide into 6 portions and form into hollowed-out nests on a greased baking pan. Put ½ tbsp. butter in each. Break in raw eggs. Season. Top with grated cheese and bake in slow oven (325°F) until eggs are set and potato delicately brown. Transfer to platter and garnish with watercress or parsley.

Spanish Omelette (6 servings)

Filling — Sauce

6 large onions
4 tbsp. butter
1 green pepper
1 red pepper
1 lb. mushrooms
3 tomatoes, or 4 oz. tomato paste
1 tbsp. Worcestershire sauce
Salt, pepper to taste

Slice onions thinly, add 2 tbsp. butter and cook over moderate heat till rings separate. Cover, allow to simmer till tender. Add peppers cut into thin strips, minced mushroom stalks, peeled and sliced tomatoes (or tomato paste). Cook until tender. Add Worcestershire sauce, salt, pepper and keep hot. Meanwhile, peel and sauté mushroom caps with 2 tbsp. butter in another pan, until brown and tender. Keep hot while preparing...

Omelette: using

6 eggs
6 tbsp, cream, milk or water
Salt, pepper to taste
1 tbsp. butter
1 tbsp. chopped parsley, chervil or watercress to garnish

When omelette starts to set, loosen from edges of pan. While it is still soft, pour half the onion-tomato-pepper filling over one side of omelette. Fold the other side over, let it stand over low heat for a moment. Invert onto hot platter, pour remaining sauce around. Arrange mushroom caps on top and cover with brown butter from mushroom pan. Garnish.

Kedgeree (4 servings)

1 lb. finnan haddie or smoked cod
1⅓ cups pre-cooked rice
4 hard-cooked eggs
⅔ cup chopped parsley
Butter
Salt
Pepper to taste

Boil fish gently, until tender. Remove skin, bones; flake. Combine with rice, prepared according to instructions. Add chopped eggs, parsley. Add generous dab of butter and mix in well. Season to taste and serve hot.

Orange French Toast (5 servings)

2 beaten eggs
1 cup orange juice
10 slices raisin bread
1½ cups (23) crushed graham crackers
Butter

Combine beaten eggs and orange juice. Quickly dip bread into mixture, then into crumbs. Fry on both sides in butter, until brown. Serve with butter and warm maple syrup.

Boodles British Cantaloupe (4 servings)

2 small cantaloupes
1½ cups fresh strawberries
1 cup frozen blueberries
2 or 3 tbsp. sugar
¼ cup Boodles British Gin
1½ tbsp. lemon juice

Halve cantaloupes, remove seeds and stringy portion. Wash, hull and cut strawberries in half; combine with blueberries, sugar, gin and lemon juice. Spoon fruit mixture into melon halves. Chill for at least 2 hours.

FONDUES AND FONDUE SAUCES 4

Fondues

For smaller, informal get-togethers, serving fondues can be fun. They are easy on the host or hostess, there is little cleaning up to do and no one need stand on ceremony. The most popular entrée-type fondues are:

1. **Cheese**
2. **Seafood** (cooked in broth).
3. **Bourguignon** (meats, fish, vegetables, etc. cooked in oil).

Please see page 39 for details on the equipment you'll need etc.

Cheese Fondue Bases

There are many excellent pre-prepared cheese fondue mixes available both in cans and foil packs. Here's another one you might like to try:

Fondue Neuchateloise (4 servings)

1 lb. shredded Swiss cheese
3 tbsp. flour
1 clove garlic, sliced in half
2 cups B&G Prince Blanc
or Graves white wine (dry)
1 tbsp. lemon juice
4 tbsp. Chemineaud Brandy
Nutmeg, freshly-ground
Pepper, to taste
2 loaves French
or Italian bread,
cut in 1½" cubes

Dredge cheese lightly with flour. Rub pot with cut clove of garlic. Pour in wine and set over low heat. When bubbles rise to surface of wine, add lemon juice. Stir with wooden spoon and add cheese by handfuls, melting each one before adding another and stirring constantly. When mixture bubbles lightly, add brandy and seasonings, stirring till blended. Serve bubbling hot.

Dunk bread in fondue with stirring motion. This soaks the bread thoroughly, and also helps keep the fondue at the right consistency. Regulate heat to keep fondue simmering. If it becomes too thick, warm some more wine and add to mixture.

Seafood Fondue Bases

Any thin seafood-based broth will do. You might also try a clear consommé or clear vegetable soup base. Here is a suggestion.

Deep Sea Fondue (4-6 servings)

4 cups clam juice
2 cups B&G Prince Blanc
  or Graves white wine
2 cups water
1 large onion, minced
½ tsp. salt
1 large carrot, minced
1 stalk celery, chopped
4 peppercorns
1 bay leaf

Bring liquids to boil in saucepan; then simmer all ingredients over moderate heat for 30 mins. Strain liquid into fondue pot, discarding solids. Keep this broth at a simmering boil. Any seafood chunks can be dipped into the hot broth and cooked to the taste of the individual. Try shrimps, lobster or crab chunks, scallops, cubes of filleted fish of any kind. Once they are cooked, seafood morsels can be dipped into a variety of sauces and then popped into the mouth.

Note: Breaded bits are not recommended for this fondue.

Bourguignon Base

This is a fondue that uses boiling hot oil to do the cooking. Use vegetable oils only (preferably peanut oil, it makes things lighter and crisper). Anything you cook in oil can be used. Morsels can either be dunked as they are, or pre-dipped in batter before cooking. Some unusual things such as ginger root and shallots are excellent when deep fried in batter. Once cooked, dip in sauces (see subsequent pages).

Black Beer Batter (8 servings)

1 cup sifted all-purpose flour
1 tbsp. baking powder
2 tsp. sugar
¼ tsp. salt
2 beaten eggs
2 tbsp. melted butter
½ cup dark beer
  (stout, not porter)
½ cup milk

Sift flour, baking powder, sugar and salt together. Stir in eggs, butter, beer and milk. Serve in bowl, with morsels prepared for the fondue dipping.

Note: If guests are frying their own batter-dipped seafood morsels, provide paper towels for draining before eating.

Fondue Sauces

Aurora Sauce (1 cup) — (Seafood or Bourguignon)

1 cup mayonnaise
2 tbsp. ketchup
2 tbsp. Chemineaud Brandy
½ tsp. Worcestershire sauce
½ tsp. lemon juice

Combine ingredients in order named and chill until ready to serve.

Avocado Sauce (1 cup) — (Seafood)

1 ripe avocado, mashed
Juice of ½ lemon
3 tbsp. mayonnaise
1 clove garlic, crushed

Blend thoroughly and serve chilled.

Bordelaise Sauce (1 cup) — (Bourguignon)

1 cup chopped mushrooms
1 tbsp. red wine
1 tbsp. butter
1 tbsp. lemon juice
1½ tbsp. cornstarch
1 tsp. powdered tarragon
1 cup beef bouillon
White pepper to taste

Sauté mushrooms in butter until tender. Mix cornstarch with some of the bouillon; add to mushrooms in pan. Cook, stirring, until mixture boils. Add wine, lemon and tarragon. Season with pepper and simmer 10 mins.

Fruit-Chutney Sauce (1½ cups) — (Seafood, Bourguignon)

1 cup apricot preserves
2 tbsp. cider vinegar
½ cup chopped chutney
1 tsp. grated lemon peel

Combine ingredients in pan; cook over low heat, stirring constantly, until mixture bubbles. May be served hot or cold.

Variations: Use pineapple, peach, plum or berry preserves in place of apricot.

Horseradish Sauce (2 cups) — (Seafood, Bourguignon)

½ cup heavy cream (35%)
1 slice dry white bread
½ cup light cream (15%)
1 tsp. sugar
½ cup prepared horseradish
¼ tsp. salt
Dash of white pepper

Blend heavy cream at low blender speed until thick. Remove to small bowl. Put remaining ingredients into blender, blend at high speed. Remove and fold into whipped cream. Chill.

Lobster Sauce (1¼ cups) — (Seafood)

Shells from lobster tails
2 cups water
2 tbsp. butter
2 tbsp. flour
2 tbsp. whipped cream
2 tsp. hollandaise sauce
Salt, white pepper to taste

Boil shells in water 20 mins., until stock is reduced by half. Strain and discard shells. Bring stock back to boil. In separate pan, melt butter over low heat. Do not brown it. Add flour and stir well. Still stirring, add boiling stock all at once. Beat briskly to blend. Bring to boil over moderate heat and, stirring, allow to boil 1 min. Simmer and stir in whipped cream and hollondaise. Blend. Season. Chill before serving.

Peanut Sauce (¾ cup) — (Bourguignon — meats only)

¼ cup heavy cream (35%)
2 tbsp. smooth peanut butter
2 tbsp. soy sauce
1 tbsp. lemon juice
4 drops Tabasco sauce

Mix together and heat gently.

Red Sea Sauce (⅔ cup) — (Seafood)

½ cup plain yoghourt or sour cream
2 tbsp. ketchup or chili sauce
2 tsp. prepared horseradish
3 drops Tabasco sauce

Blend and mix well. Chill before serving.

Spanish Sauce (1¼ cups) — (Bourguignon)

4 cloves garlic, peeled
2 egg yolks
1 cup olive oil
1 tsp. lemon juice
¼ tsp. fresh ground pepper
¾ tsp. salt

Mash garlic with egg yolks, blending well. Add oil, drop by drop, while beating. When sauce is consistency of mayonnaise, stir in remaining ingredients.

Super-Supper Sauce (2½ cups) — (Seafood or Bourguignon)

1 cup mayonnaise
1 cup sour cream
2 tsp. curry powder
1 tsp. chopped capers
1 tsp. dry mustard
1 tsp. onion flakes
1 tsp. parsley flakes
1 tsp. coarse salt
1½ oz. Chemineaud Brandy

Stir all ingredients together, except brandy. Let stand for 20 mins. Add brandy and stir again.

Sweet-and-Sour Fondue Sauce (2 cups) — (Bourguignon)

½ cup minced onion
½ cup minced green pepper
2 tbsp. butter
1 tbsp. cornstarch
½ cup water
7½ oz. tomato sauce
2 tbsp. orange marmalade
2 tbsp. vinegar
½ tsp. powdered ginger

Sauté onion and green pepper in butter, over medium heat, until tender. Blend cornstarch with water. Add to vegetables. Add remaining ingredients. Simmer 10 mins.

Tartar Sauce (1½ cups) — (Seafood)

4 green onions (white parts only), finely chopped
1 small sour pickle, minced
¼ cup stuffed green olives, minced
1 cup mayonnaise
2 tbsp. chopped parsley
Salt
White pepper

Combine onions, pickle, olives. Blend thoroughly with mayonnaise. Stir in parsley. Season to taste.

5

SOUPS

Bloody Mary Soup (6 servings)

1 medium onion, diced
3 celery ribs, diced
2 tbsp. butter
2 tbsp. tomato purée
1 tbsp. sugar
5 cups tomato juice
1 tbsp. salt
2 tsp. Worcestershire sauce
¼ tsp. pepper
1 tbsp. lemon juice
4 oz. Bolshoi Vodka
Chives or chopped parsley, to garnish

Sauté onion and celery in butter until light brown. Add tomato purée and sugar. Sauté 1 min. Add tomato juice; simmer 8 mins. Add other ingredients. Strain. Serve either hot or well-chilled. Sprinkle with chives or chopped parsley.

Borscht (8 servings)

2 small bunches fresh beets
6 cups beef stock
2 tsp. sugar
3 tsp. lemon juice
1 cucumber
Salt
1 cup sour cream
Chopped fresh dill

Wash, trim, scrape beets. Dice into stock and simmer, covered, about 45 mins. Strain liquid, discard beets. Stir in sugar and lemon juice. Chill. Peel and halve cucumber, remove seeds and cut flesh into thin strips. Add to soup, with salt to taste. Serve topped with sour cream and sprinkled with dill.

Chilled Salmon Bisque (4 servings)

½ clove garlic
1 small onion, sliced
½ green pepper, chopped
1 tbsp. butter
7¾-oz. can salmon
1½ cups milk
¼ cup chopped dill
¼ tsp. Tabasco sauce
1 tsp. salt
¼ tsp. ground black pepper
½ cup heavy cream (35%)
2 tbsp. dry sherry
Red food colouring (optional)

Sauté garlic, onion, green pepper in butter. Put sautéed vegetables, salmon, milk, dill, seasonings in blender, on high speed for 15 secs. (Or mix ingredients thoroughly and force through strainer.) Add cream and chill. Just before serving stir in sherry. To improve colour, add a few drops of red food colouring with cream.

Crab Soup (4 servings)

10-oz. can cream of mushroom soup
10-oz. can asparagus soup
1 cup milk
6-oz. can crabmeat
½ cup cream
3 tbsp. sherry

Combine and heat — but don't boil — the two soups, milk and crabmeat. Add cream. Lastly, add sherry.

French Onion Soup (10 servings)

½ cup butter
2 lbs. sliced onions
1 tbsp. flour
2 qts. chicken or beef stock
Salt and white pepper
1 loaf sliced French bread
2 cups B&G Prince Blanc or Graves white wine
¼ lb. grated Swiss cheese
¼ lb. sliced Swiss cheese

Melt half the butter in a pan. Sauté onions till golden and transparent. Add flour and stir. Cook for 3 mins. Add stock and simmer 30 mins. Salt and pepper to taste. Toast bread slices and spread with remaining butter. Pour soup into large earthenware casserole. Add wine and half the grated cheese. Cover surface with pieces of buttered toast. Sprinkle all with remaining grated cheese, add slices of cheese — so that liquid is completely covered with toast and cheese. Bake, uncovered at 375°F for 15 mins., or until cheese and bread are brown and crusty.

Gazpacho (8 servings)

1 clove garlic
2 tsp. salt
⅓ cup chopped mushrooms
3 tbsp. olive oil
1 cup chopped onions
2 cups chopped tomatoes
1¼ cups chopped green peppers
1 cup finely chopped celery
1 cup finely chopped cucumber
1 tbsp. chopped parsley
1 tsp. ground black pepper
¼ tsp. Tabasco sauce
1 tsp. Worcestershire sauce
½ cup tarragon wine vinegar
3 cups tomato juice
2 tsp. chopped chives

Crush garlic in 1 tsp. of the salt. Sauté mushrooms in olive oil till lightly browned. Combine mushrooms and garlic with remaining ingredients (except chives) in stainless steel or glass bowl. Cover and chill at least 3 hrs., or overnight. Serve with plain or garlic croutons (see page 101), if desired. Sprinkle with chopped chives.

Senegal Soup (4 servings)

2 tbsp. butter
1½ tsp. curry powder
1½ tbsp. flour
3 cups chicken broth
Paprika
2 egg yolks
½ cup milk or cream
½ cup chopped cooked chicken
3 tbsp. chutney
Chopped chives

Melt butter, add curry powder and stir until blended. Add flour, stir. Blend in broth, bring to a boil and season with paprika to taste. Reduce heat. Beat together egg yolks and milk or cream. When soup is no longer boiling, add egg mixture and stir over low heat till slightly thick. Add chicken meat and chutney. To heat for serving: be careful not to allow soup to boil. Garnish with chopped chives.

6 SALADS AND DRESSINGS, SAUCES

SALADS

Belgian Salad (6 servings)

6 heads Belgian endive
½ cup walnut meats
2 sweet apples
Juice of 1 lemon
6 tbsp. olive oil
Salt

Cut endive into bite-sized pieces, rinse thoroughly and dry. Place in bowl, sprinkle with walnuts. Add bite-sized pieces of peeled apple and sprinkle with lemon juice at once, to preserve colour. Add oil and salt. Toss. Serve immediately.

Bloody Mary Aspic (4 servings)

1½ cups tomato juice
½ tsp. sugar
1 envelope (1 tbsp.) unflavoured gelatin
1 tsp. fresh or dried basil
1 small bay leaf
1 tsp. lemon juice
¼ cup Bolshoi Vodka
½ tsp. salt
¼ tsp. pepper

Mix ¾ cup tomato juice, sugar, gelatin, basil and bay leaf in pan. Stir over moderate heat until gelatin dissolves. Remove from heat, strain and add remaining ¾ cup tomato juice, lemon juice, Bolshoi Vodka, salt, pepper. Pour into pint mould, chill until firm.

Caesar Salad (4 servings)

3 anchovy fillets, cut into small pieces
1 clove crushed garlic
½ tsp. hot, dry English mustard
5 dashes Worcestershire sauce
2 tbsp. dry breadcrumbs
Juice of ½ lemon
2 egg yolks
3 tbsp. grated Parmesan cheese
½ cup + 2 tbsp. olive oil
1 large head romaine lettuce
1½ cups croutons (see below)

Put anchovies, garlic, mustard, Worcestershire in large salad bowl and mix thoroughly. Add dry breadcrumbs. With spoon, crush and mash ingredients vigorously for about 7 mins., or until mixture blends into very thick paste. Add lemon juice and egg yolks, beat again. Add 1 tbsp. of the Parmesan. Pour oil in very slowly, beating fast until mixture is thick and creamy. Wash lettuce, dry between paper towels, tear into bite-sized pieces and add to bowl. Add remaining cheese. Toss lightly, so every piece of lettuce is coated with dressing. At very last minute, add croutons — toss and serve immediately.

Croutons (for Ceasar Salad above or Gazpacho, page 98)

Prepare by frying cubes of good rye bread over low flame, in butter with a split clove of garlic. Toss frequently, so that all sides are browned. Remove from pan, spread on baking tray and bake at 250°F for 30 mins.

Guacamole Salad (10 servings)

1 envelope "Good Seasons" garlic dressing mix
1½ tsp. chili powder
3 tbsp. chili sauce
4 dashes Tabasco sauce
½ cup mayonnaise
1 tbsp. lemon juice
1 small onion, grated
2 large avocados, peeled
3 large heads lettuce or romaine

Combine all ingredients (except lettuce or romaine) in blender and blend. Spoon into a quart jar. Seal tightly and chill 1 hr. (Avocado will darken if not properly covered.) Spoon over shredded lettuce or romaine.

Jellied Chicken Salad (25 servings)

4 3-oz. packages lemon flavoured jelly powder*
1½ tbsp. garlic salt
3 cups hot water
2 tbsp. grated onion
⅛ tsp. pepper
¼ cup wine vinegar
1 pint sour cream
2 cups mayonnaise
1 cup chopped pecans
8 cups diced cooked chicken
2 cups diced celery
2 heads lettuce
2 heads escarole
2 heads romaine
2 bunches watercress
1 cup sliced olives
2 cups diced pineapple
8 medium tomatoes, diced
Sour Cream Garlic Dressing (see page 104)

*Note: Use commercially flavoured products. Do *not* use unflavoured packaged gelatines adding your own flavouring.

Dissolve jelly and garlic salt in hot water. Add onion, pepper, vinegar. Cool. Blend in sour cream and mayonnaise. Chill until slightly thickened. Fold in pecans, chicken, celery. Pour into shallow pans to depth of about 1¼″. Chill until firm, then cut into cubes. Tear salad greens into bite-sized pieces. Combine with olives, pineapple, tomatoes. Mix in Sour Cream Garlic Dressing, tossing lightly. Arrange salad cubes on top and serve.

Kidney Bean Salad (10 servings)

½ tsp. salt
2 14-oz. cans kidney beans
1½ cups sliced celery
⅔ cup sliced onions
½ cup chopped dill pickle
½ cup chopped green pepper
½ cup French dressing

Salt the drained beans and let stand while preparing vegetables. Combine all ingredients and toss well. Marinate 2 to 3 hrs. before serving.

Mimosa Salad (6 servings)

4 cups mixed salad greens
Watercress sprigs
French dressing
2 small (or 1 large) hard-cooked egg

Toss salad greens and watercress with French dressing. Distribute on chilled salad plates. Chop egg whites and sieve yolks. Combine and sprinkle on salad. Serve at once.

Puffed Chicken Salad (4 dozen)

½ cup butter
1 cup boiling water
1 cup sifted all-purpose flour
4 unbeaten eggs
3 cups finely chopped cooked chicken
3 cups finely chopped celery
¾ cup mayonnaise
¾ cup French dressing
1 tbsp. minced parsley

To make the puffs: Add butter to water in pan and bring to boil. Reduce heat. Add flour all at once, stirring rapidly. Cook and stir until mixture thickens and leaves sides of pan — about 2 mins. Remove from heat. Add eggs, one at a time, beating well after each addition. Then beat until mixture looks satiny and breaks off when spoon is raised. Drop by teaspoonfuls on an ungreased baking sheet, about 1″ apart. Bake at 425°F for 30 mins. Cool.

Combine remaining ingredients. Cut shallow piece from top of each puff and fill with salad mixture. Replace tops and chill before serving.

Tomato and Onion Salad (8 servings)

1 clove garlic, minced
1 tsp. salt
1 tsp. sugar
¼ tsp. pepper
2 tsp. prepared mustard
¼ cup olive oil
2 tbsp. tarragon vinegar
6 sliced tomatoes
1 thinly sliced onion
Chopped parsley

Combine garlic and salt in small bowl. Stir in sugar, pepper, mustard, oil and vinegar. Pour over tomato and onion slices. Sprinkle with parsley. Chill. Serve as relish salad. Or on crisp greens.

DRESSINGS, SAUCES

Hot Mustard Sauce (1/4 cup)

Gradually add 2 tbsp. water to 1/4 cup dry mustard, stirring until it is creamy and smooth.

Martini French Dressing (3/4 cup)

1/2 cup olive oil
1 tbsp. wine vinegar
1 tbsp. Noilly Pratt French Vermouth
1 tbsp. King Arthur Gin
1 tsp. salt
1/2 tsp. sugar
1/4 tsp. dry mustard
1 garlic clove, squeezed through press

Combine all ingredients in jar with tight lid. Shake well before using.

Mustard French Dressing

1 cup olive oil
1 tsp. salt
1 tsp. sugar
1 tsp. dry mustard
1 tbsp. finely chopped shallots
1/4 tsp. fresh ground black pepper
3 tbsp. wine vinegar

Combine oil with salt, sugar, mustard, shallots and pepper; let stand for at least 1 hr. Add vinegar, beat vigorously with fork or rotary beater.

Sour Cream Garlic Dressing (4 cups, 25 servings)

1 cup sour cream
1 cup mayonnaise
2 cups commercial garlic salad dressing

Blend sour cream and mayonnaise. Gradually add salad dressing, stirring until mixture is smooth and creamy.

Sweet-and-Sour Tempura Sauce (3/4 cup)

5 tbsp. finely chopped chutney
1/4 cup currant jelly
1 1/2 tsp. sugar
1 tsp. vinegar

Combine all ingredients in small pan and heat, stirring frequently, until jelly is melted.

Cayman Lobster (12 servings) (You can substitute shrimp, crab, or scallops.)

10-oz. can of mushrooms
¼ cup chopped green pepper
¼ cup chopped onion
6 tbsp. butter
4 cups cooked lobster
¼ cup chopped pimento
2 tsp. dry mustard
½ tsp. pepper
2 eggs
1⅓ cups mayonnaise
4 slices white bread

Drain and slice mushrooms. Cook with green pepper and onion for 5 mins., in 2 tbsp. of the butter. Combine with lobster. Add pimento and seasoning. Beat eggs, mix with mayonnaise and pour over mixture. Stir well, transfer to shallow baking dish. Cut 12 small rounds from bread slices, sauté in remaining butter and lay on top of lobster dish. Bake at 350°F for 20 mins., or until bubbly.

Ceviche Mary — a refreshing dish for hot summer days (8 servings)

1 lb. scallops
Juice of 2 limes
1 oz. Bolshoi Vodka
½ cup ketchup
2 tsp. prepared horseradish
Few dashes Tabasco sauce
Salt to taste
2 tsp. minced dried onion
⅛ tsp. garlic powder
2 oz. Bolshoi Vodka

Rinse and dry scallops, (thin strips of filleted raw fish can be substituted). Marinate in lime juice and 1 oz. vodka in refrigerator for 4 hrs.

Sauce: Combine remaining ingredients and mix thoroughly. Correct seasonings: should be fairly sharp and just a little saltier than usual, to allow for blandness of fish. Drain fish well and combine with sauce. Serve very cold, garnished with stuffed olive or lime wedges.

Coquille St. Jacques (4 servings)

- $1/2$ cup clam juice
- $1/4$ cup Trelawny Classic White Rum
- $1/4$ cup water
- 1 sprig parsley
- 2 tbsp. chopped onion
- $1/2$ bay leaf
- Pinch thyme
- $1/2$ tsp. salt
- Dash pepper
- $1/4$ tsp. sugar
- $3/4$ lb. scallops or fish chunks
- $1/4$ lb. sliced mushrooms
- 3 tbsp. butter
- 1 tbsp. lemon juice
- 2 tbsp. flour
- $3/4$ cup light cream (15%)
- 1 cup mashed potatoes
- $3/4$ cup soft, buttered, white breadcrumbs
- 2 tbsp. grated Parmesan cheese

Combine clam juice, rum, water, parsley, onion, bay leaf, thyme, salt, pepper, sugar in pan. Bring to boil. Add seafood cut into thumbnail-sized chunks. Over low heat, simmer 5-7 mins., or until tender. Remove seafood, strain broth and reserve. Sauté mushrooms in 1 tbsp. butter until golden. Add lemon juice and set aside. Melt remaining 2 tbsp. butter in pan, add flour. Gradually stir in $3/4$ cup of reserved broth and $3/4$ cup cream. Cook until smooth and thickened, stirring constantly. Add seafood and mushrooms. Spoon mixture into individual scallop shells that have previously been circled around the outer edges with the mashed potato thus making a nest for the seafood. (Your squeeze bag cake icer is ideal for this, and makes the dish even more attractive.) These scallop shells are available in gourmet stores — they can be washed and re-used. Top with crumbs, sprinkle with cheese. Bake at 400°F for 10 mins.

Crab and Mushroom Casserole (6 servings)

- 1 lb. sliced mushrooms
- $2/3$ cup butter
- $1/3$ cup flour
- 10 oz. chicken broth
- $1\,1/2$ cups light cream (15%)
- Salt, pepper to taste
- $1\,1/2$ lbs. crabmeat
- Buttered breadcrumbs
- Grated Cheddar cheese

Sauté mushrooms in 2 tbsp. butter for 5 mins., then set aside. Melt remaining butter, remove from heat and blend in flour. Add broth, cream; season with salt and pepper. Return to heat and cook till thick and smooth, stirring constantly. In 6-cup casserole, arrange alternate layers of mushrooms, sauce, crabmeat; sprinkle with breadcrumbs and cheese. Bake at 350°F for 30 mins. If frozen uncooked, bake at 325°F for 45 to 60 mins.

Lobster Thermidor (6 servings)

6 cooked lobsters (excluding claws)
2 tbsp. dry sherry
2 tbsp. Chemineaud **Brandy**
½ cup butter
¼ cup flour
½ tsp. salt
Pinch of nutmeg
Pinch of paprika
1½ cups half and-half (milk and cream)
1 lightly-beaten egg yolk
⅓ cup grated Parmesan cheese

Remove lobster meat from shells, keeping shells intact. Cut meat into pieces. Mix in large bowl with sherry and brandy. Cover, set aside. Wash and dry lobster shells and reserve. Prepare sauce by melting butter in large pan. Remove from heat. Stir in flour, salt, nutmeg, paprika. Gradually stir in half-and-half. Bring to boil, stirring. Reduce heat, simmer for several minutes. Stir some of hot mixture into egg yolk, and pour this into pan. Add lobster meat. Cook, stirring, over low heat until sauce thickens and lobster is heated through. Fill shells with mixture, piling it high. Sprinkle with Parmesan. Place filled shells on baking sheet and bake at 450°F until cheese melts and tops are brown, 8-10 mins.

Shrimp Creole (18 servings)

½ cup butter
1⅓ cups diced green pepper
1⅓ cups chopped onions
2½ cups diced celery
½ cup flour
10 cups canned tomatoes
1½ tbsp. salt
½ tsp. pepper
2 tbsp. firmly-packed brown sugar
3 bay leaves
8 whole cloves
8 cups fresh shrimp
2 tbsp. Worcestershire sauce
⅛ tsp. Tabasco sauce
1 tbsp. lemon juice
⅔ cup B&G Prince Blanc or Graves white wine
3½ qts. (18 cups) hot cooked rice (6 cups uncooked)

Melt butter in heavy 8-qt. saucepan. Add peppers, onions, celery and sauté till tender (about 10 mins.). Remove from heat. Add flour, blend thoroughly. Add tomatoes gradually, stirring constantly. Add salt, pepper, sugar, bay leaves, cloves. Bring to a boil. Reduce heat and simmer, uncovered, over low heat about 45 mins., stirring occasionally. Shell, clean and rinse shrimp. Add to thickened sauce and cook about 5 mins. Stir in Worcestershire, Tabasco, lemon juice, wine. Serve over rice.

Tempura (4 servings)

¾ lb. fresh shrimp
¾ cup sifted flour
1 tsp. baking powder
½ tsp. salt
1 egg
½ cup water

Shell and devein shrimp, leaving tails on; rinse and dry. Sift flour, baking powder, salt together. Beat egg slightly, add dry ingredients and blend. Add water, tablespoonful at a time, until batter is the consistency of custard sauce. Dip shrimp in batter and fry in hot fat (350° to 360°F) about 3 mins. Serve with Sweet-and-Sour Tempura Sauce (page 104).

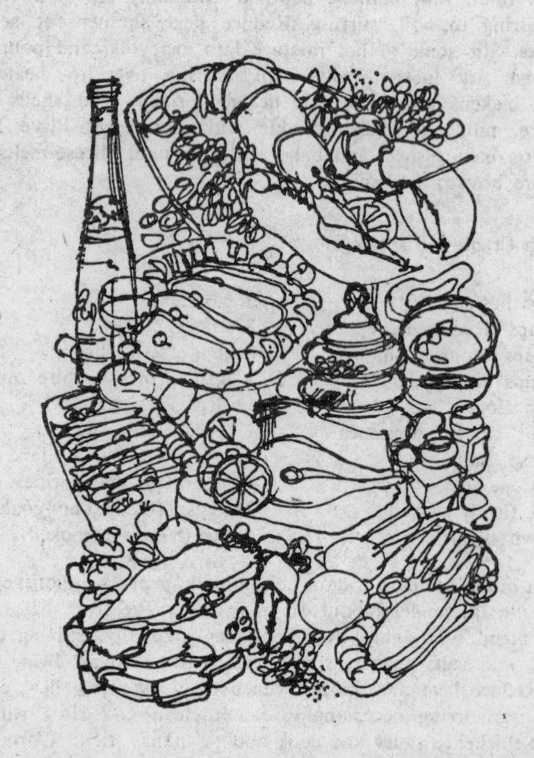

Almond Chicken (8 servings)

4 lbs. frying chicken, cut up
⅓ cup flour
2 tsp. salt
¼ tsp. pepper
6 tbsp. peanut or vegetable oil
¾ cup blanched, sliced almonds
4½ cups chicken stock
1 clove garlic, chopped
1 tsp. ginger
6 tbsp. cornstarch
3 tbsp. water
¼ cup soy sauce
⅓ cup sliced green onions
1 cup sliced celery
5-oz. can water chestnuts
½ cup bamboo shoots
10-oz. can mushrooms
1 cup diced cucumber

Dredge chicken in flour seasoned with 1 tsp. salt and ⅛ tsp. pepper. Sauté in 3 tbsp. of the oil until lightly browned. Remove to heavy pan or Dutch oven for cooking. Add almonds to drippings, sauté lightly and reserve. Add chicken stock, remaining salt and pepper, garlic, ginger to chicken. Cover, bring to boil. Reduce heat and simmer about 30 mins., until chicken is tender. Remove chicken to shallow casserole or oven-proof platter. Cover and keep warm. Make a paste of cornstarch, water, soy sauce; add to chicken stock, stirring constantly, until blended. Cook and stir about 5 mins., until thickened. Sauté onions, celery, water chestnuts, bamboo shoots, mushrooms, cucumber in remaining 3 tbsp. oil, until tender. Pour thickened sauce over chicken. Top with sautéed vegetables and sprinkle with almonds.

Beef with Dumplings (6 servings)

2 cups finely chopped onions
¼ cup clarified butter
1 cup all-purpose flour
Salt, black pepper
3 lbs. chuck beef, in 2" cubes
2 tbsp. Chemineaud Brandy
1 large bay leaf
1-1½ qts. (approx.) boiling beef stock
½ lb. mushrooms
2 cups sour cream
Dumplings (recipe follows)

Cook onions in clarified butter* till transparent. Remove from pan and reserve. Use ¾ cup flour, seasoned, to dredge beef. Brown in same pan in which onions were cooked. When thoroughly brown, add brandy and ignite. When flames die down, return onions to pan, add bay leaf and enough beef stock to cover meat. Cover, reduce heat, simmer about 1½ hrs. till meat is almost tender. Add mushrooms. Combine sour cream with the remaining ¼ cup flour; gradually add a little hot sauce from the pan. Spoon this mixture over top of meat but do not stir. When sauce starts to bubble around the sides, add dumplings. Cover pan and cook 30 more mins.

*See your favourite cookbook for instructions.

Dumplings (Makes 12)

1 24-oz. loaf sliced white bread
¼ cup water
6-8 beaten eggs
Salt
½ cup chopped parsley
½ cup chopped onion
½ tsp. grated nutmeg

Trim crusts from bread and use remainder to make crumbs. Sprinkle enough water to barely moisten, tossing with fork. Add eggs, blend; add salt to taste, then remaining ingredients. Drop by tablespoons on top of bubbling stew.

Chicken à la King (4 servings)

½ lb. sliced mushrooms
1 small chopped onion
2 tbsp. butter
¼ cup flour
1½ cups milk
½ tsp. salt
⅛ tsp. pepper
⅛ tsp. garlic powder
1 tbsp. chopped parsley
1 tbsp. chopped pimento
2 cups diced cooked chicken
½ cup Leroux Triple Sec
Hot toast points

Sauté mushrooms and onion in butter for 10 mins. Remove from heat. Blend in flour. Return to heat; add milk slowly, stirring until thickened. Add salt, pepper, garlic powder, parsley, pimento, chicken. Cover and cook slowly for 10 mins. Stir in Triple Sec and cook, uncovered, 5 more mins. Serve on hot toast points.

Chicken Cashew (8 servings)

2 broiler chickens (3 lbs. each), quartered
1 cup crushed cashew nuts
¼ cup butter
Shortening to brown
Salt and pepper to taste
¼ cup Chemineaud Brandy
1 cup light cream (15%)

Roll each chicken quarter in crushed cashews mixed with butter. Brown quickly in hot shortening. Sprinkle with salt and pepper, cover and simmer till tender (35-45 mins.). Add brandy and cream, cook on low heat till sauce thickens.

Chili Con Carne (8 servings)

3 tbsp. salad oil
¼ cup chopped green pepper
1 cup chopped onions
1 clove garlic, chopped
2 lbs. ground beef
2 cups diced cooked ham
2 19-oz. cans kidney beans
2 19-oz cans tomatoes
1½ tsp. salt
1½ tbsp. chili powder (or to taste)
½ cup water

Heat oil in large skillet. Add green pepper, onions, garlic, beef. Sauté, stirring frequently, till lightly browned. Add ham, beans, tomatoes, salt, chili powder; mix well. Simmer about 30 mins., stirring occasionally. If mixture becomes too thick, gradually stir in water.

Chicken Tang (8 servings)

2 10-oz. cans cream of chicken soup
¼ cup chopped onion
1 tsp. celery flakes
¼ tsp. thyme
2 tsp. salt
⅛ tsp. pepper
1 tsp. parsley flakes
2⅔ cups water
2⅔ cups instant rice
3 cups diced cooked chicken
½ tsp. paprika

Combine soup, onion, seasonings in pan, mixing well. Gradually add water, blend and bring to boil over medium heat, stirring constantly. Pour half soup mixture into 3-quart casserole. Add half the rice, then half the chicken, remainder of rice and remainder of chicken. Top with remaining soup mixture. Cover and bake at 375°F for 15-20 mins. Stir well after 10 mins. Sprinkle with paprika.

Coq Au Vin (6 generous servings)

4½ lbs. frying chicken, cut up
¼ cup Chemineaud Brandy
⅓ cup flour
1 tsp. salt
¼ tsp. pepper
¼ cup butter
1 tbsp. salad oil
2 cups water
2½ cups dry red wine
½ tbsp. peppercorns
1 sprig parsley
1 bay leaf
1 sprig thyme
1 clove garlic, crushed
¼ lb. salt pork
6 small onions
½ lb. fresh mushroom caps or drained canned mushrooms

Place chicken pieces in large skillet. Pour brandy over and ignite. Then dredge singed chicken with mixture of flour, salt, pepper. Add butter and oil to skillet, and sauté chicken until lightly browned. Remove chicken to baking dish. Add 1½ cups of the water to drippings, heat until all browned particles are loosened. Pour drippings mixture and wine over chicken. Prepare a bouquet garni by tying peppercorns, parsley, bay leaf, thyme in piece of cheesecloth. Add bouquet garni and garlic to chicken; cover and bake at 325°F about 30 mins. Meanwhile, simmer pork in remaining ½ cup of water for 5 mins. Drain and dice. Sauté salt pork in skillet with onions and mushrooms, till onions are glazed. Place sautéed vegetables and salt pork in baking dish with chicken. Cover and continue baking about 2 hrs. Serve on hot platter.

Crêpes (12 crêpes)

¼ cup all-purpose flour
1 egg
1 egg yolk
3 tbsp. milk
1 tbsp. vegetable oil
1 cup milk

Beat with a whisk the flour, egg, egg yolk, the 3 tbsp. milk and the oil. Add enough from the 1 cup milk to make a thin batter. Refrigerate 3-4 hrs. Remove and add enough milk to reduce consistency to that of light cream. Heat pan and when very hot, wipe with piece of buttered paper. Lower heat. Cover bottom of pan with very thin layer of batter. Cook until golden on one side. Turn and cook other side.

Fill crêpes with crabmeat, chopped ham, chopped chicken, cold curry, or flaked fish. Fold ends under. Butter tops. Bake in buttered dish at 375°F for 30 mins.

NOTE: Addition of 1 tbsp. curry powder to crêpe batter goes well with fish filling.

Curried Chicken (4 servings)

2 tbsp. minced green onions
1 tbsp. beef drippings
1 tbsp. curry paste*
1 tbsp. flour
2 tbsp. curry powder
2 cups chicken stock
1 lb. cooked chicken
1 tbsp. butter
½ coconut, grated (or 1 cup dessicated coconut)
½ cup boiling water
½ tsp. lemon juice
1 tbsp. red currant jelly

Sauté green onions in drippings; stir in curry paste, flour, curry powder and cook gently for 5 mins. Gradually add stock, stirring all the time. Bring to a boil and simmer for 15 mins. Cube chicken meat and brown it in butter. Grate coconut flesh, cover with boiling water and set aside to infuse. Add sautéed chicken to curried stock and set it aside for 60 mins. Then heat it gradually — do not boil. Stir in lemon juice, red currant jelly and coconut water. Serve on hot dish, with plain boiled rice.

*Available from many special stores. If unavailable, substitute 1 extra tbsp. curry powder.

Ham Rolls au Gratin (8 servings)

2 10-oz cans cream of mushroom soup
1 pint sour cream
12-oz. package frozen chopped spinach
2 cups creamed cottage cheese
2 lightly beaten eggs
½ cup chopped green onions
1 tsp. dry mustard
½ tsp. salt
24 slices cooked ham

Combine soup and ½ cup of sour cream in bowl and set aside. Cook and drain spinach. Sieve cottage cheese. Combine remaining sour cream with cheese, eggs, green onions, spinach, mustard and salt. Mix well. Spoon about 2 tbsp. filling onto each slice of ham; roll up, folding in edges. Place in shallow baking dish and cover with sour cream sauce. Bake at 350°F for 20-25 mins.

Highland Chicken (4 servings)

4 whole chicken breasts, left on bone
4 tbsp. 100 Pipers Scotch
½ cup fine dry breadcrumbs
½ tsp. salt
⅛ tsp. Ac'cent
½ tsp. paprika
⅛ tsp. pepper
¼ cup sour cream

Split chicken breasts in half and remove skin. Pour 2 tbsp. Scotch into shallow pan and place chicken, flesh side down, in pan. Spoon Scotch over backs. Marinate 1 hr., basting occasionally. Preheat oven to 350°F. Combine crumbs with salt, Ac'cent, paprika, pepper. Add remaining 2 tbsp. Scotch to sour cream. Pat chicken dry with paper towels. Spread sour cream over each piece, front and back; dip chicken in seasoned breadcrumbs, shaking off excess crumbs. Place on oiled shallow pan and bake for 1¼ hrs.

Old Thyme Pork Chops (4 servings)

4 thick loin pork chops
2 tbsp. butter
½ cup chopped onion
1½ cups tomato purée
1 cup B&G Prince Blanc
or Graves white wine
Pinch of ground thyme
½ bay leaf
Salt, black pepper to taste
½ cup chopped parsley
2 minced garlic cloves
2 tsp. grated lemon rind

Brown chops on both sides in the butter. Transfer to platter and keep warm. Pour off most of the fat. To remaining fat, add onion and sauté lightly. Add tomato purée, wine, thyme, bay leaf, salt and pepper. Return chops to skillet and turn them in the sauce. Cover and bake at 350°F for one hour, basting occasionally, until chops are tender. Mix parsley, garlic, lemon rind and sprinkle over chops. Cover and keep warm until ready to serve.

Paella (4 servings)

2 cups long-grained rice
½ tsp. saffron
2 tbsp. olive oil
1 medium onion, chopped
1 green pepper, chopped
1 large tomato, finely chopped
1 clove garlic, minced
1 tsp. salt
4¼-oz. can drained shrimp
1 cup chicken meat
1 cup chicken stock
5-oz. can clams
14-oz. can drained artichoke
hearts (optional)
12-oz. package frozen peas
Pimento strips

Simmer rice, with saffron added, until barely done (10 mins.). Drain. Add oil, onion, green pepper, tomato, garlic, salt. Mix well and transfer to casserole. Add shrimp, chicken; then add stock and juice drained from clams. Cover, bake at 350°F for 45 mins. Remove cover. Add drained clams, artichoke hearts, peas (cooked for 5 mins.), garnish with pimento and bake another 20 mins.

Sauerbraten (8 servings)

3½ to 4 lbs. boned rump or shoulder of beef

Marinade

4 cups beer
2 cups water
1 lemon, quartered
1 bay leaf
1 sliced onion
2 whole cloves
1 chopped tomato
5 peppercorns

Sauce

3 tbsp. flour
3 tbsp. butter
1 sliced lemon
Sugar to taste
Salt to taste
½ cup sour cream

Marinate meat for 2 to 3 days in refrigerator, turning several times. Remove (strain marinade and reserve), dry meat and dredge with flour. Brown in butter, add 1 cup strained marinade, lemon, sugar and salt. Cook covered until meat is very tender (2½ to 3 hrs). Remove. Strain sauce and skim off fat. Add sour cream, blend well and reheat slowly. Serve sauce over sliced meat.

Swiss Mozzarella Steak (8 servings)

4 lbs. beef (round steak) ½" thick
¾ cup flour
4-6 tbsp. shortening
1 tbsp. salt
¼ tsp. pepper
½ tsp. savory
2 cups water
1 cup chopped celery
1 cup chopped green pepper
4 cups canned tomatoes
½ lb. thinly sliced Mozzarella cheese

Cut meat into 8 serving pieces. Dredge in ½ cup of the flour. Brown in hot shortening. Remove meat to large roasting pan. Blend remaining ¼ cup flour with hot drippings; add seasonings. Gradually blend in water. Add vegetables. Cook and stir until slightly thickened. Pour mixture over meat and bake, uncovered, at 325°F for 2½ to 3 hrs., until meat is tender. Top meat with slices of cheese; return to oven until cheese melts and serve at once.

Shish Kebab (6 servings)

1 tsp. curry powder
1½ tbsp. salt
3 bay leaves
8 peppercorns
2 tbsp. grated onion
1 large garlic clove, crushed
¼ cup lemon juice
¼ cup B&G Prince Noir red wine
⅓ cup olive oil
2 lbs. lamb, cut in 1½" cubes
Green pepper squares
Small white onions, semi-cooked
Tomato wedges

Combine seasonings, lemon juice, dry wine and oil in bowl. Place lamb, green pepper and onions in mixture; marinate 4 to 12 hrs. Drain and reserve marinade. Alternately place marinated meat, pepper, onions and tomatoes on skewers. Line broiler tray with foil. Place kebabs on foil, brush with marinade. Broil 20 to 30 mins., turning and basting often, until kebabs are brown on all sides. Serve with Pilaf (recipe follows).

Pilaf (6 servings)

2 cups canned condensed beef bouillon
1½ tbsp. butter
2 cups pre-cooked rice

Boil beef bouillon with butter; then add the rice. Mix to moisten, cover and remove from heat. Let stand 5 mins. Fluff with fork. Spoon pilaf into oblong serving dish and arrange hot Shish Kebab across it.

Sukiyaki (4 servings)

½ cup sliced onions
¼ cup butter
1 lb. beef sirloin, cut in strips
Salt and pepper
½ lb. sliced mushrooms
½ cup sliced celery
2 cups drained bean sprouts
¼ cup water chestnuts, sliced
2 tbsp. soy sauce
2 cups fresh spinach or watercress
1 beef bouillon cube
1½ cups hot water
1⅓ cups pre-cooked rice
½ cup chopped green onions

Sauté onions in butter until transparent. Season beef with salt and pepper; add to onion and brown on all sides. Stir in mushrooms, celery, bean sprouts, water chestnuts and soy sauce. Cook 5 to 10 mins. Then add spinach or watercress and cook 2 mins. Meanwhile, dissolve bouillon cube in hot water in pan; stir in rice. Pour into center of other ingredients; sprinkle with chopped green onions. Cover and let simmer over low heat for 5 mins. Do not overcook.

Swedish Meat Balls (12 servings)

1 cup fine breadcrumbs
1 cup milk
2 lbs. ground beef
1 cup chopped onions
2 eggs, slightly beaten
1½ tsp. salt
¼ tsp. pepper
1 tsp. nutmeg
½ cup butter
¼ cup flour
3 beef bouillon cubes
3 cups hot water
1½ cups milk
1½ cups light cream (15%)

Soften crumbs in 1 cup of milk; add beef, onions, eggs, seasonings. Mix thoroughly, shape into 1″ balls. Heat butter in large pan; add meat balls and brown on all sides. Remove and stir flour into drippings, blending well. Dissolve bouillon cubes in hot water. Gradually add to pan, stirring till smooth. Add milk and cream. Cook over low heat, stirring constantly, about 3 mins. Add meat balls to sauce and simmer 10 to 15 mins., stirring occasionally, until sauce is desired consistency. Transfer to covered dish and serve.

Veal Parmesan (6 servings)

2 cloves garlic, crushed
½ cup chopped onion
1 lb. ground beef
¼ cup olive oil
28-oz. can tomatoes
1 bay leaf
2 5½-oz. cans tomato paste
2 tsp. salt
2 lbs. veal cutlets, thin
Parmesan cheese
3 beaten eggs
¼ tsp. pepper
Seasoned breadcrumbs
Sliced Mozzarella cheese

Sauté garlic, onion, and beef in oil. Add tomatoes, bay leaf, tomato paste and 1½ tsp. salt. Simmer, covered, 2½ to 3 hrs., until thickened and reduced. Dip cutlets in Parmesan cheese, then dip into mixture of eggs, remaining ½ tsp. salt and pepper. Dip once again in crumbs; brown on both sides in oil. In casserole, make alternate layers of veal, sauce and sliced Mozzarella. Top with sauce and bake at 375°F until cheese is browned (20 to 30 mins.). If frozen: defrost before baking at 350°F for 30 to 45 mins.

Veal Scaloppine (6 servings)

2 lbs. thinly sliced veal cutlets
2 tbsp. flour
1¼ tsp. salt
¼ tsp. pepper
1 clove garlic
¼ cup butter
2 tbsp. salad oil
½ lb. sliced mushrooms
½ cup water
1 cup dry sherry

Pound cutlets very thin; sprinkle lightly with mixture of flour, ¼ tsp. of the salt, the pepper. Brown garlic in 3 tbsp. of the butter and salad oil. Remove garlic, add cutlets to hot fat and cook quickly till brown on both sides. Place in shallow baking dish. Melt remaining 1 tbsp. butter in skillet; add mushrooms and sauté till golden. Add water, remaining salt and sherry, scraping bottom and sides of pan. Bring to boil and simmer 2 mins., to blend flavours. Pour mushroom sauce over veal. Cover and bake at 350°F for 30 mins., basting twice during baking.

VEGETABLES 9

If you turn back to page 33, you'll find many more ideas about vegetable cooking, under the heading "Some Tricks of the Trade."

Cucumber in Yoghourt (6 servings)

½ clove garlic
¾ tsp. salt
1½ cups yoghourt (plain)
2 tbsp. vinegar
¼ tsp. pepper
2 medium cucumbers

Finely chop garlic in salt. Combine in bowl with yoghourt, vinegar and pepper. Mix well. Peel and slice cucumbers; add to mixture and toss lightly. Chill before serving.

Marinated Eggplant (6 servings)

1 small eggplant
½ cup chopped celery
⅓ cup chopped pimento
1 small clove garlic, minced
2 tbsp. chopped capers
2 tbsp. chopped parsley
⅛ tsp. powdered dill
¼ tsp. oregano
½ tsp. salt
⅛ tsp. pepper
⅓ cup salad oil
⅓ cup vinegar

Cook eggplant in boiling salted water about 20 mins., or until tender. Drain. Cool. Peel and cut in 2" lengths. Add remaining ingredients and mix well. Cover tightly and store in refrigerator.

Peas in Lettuce (4 servings)

12-oz. package frozen peas
2 outside lettuce leaves
½ tsp. salt
1 tbsp. butter
½ garlic clove

Place one lettuce leaf in bottom of 1-qt. pan. Add peas (break frozen block into several pieces), salt, butter, garlic. Cover with second lettuce leaf and lid. Place over medium heat. When lid is hot to the touch, reduce heat and cook for 15 mins. Remove lettuce and garlic before serving.

Hawaiian Rice (4 servings)

1⅓ cups pre-cooked rice
½ tsp. salt
1⅓ cups boiling water
½ cup drained canned crushed pineapple

Add rice and salt to boiling water in saucepan. Mix to moisten. Cover, remove from heat and let stand 5 mins. Add pineapple and mix lightly with fork.

BISCUITS ETC.

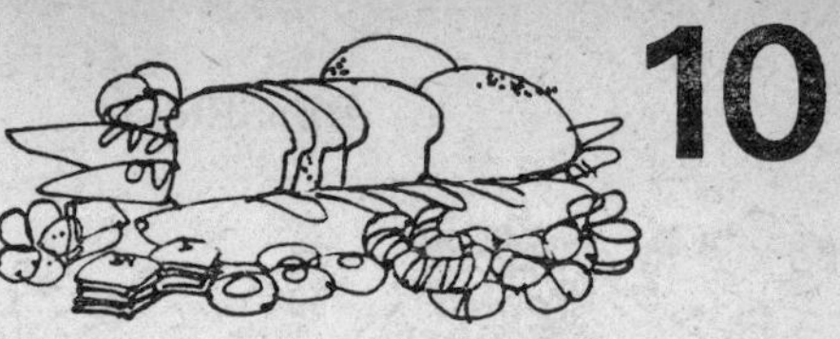

10

Cheese Biscuits (4 dozen)

8 cups sifted cake flour
3½ tbsp. baking powder
3 tsp. salt
¾ cup shortening
4 cups grated cheese
2¼ cups milk

Measure sifted flour, add baking powder and salt, sift again. Cut in shortening until finely divided. Add cheese and mix lightly with fork. Then add milk and stir until soft dough is formed. Divide into four parts. Turn each part out on lightly floured board, knead for 30 seconds. Pat or roll ½″ thick and cut with 2″ biscuit-cutter. Bake on ungreased baking sheet at 450°F 10 to 12 mins.

Herb Biscuits (28 biscuits)

4 cups sifted all-purpose flour
5 tsp. baking powder
1½ tsp. salt
½ cup + 2 tbsp. shortening
½ tsp. grated onion
1½ cups milk
1 tbsp. chopped parsley
⅓ tbsp. celery seed

Measure sifted flour, add baking powder and salt, sift again. Cut in shortening. Add grated onion to milk. Add parsley, celery seed to flour mixture; add milk-and-onion and stir with fork until soft dough is formed. Turn out on lightly floured board and knead 20 turns. Pat or roll till ½″ thick, cut with 2″ cookie cutter. Bake on ungreased sheet at 450°F 12 to 15 mins.

Tortillas (24 servings)

2 cups cornmeal
1 tsp. salt
1 cup flour
Water

Mix cornmeal and salt with enough warm water to form a stiff dough. Add flour, then set aside for 20 mins. Wet hands, form dough into egg-sized balls. Pat into wafer-thin cakes. Cook both sides lightly on greased griddle. Don't let them get brown.

Folded in half, filled with seasoned chopped ham (oregano, cumin, garlic, chili peppers or chili powder), the tortillas become **Quesadillas.**

Fold tortillas in half, fry till crisp, stuff with seasoned (as above) shrimp, top with sour cream, and they become **Tacos.**

Fry unfolded tortillas; stack with minced chicken, avocado, chopped tomatoes, shredded lettuce and radish, and they are **Tostados.**

11

DESSERTS

For other dessert ideas, be sure to check under the headings "Be A Spirited Cook" p.34 (all about cooking with liquor), and "The Burning Question" p.38 (dealing with flambéing), in the first section of the book, "Let's Have a Party!"

Amber Cream (2 cups)

1 cup whipping cream
1/2 tsp. vanilla
2/3 cup brown sugar, firmly packed

Combine ingredients and chill for 1 hour. Place in chilled bowl and beat until cream holds its shape. Don't over-beat. Serve on any fruit pie or pudding.

Variations: Add 1/4 tsp. nutmeg, or grated rind or an orange.

Baked Alaska (6 servings)

1 qt. ice cream (brick or moulded)
Sponge cake
Meringue topping for 9″ pie
1 tbsp. granulated sugar

Freeze ice cream as hard as possible. Trim layer of sponge cake to the same shape as the base of the ice cream. Preheat oven to 450°F. Cover a thick wooden board with heavy unglazed paper, place trimmed sponge cake in middle. Place ice cream in center of cake. Cover both ice cream and cake with layer of meringue, sealing ice cream inside. Dust with sugar. Bake about 5 mins., until meringue is delicately brown. Slip onto a chilled platter and serve immediately.

Banana Meringue (6 servings)

3 egg whites
3/4 cup sugar
1 tsp. vanilla
1/4 tsp. vinegar
1 cup crushed ripe bananas
1/4 tsp. salt
1 1/2 tbsp. lemon juice
1/4 cup icing sugar
1 cup heavy cream (35%), whipped

Beat egg whites, sugar and vanilla until peaks form. Then add vinegar. Beat again for a couple of minutes. Spoon meringue into metal ice trays and bake at 275°F until light brown (40 to 55 mins.). Cool. Combine bananas, salt, lemon juice. Fold in icing sugar to whipped cream; add to banana mixture. Place this filling between the 2 baked meringues; cover with waxed paper and freeze till center is firm. Slice and serve.

Brandy Flan (6 servings)

5 eggs
$^2/_3$ cup sugar
$^1/_8$ tsp. salt
1 large can evaporated milk
2 tbsp. Chemineaud Brandy
$^1/_3$ cup light-brown sugar, firmly packed

Beat eggs with sugar and salt until blended. Scald milk, gradually beat into egg mixture. Stir in brandy. Sift brown sugar into bottom of 3-cup baking dish. Pour egg-milk mixture gently over. Place in shallow pan of hot water and bake at 350°F about 30 mins. Refrigerate. Before serving, run knife around edge of pan and turn out on serving platter.

Caramel Flan (8 servings)

$1^1/_2$ cups sugar
8 eggs
4 cups milk
1 stick cinnamon
1 tsp. vanilla

Cook $^1/_2$ cup sugar in large heavy skillet over low heat, stirring constantly, until it is melted and golden brown. While still hot, spread evenly over bottom of shallow 2-qt. casserole. Cool. Beat eggs until foamy. Gradually add remaining 1 cup sugar, beating well after each addition. Meanwhile, heat milk with cinnamon stick till just below boiling point. Remove cinnamon stick. Gradually add hot milk to egg mixture, stirring until sugar is completely dissolved. Strain this mixture. Add vanilia and pour into caramel-lined casserole. Place in pan of hot water and bake at 350°F about 70 mins., or until inserted knife comes out clean. Cool and unmould before serving.

Champagne Carnival Cups (18 servings)

4 3-oz. packages lemon flavoured jelly powder (not unflavoured gelatin)
3 cups hot water
28 ice cubes
2 27.5-oz. bottles Mumm Extra Dry Champagne

Dissolve jelly in very hot water. Add ice cubes and stir until gelatin thickens slightly. Remove unmelted ice cubes, stir in champagne. Pour into stemmed sherbet glasses; chill until set.

Garnish with fruit or whipped cream.

NOTE: be sure gelatin mixture is slightly thickened when champagne is added. Then bubbles will stay suspended.

Variations: Use sparkling Burgundy instead of champagne.
Or ginger ale and white wine.
Or sparkling apple cider.

Cheesecake De Luxe (8 servings)

Crust

1 cup sifted all-purpose flour
1/4 tsp. sugar
1 tsp. grated lemon rind
1/2 cup butter
1 egg yolk, lightly beaten
1/4 tsp. vanilla extract

Filling

2 1/2 lbs. cream cheese
1/4 tsp. vanilla extract
1 tsp. grated lemon rind
1 3/4 cups sugar
3 tbsp. all-purpose flour
1/4 tsp. salt
5 eggs
2 egg yolks
1/4 cup heavy cream (35%)

Glaze

2 lbs. whole frozen strawberries
Cherry juice or water
2 tbsp. cornstarch

Preheat over to 400°F. Prepare crust by combining flour, sugar, lemon rind; cut in butter until mixture is crumbly. Add egg yolk and vanilla. Mix. Pat 1/3 of the dough over bottom of 9″ spring-form pan with sides removed. Bake about 6 mins. until golden. Cool. Butter the sides of the pan and attach to the bottom. Pat remaining dough around sides to a height of 2″. Increase oven heat to 475°F.

Prepare filling by beating cream cheese until fluffy. Add vanilla and lemon rind. Combine sugar, flour, salt. Blend gradually into cheese mixture. Beat in eggs and egg yolks, one at a time. Beat in cream. Beat thoroughly. Pour mixture into prepared pan and bake 8 to 10 mins. Reduce oven heat to 200°F and bake a further 1 1/2 hrs., or until set. Turn off heat. Allow cake to remain in oven with door ajar for 30 mins. Cool on rack. Chill.

Prepare glaze by thawing and draining strawberries very well, reserving any juice. Add cherry juice or water until liquid makes 2 cups. Reserve berries. Slowly mix cornstarch with juice in small pan; gradually bring to a boil, stirring, and cook 2 to 3 mins. or until thick and transluscent. Cool and chill. Fold in strawberries and spread on chilled cake.

(Contiuned following colour Section)

For successful entertaining say Seagram's and be sure

Starting on page 147, you will find a selection of drink recipes. Whether you are an experienced mixologist or just a beginner, we think you will enjoy trying many of them and experimenting a little. But, there is one ingredient that you should not experiment with, and that is your choice of spirits. Any good bartender knows Seagram quality products are truly the spirits of hospitality — Say Seagram's and be sure.

SEAGRAM'S CROWN ROYAL

A regal blend of whiskies, aged from ten to thirty years, that is smooth, sippable, with a full bouquet. The perfect whisky for gift-giving.

SEAGRAM'S 83

Made exclusively for Canada and Canadian tastes. First introduced in 1883 by Joseph E. Seagram, 83 is a fully matured, mellow 6-year old that Canadian whisky drinkers have enjoyed for ove 90 years.

BLACK WATCH SCOTCH WHISKY

A distinguished blend of the finest 10-year old Scotch whiskies.

SEAGRAM'S V.O.

Seagram's V.O. is Canada's most respected 8-year old whisky. Its perfect balance of smoothness and flavour is unmatched by any other whisky in the world. Only V.O. is V.O.

SEAGRAM'S FIVE STAR

It's Canada's Choice, Naturally. Five Star's fine, bright taste has made it Canada's favourite 5-year old whisky.

SEAGRAM'S 100 PIPERS SCOTCH WHISKY

For the man who calls the tune. Now sold in 102 countries around the world.

CAPTAIN MORGAN DE LUXE

Age: that's the essential ingredient behind this rich, smooth rum. Captain Morgan De Luxe is a blend of the finest procurable rums, aged between 6 and 10 years for unequalled excellence.

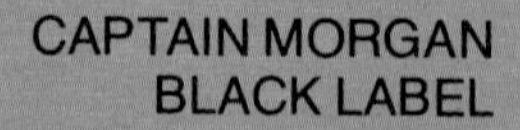

CAPTAIN MORGAN BLACK LABEL

Its clean, robust flavour has made Captain Morgan Black Label a Canadian favourite from coast to coast. The true Demerara flavour is equally enjoyable with cola, juices or in a punch.

TRELAWNY CLASSIC WHITE ESTATE RUM

A blend of premium dry and delicate rare rums for a subtle flavour and bouquet.

MORGAN WHITE RUM

The clean, smooth-tasting rum. A perfect blend of the world's choicest rums, carefully selected at the peak of maturity. Complements a cola, livens up a fruit juice, adds zing to a zombie.

CAPTAIN MORGAN GOLD LABEL

A rum rich in flavour, yet mellow in character. Captain Morgan Gold Label is blended from the world's largest stocks of maturing rums. Perfect on the rocks, or with any mix.

CHEMINEAUD BRANDY

Chemineaud is a delightfully smooth and enjoyable blend of imported and domestic brandies that have been aged four to eight years.

BOODLES BRITISH GIN

The Great Gin imported from Great Britain comes in an elegant crystal-clear decanter-style bottle.

SEAGRAM'S KING ARTHUR LONDON DRY GIN

Heroically dry with a fresh, clean taste. Taste King Arthur Gin and you'll discover a very special pleasure.

OLD BUSHMILLS*** IRISH WHISKEY

The true flavour of Irish whiskey. From the world's oldest operating distillery, established in 1608. Perfect on the rocks, with soda or in an Irish coffee.

SEAGRAM'S EXTRA DRY GIN

The only gin that is aged in white oak casks. The perfect martini gin because it doesn't require vermouth to make it taste smooth.

BOLSHOI VODKA

The Vintage Vodka. Mellowed for a full two years for exceptional smoothness.

"BLACK BUSH" SPECIAL OLD IRISH WHISKEY

A truly unique taste sensation. Twelve years of ageing results in a whiskey of exquisitely refined character — so smooth, so sippable. Limited availability through specialty liquor stores.

Chocolate Mousse Supreme (4 servings)

1/4 lb. semi-sweet chocolate
1/2 cup sugar
1/4 cup water
4 separated eggs
2 tbsp. Captain Morgan Black Label Rum
Chopped pistachio nuts

Melt chocolate in top of double boiler. Cómbine sugar and water, cook 10 mins. (to the syrup stage). Stir syrup into melted chocolate. Add wgg yolks, one at a time, beating well after each one. Remove mixture from heat and stir in rum. Cool. Beat egg whites till stiff and fold into mixture. Heap into serving dish or individual dishes and sprinkle with shelled pistachio nuts.

Coconut Pralines (24 servings)

2 cups granuled sugar
1 cup brown sugar, firmly packed
3 tbsp. light corn syrup
1 cup light cream (15%)
2 2/3 cups flaked coconut
1 tsp. vanilla
1/2 cup butter

Combine sugars, corn syrup, cream in heavy saucepan. Bring to a boil over low heat, stirring constantly. Boil gently, without stirring, to temperature of 236°F (until mixture forms soft ball in cold water). Remove from heat. Add coconut, vanilla, butter. Blend well. Cool to lukewarm (110°F) without stirring. As candy begins to thicken (1 to 2 mins.), beat vigorously. Drop by spoonfuls onto waxed paper, allow to stand 3 hrs. To store, wrap individually in waxed paper.

Dessert Crêpes

(See page 112 for crêpe recipe)

Stuff with raspberry or cherry pie mixture, blended with sour cream. Place in buttered dish and bake at 375°F for 30 mins.

Fresh Lime Cream (6 servings)

1 cup sugar
2 tbsp. cornstarch
1/8 tsp. salt
1 cup water
1/4 cup fresh lime juice
1 egg, lightly beaten
1 tsp. grated lime rind
1 tsp. vanilla extract
1 cup whipping cream, whipped
Additional whipped cream, and grated lime rind for garnish

Combine sugar, cornstarch and salt in pan or top part of double boiler. Gradually stir in water. Cook over low heat (or hot, not boiling, water) until thickened, stirring constantly. Add lime juice. Add a little of hot mixture to beaten egg, then stir that into remaining hot mixture. Cook for a couple of minutes over low heat, stirring. Remove from heat, add grated lime rind and vanilla. Cool. Fold in whipped cream. Serve in sherbet glasses, decorate with more whipped cream and a sprinkle of lime rind.

Frozen Lime Foam (4 servings)

3 separated eggs
1/2 cup sugar
Grated rind of 1 lime
Juice of 1 or 2 limes
1 cup whipping cream, whipped
3/4 cup graham cracker crumbs

Combine egg yolks, sugar, lime rind and juice in top of double boiler. Cook over hot water, stirring, until slightly thickened. Cool. Fold in stiffly beaten egg whites. Fold in whipped cream. Sprinkle half the crumbs into large refrigerator tray. Pour in lime mixture. Top with remaining crumbs and freeze until firm.

Maple Mousse (6 servings)

1 cup maple syrup
4 egg yolks
2 cup whipping cream, whipped

Pour maple syrup into saucepan; beat egg yolks and stir into syrup. Heat on low burner until mixture thickens — being careful not to let it burn. Remove from heat and chill. Fold in whipped cream, turn into mould and chill thoroughly.

Nesselrode Bavarian (8 servings)

2 envelopes (2 tbsp.) unflavoured gelatin
1/4 cup sugar
1/4 tsp. salt
1 1/2 cups milk
4 separated eggs
1 tsp. vanilla
1/4 cup Captain Morgan Gold Label Rum
1/4 cup blanched chopped almonds
2 tbsp. raisins
2 tbsp. chopped candied citron
1/4 cup chopped dates
1/2 cup candied cherries, halved
1/2 cup whipping cream, whipped

Mix gelatin, 1/4 cup sugar and salt in top of double boiler. Add milk, egg yolks; beat until blended. Set over simmering water and cook, stirring constantly, until mixture thickens enough to coat a metal spoon. Remove from heat; add vanilla, rum, almonds, fruits. Chill until thickened, but not firm. Beat egg whites till frothy. Gradually add 1/2 cup sugar and beat until stiff. Fold into fruit-nut mixture, along with whipped cream. Pour into 1½-qt. mould and chill until firm.

Zabaglione (8 servings)

2 cups cold milk
3 cups cold light cream (15%)
2 3¼-oz. packages vanilla instant pudding mix
2 egg whites
¼ cup sugar
⅓ cup sherry

Pour milk and cream into mixing bowl; add pudding mix and beat by hand slowly about 1 min., until well blended. Do not over-beat. Let stand about 5 min. Meanwhile, beat egg whites until stiff but not dry. Gradually beat in sugar, a little at a time. Continue beating till mixture is smooth and glossy. Fold egg white into pudding. Chill. Just before serving, stir in sherry. Serve in sherbet or dessert glasses.

Zitronencreme (6 servings)

3 separated eggs
2 tbsp. sugar
Grated rind of 1 lemon
2 tbsp. Chemineaud Brandy
3-oz. package lemon jelly powder
1 cup hot water
½ cup orange juice, strained
2 tbsp. fresh lemon juice
1 cup whipping cream, whipped

Beat egg yolks with sugar and lemon rind until thick and light. Stir in brandy. Dissolve gelatin in hot water; add orange and lemon juices, egg yolks. Chill until mixture thickens to consistency of unbeaten egg white. Beat egg whites till stiff. Beat gelatin mixture till thick, but not stiff. Fold whipped cream into gelatin. Fold egg whites into gelatin. Pour into mould or serving dish and chill until firm. Garnish with whole strawberries or black cherries.

Turkish Coffee (6 servings)

2 cups water
6 sugar lumps
6 heaping teaspoons of finest ground coffee

Place water, sugar and coffee in small saucepan. Bring just to boil. Remove from heat and cool slightly. Repeat boiling process twice more, before draining syrup from the grounds. Serve in demitasses.

MOVING TOWARD METRICS

In preparing this revision of "The Spirit of Hospitality"; we decided not to change any of the measurements used throughout the book to metrics because —

- Chances are you'll want to continue using your "old favourite" recipes, along with your present baking pans, glasses and measuring utensils for quite some time to come.
- There is still some indecision as to which new metric sizes will become "standards" for measuring utensils, cans, glass, metal and cardboard containers etc. It appears these wrinkles will not all be ironed out for quite a while.

But because we *do* want this to become your *complete* bartending and entertaining handbook we have outlined below some of the basic things you will want to know about metric conversion when it comes along. Particularly as it applies to recipe preparation — in the kitchen, or behind the bar.

THINKING METRIC

Metrics are actually much simpler than the somewhat confusing system we have learned to live with. Measurements are based on multiples of 10. (The "decimal system" — which is the way we now calculate dollars and cents.) For instance:

Weights: 1,000 grams (symbol = g) = 1 Kilogram (Kg)
Volume: 1,000 millilitres (ml) = 100 centilitres = 1 litre (l) (liquids & solids)
Temperatures: A temperature scale measured in °Celsius, where 0°Celsius is the freezing point of water and 100° is the boiling point of water.

It's probably easier still to understand these new measurements if we can get an idea of what they look like in comparison to measurements we are now using.

Weights: 1 Kilogram (Kg) = 2 lb. 3 oz.
Volume: 1 litre (l) — 35 oz. or about 4½ measuring cups.
Temperatures: 0°Celsius =32°F (freezing)
100°Celsius = 212°F (boiling)

Here are some of these equivalents in chart form.

OVEN TEMPERATURE COMPARISONS

Fahrenheit Degrees	Celsius Degrees (Centigrade)	Oven Temperature Terms
212	100	(Boiling point of water)
240-250	116-121	Very slow
290-300	143-149	Slow
350-355	177-179	Moderate
400-405	205-208	Moderately Hot
428	220	Hot
470	243	Very Hot

LIQUID COMPARISONS (Volume)

Present Day Ounces (Vol.)	Metric Volume	Equivalent in Frequently Used Standard Measures
1/6 oz.	5 ml	1 tsp.*
1/2 oz. (1/16 cup)	15 ml	1 tb.*
1 oz.	28 ml	2 tb.*
1 1/4 oz.	35 ml	Standard measure for spirits
1 1/2 oz.	43 ml	1 jigger
8 oz.	240 ml	1 cup
12 oz.	340 ml	Standard spirit bottle size
16 oz.	470 ml	2 cups
20 oz.	570 ml	1 pint (imperial)
25 oz.	710 ml	Standard spirit bottle size
35 oz.	1. l	
40 oz.	1.14 l	1 quart (imperial) Standard spirit bottle size

WEIGHT COMPARISONS

Present Day (pounds & ounces) (approximate)	Metrics grams (g) & Kilograms (Kg) (approximate)	Equivalents in Frequently Used Standard Measures: Flour (Unsifted)	Sugar & Salt	Butter
	5 g		1 tsp.*	1 tsp.*
	7.5 g	1 tb.*		
1 oz.	30 g	4 tb.*	2 tb.*	2 tb.*
4 oz.	115 g	3/4 cup		
5 oz.	140 g	1 cup	3/4 cup	3/4 cup
	190 g		1 cup	1 cup
8 oz. (1/2 lb.)	225 g	1 1/2 cup		
1 lb.	450 g	3 1/4 cups	2 1/2 cups	2 1/2 cups
1 lb. 2 oz.	500 g	3 1/2 cups		
2 lbs. 3 oz.	1 Kg	7 cups	5 1/4 cups	5 1/4 cups

*tsp = teaspoon, tb = tablespoon

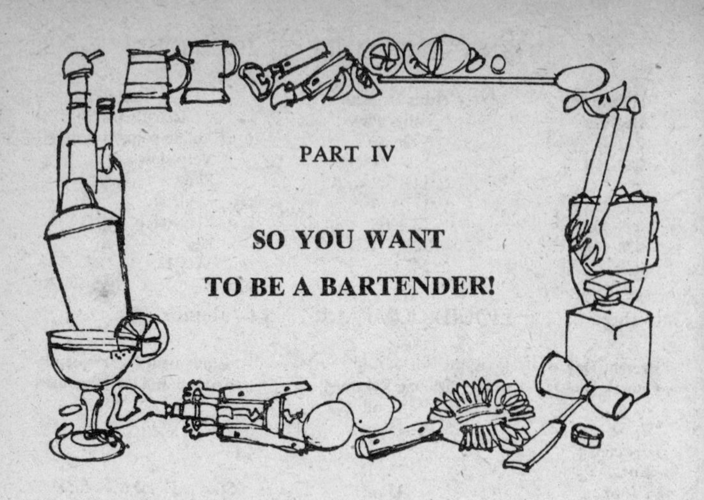

PART IV

SO YOU WANT TO BE A BARTENDER!

Every time you sit at your favourite bar, does the thought flit through your mind, that it might be great to give up the rat race and become a bartender?

Sure it does, it's part of the Walter Mitty in all of us. Have you ever stopped to think why the bartender's job looks so appealing? Basically, it's because he is surrounded by people enjoying themselves, and most good bartenders appear to be having as much fun as their customers.

In short, your favourite "maestro of the mixes" is exhibiting his talents as the perfect host, and that's what this book is all about.

Another thing that usually intrigues us about the art of bartending is the alchemy of it all. A jigger of this, a dash of that, a vigorous shake and presto — a bubbling, frothy liquid is poured with gusto into a tantalizingly frosted glass until it appears about to surge over the top, but by some miracle the shaker runs dry just at that critical instant. It always looks like fun, and it is. With a little practice, and using some of the hints on the following pages, there is no reason why you can't become the best amateur bartender in town.

Mixing all of today's popular drinks is easy and worth learning because, besides having fun, you'll have the double satisfaction of being able to please your own taste and that of your guests.

In the following chapters we'll discuss the equipment you'll need (including glassware) and the various types of drinks and how to mix them, along with many other tricks of the trade.

To make it a little easier, you'll we've divided things up into three categories, using asterisks.

* Indicates basic essentials in the bar, or the easiest of mixed drinks.

** Equipment, glasses and drinks that you might consider once you-ve covered the basics.

*** Appears beside those items or mixed drinks that perhaps "experts" would like to consider.

With that little bit of instruction, let's get on with the business at hand.

1

THE BARTENDER'S TOOL KIT

With any skill there are basic tools of the trade that help make the job easier and the finished product better. Bartending is no exception.

Chances are, many of the items you need are already somewhere around the house, but don't start getting them together five minutes after the first guests arrive and you have just asked them what they would like to drink. Do it now. Round up the things you need for that Bartender's Tool Kit, and come to think of it, that's not a bad idea. Why not buy yourself a small tool kit and set it aside just for that purpose? You can even lock it when not in use so that your razor-sharp paring knife doesn't find its way into junior's room as a balsa splitter for model airplanes.

* The Basics *

If you went in for all the available bar equipment — blenders, midget refrigerators, electric ice crushers and juicers, etc. — you'd have no money left for the liquor! So here are the 12 items you can't really do without. All can be inexpensively bought from your local store.

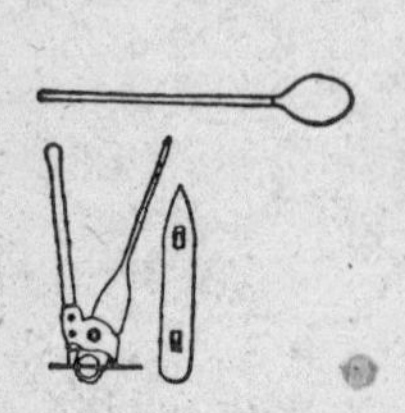

Bar Spoon, long handled — for stirring drinks and fishing for olives, onions, cherries, etc.

Bottle Opener — sturdy and simple.

Can Wedge — the kind that makes the triangular openings in cans containing liquids.

Can Opener.

Corkscrew — any one of the four listed below.

- *The Twist and Pull* — the simplest and probably most often used. Look for a good heavy thread and solid metal with no sharp edges. One that will really screw in and grab hold of the cork. The spindly ones often just ream out the center of the cork at the first yank, leaving the balance in place. Then you're in trouble.

- *The Twist and Pry* — the professional waiter's constant companion. It usually comes as a corkscrew, bottle opener, penknife combination. (Useful for taking off the lead foil that is on the neck of many wine bottles.)

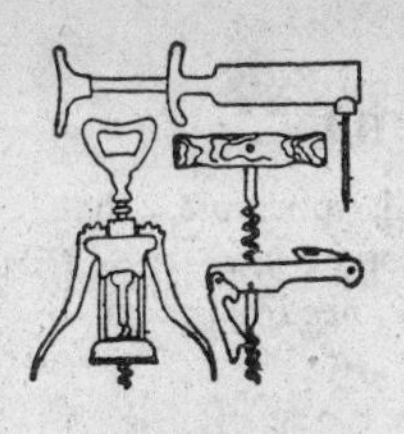

- *The Italian Angel* — somewhat more elaborate, but very effective.
- *The Syringe Type* — not cork "screws," but rather hollow syringe-type needles that are pushed through the cork so that the air hole in the needle is between the bottom of the cork and the liquid. Air is then pumped in, forcing the cork to pop out. There are two types available — one uses a little seltzer cylinder of CO_2 to provide the air pressure, the other you pump by hand like a football pump.

A WORD OF CAUTION: It's amazing the air pressure these syringe-type openers can build up. Presumably, the thing that gives is the cork. Unfortunately, this is not always the case. If the cork is dry and sticks to the neck of the bottle, or if there is a serious flaw in the bottle, the bottle itself could give first. Then, watch out. Bottles with broad shoulders are particularly susceptible. It's not a bad idea to wrap any bottle in a towel while using this type of opener — just in case.

Ice Bucket — pick a big one with a non-metallic, easy to clean interior. Make sure it will hold at least three or four trays of cubes (40 - 50), is well insulated and has a tightly fitting lid.

Ice Cube Tongs or a **small ice scoop.**

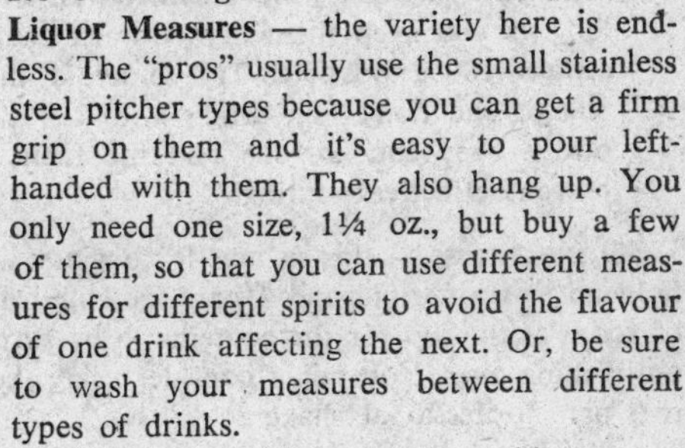

Liquor Measures — the variety here is endless. The "pros" usually use the small stainless steel pitcher types because you can get a firm grip on them and it's easy to pour left-handed with them. They also hang up. You only need one size, 1¼ oz., but buy a few of them, so that you can use different measures for different spirits to avoid the flavour of one drink affecting the next. Or, be sure to wash your measures between different types of drinks.

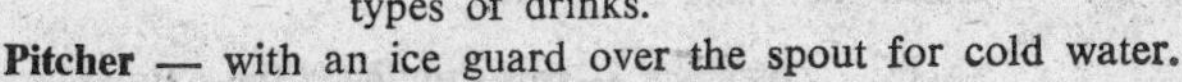

Pitcher — with an ice guard over the spout for cold water.

Sponge — large and absorbent.

Small Terry Cloth Towel.

Tray — with a non-slip surface.

With the above 12 items, you are equipped to handle the basic drinks — On The Rocks, Highballs, Martinis, Manhattans, etc. To easily enlarge your repertoire to include the Sours, Gimlets, Alexanders, etc. —

** Add The Following Items **

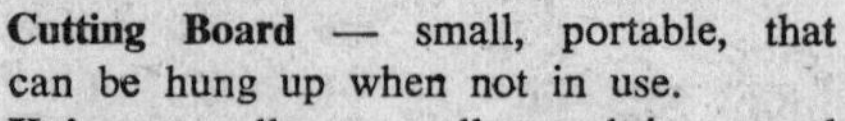

Cutting Board — small, portable, that can be hung up when not in use.

Knives — all you really need is a good sharp paring knife.

Shaker — there are two types:

- *The professional style,* which is made up of two parts: A) a large stainless steel, slope-sided container, and B) a smaller, strong, slope-sided glass. The rim of this glass should be wide enough so that when it is inserted top first inside the metal container, the rim will fit in snugly all around the sides when it is about ¼ of the way inside.

  A strong, uniform, bevelled edge is best. Buy two or three glasses — they sometimes get broken, and it will also save the constant washing when you are mixing a variety of drinks.

- *The glass or metal cocktail shaker* with the detachable top and screw top spout. Possibly you were given one of these as a gift. They work sometimes, and do a good job as long as you keep them dry between uses — but this is not always 100% possible. Try to avoid those that are silver plated, and don't mix drinks with citrus fruits in them too often. They can corrode and the fruit particles sometimes prevent effective pouring.

Stirring Glass — this is any large glass with the capacity to hold up to 6 oz. fluid and 3 or 4 ice cubes and still have plenty of room at the top for the contents to be stirred vigorously without spilling over. You might consider using the glass part of your two part professional shaker.

Strainer — this should be the stainless steel spring type. The spring expands or contracts to fit snugly inside the rim of the pouring glass. The two metal clips and the handle sit over the top of the glass edge. Buy two sizes, one for small glasses, the other for larger ones.

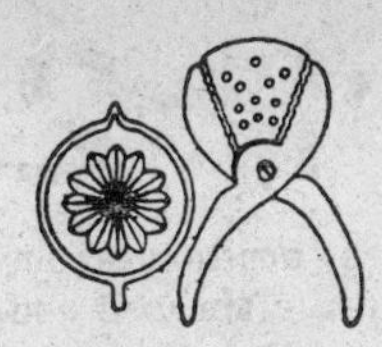

Squeezer — for oranges and lemons, either hand, electric or battery operated and, if possible, the small scissors type lime squeezer. Remember, when squeezing fresh citrus fruit, do not squeeze too hard as some of the bitter oils of the skin might get in with the juice.

A Plastic Waste Paper Basket — with a small kitchen garbage bag in it. Don't use a metal one, chances are it will rust.

*** For The Expert ***

To have the best equipped home bar in town and be prepared to handle almost any cocktail requested, here are a few extra items you may wish to consider.

Muddler — made of hardwood, not glass, for muddling sugar cubes and crushing mint leaves, etc.

Blender — this can be a real aid in mixing up all kinds of exotic drinks in a flash.

Electric Ice Crusher — a great time saver if you are partial to frappés or like to use crushed ice in your shaker or blender. Preferably, it should have three settings — "fine," "medium," and "coarse." Otherwise, an ice bag and mallet do a great job. Basically, any small canvas or heavy cotton bag and wooden hand mallet will do. Don't use your blender for crushing ice. Most manufacturers don't recommend it.

If you are wondering why we have not even mentioned glasses up to now, it is because they warrant a chapter unto themselves. The next . . .

2 WHY DO WE NEVER HAVE ENOUGH GLASSES?

That's probably the most frequently asked question about glasses. The answer is, because they are the most often used and most often broken item in any household. So, usually when party time comes, the shortage of glassware becomes a pressing problem.

How Many Do You Need?

That depends on how many people are coming and what you are serving. If you are having a relatively small group and plan on serving cocktails, wine with the meal and liqueurs with coffee, one glass of each type per person is about all that is required.

For a cocktail party, you will need an assortment of highball, on the rocks and cocktail glasses. A good rule of thumb is to allow for a total glass count of two glasses per person, equally divided between the glass types required for the drinks being offered. This should ensure that you have sufficient of any one type.

If you have a big party coming up and if you don't entertain on this scale at least four times a year, why not rent? (See page 22.)

Some Basic Buying Rules

- For party use, or everyday entertaining, don't buy hand blown or crystal glasses. But don't buy plastic cups either (unless for use on the patio or around the pool).
- Do buy good quality, machine blown glassware, in a style that can be easily replaced. Clear, not coloured, and unpatterned.
- Buy the right sizes and shapes you need, because each type of glass is designed to do a specific job.

What Sizes To Buy?

Described below are 10 different sizes and shapes of glasses, each designed for a specific type of drink. The first five are the ones we'd pick as doing almost any entertaining job admirably. Regardless of what sizes you decide to buy, get at least a dozen of each. This is the bare minimum you'll need for eight people, and allows for inevitable breakage.

* The Top Five *

These five types of glasses cover the vast majority of home ente.taining needs, from cocktails, through dinner to after dinner.

Highball Glass: 8 to 12-oz. A heavy-based, straight-sided glass for straightforward mixes on ice, such as "with soda," "with water," etc.

Old Fashioned or On the Rocks Glass: 6 to 10-oz. Low slung, rugged and very versatile. It can be used to serve just about any iced drink. It can be purchased with or without a stem.

Cocktail Glass: 3 to 4½-oz. Broad V or bellshape with a stem. This is probably going to be your most frequently used glass (along with the highball glass) . . . for most stirred or shaken cocktails.

Sherry Glass: 2 to 2½-oz. V-shaped with a stem. Ideal for of course sherry, but also ports and other fortified wines, and liqueurs served straight.

Large Universal Wineglass: 8-oz. Bell-shaped with a stem. This glass can also, in a pinch, be used for extra large cocktails. This is a large glass, and should only be half filled with wine so that you leave sufficient space at the top for swirling and inhaling the bouquet of the wine. This glass is also far better for champagne or sparkling wines than the traditional champagne glass. It holds the bubbles and sparkle longer.

** The Welcome Additions **

The following glasses tend to be used less frequently by the average home bartender. But, they have such attractive shapes and are so ideally suited for certain types of liquor and mixed drinks, that they are certainly a welcome addition to any bar. Consider the possibility of adding even a few of these to your glass supply.

Delmonico or Sour Glass: 5 to 7-oz. Ideal for all cocktails that have a frothy head.

Cordial, Liqueur or Pony Glass: 1-oz. It's small, petite and feminine and adds to the appearance of the liqueur but it doesn't help the enjoyment factor. Used for Pousse Café.

*** Completing the Lineup ***

To be able to produce the right glass for the right drink on every occasion, you should add these final three to your stock.

The Brandy Snifter: 8 to 12-oz. Its broad, "hold in the palm" shape makes it just great for savouring the bouquet of good cognac or brandy and just about any whisky straight. It also does something for the variety of colourful liqueurs.

Zombie or Sling Glass: 14-oz. Tall, very slim, straight-sided. For those multi-coloured drinks.

Champagne Glass: 5 to 6-oz. Broad, open shape with a stem. It's not the best glass for champagne despite its name, but it is traditional. Also a nice glass for frothy drinks.

Washing Glasses

It's an appealing sight! A tray of frosty drinks in sparkling glasses, brimming with crystal-clear ice cubes. Here are the three simple steps needed to give your glasses that extra gleam.

- As soon as possible after use, wash with warm water and lots of soap.
- Then, rinse with scalding water.
- Dry with a lint free towel.

A WELL-STOCKED BAR SAYS "WELCOME" 3

Now that you have finished setting up the best equipped bar in town, let's consider the most essential ingredient — the liquor.

You probably have your own preferences, which you'll naturally put at the top of your shopping list. But, as the perfect host, you'll want to consider your guests' tastes too.

Liquor preferences do follow somewhat of a geographical pattern in Canada. Rum is a great favourite in the Atlantic provinces, gin in Quebec, and whisky just about everywhere else. But no matter which province one is in, Canadian whisky is always in demand (which suggests that perhaps you should have two bottles of Canadian whisky in your basic bar).

These regional differences ares mentioned as a guideline only. There is a wide choice of liquors available today, and the emphasis is on individual preference. So your guests will appreciate your talents as a host if they find their particular favourite in your well-stocked bar.

So, using our *, **, *** system, here is a suggested list of what your bar should contain.

* Basics *

1 bottle **Seagram's V.O. Canadian Whisky**
1 bottle **Seagram's 83 or Five Star Canadian Whisky**
1 bottle **King Arthur Dry Gin**
1 bottle **Morgan White Rum**
1 bottle **Seagram's 100 Pipers Scotch**
1 bottle **Bolshoi Vodka**
1 bottle **Noilly Pratt French Vermouth (white)**
1 bottle **Noilly Pratt Italian Vermouth (red)**

With these six brands and the two vermouths, you can satisfy the tastes of about 85% of Canadians.

** Adding To The List **

1 bottle **Boodles British Gin** (Great gin from Great Britain)
1 bottle **Captain Morgan Black Label Rum**
1 bottle **Chemineaud Brandy**
1 bottle **Black Watch Scotch** (10 year old Scotch)
1 bottle **Leroux Green Crème de Menthe**
1 bottle **Leroux Crème de Café**
1 bottle **Leroux Triple Sec**

***** Then, To Make Your Lineup Complete *****

1 bottle **Seagram's Extra Dry Gin** (it's the distinctively different Martini gin — no need to add Vermouth).
1 bottle **Captain Morgan Gold Label Rum**
1 bottle **Trelawny Classic White Estate Rum**
1 bottle **Leroux White Crème de Menthe**
1 bottle **Leroux Apricot Brandy**
1 bottle **Leroux Cherry Brandy**
1 bottle **Leroux Cherry Whisky**

And for those special occasions . . .

1 bottle **Seagram's Crown Royal Canadian Whisky**
1 bottle **Mumm Cordon Rouge Brut Champagne or Mumm Extra Dry**

You might also want to add any of the specialties you and friends might have a particular preference for, such as **"Old Bushmills" Irish Whiskey, Lochan Ora, Sabra, Vandermint,** etc.

Once you have your bar set up, remember to constantly check your stock. There is nothing worse than inviting a group of martini-drinkers over only to find you have run out of gin.

That's Quite A List — Think Of The Cost

If you decided to go all out and purchase the complete list of suggestions above, the total cost would be just over $200. But more realistically, the basic bar can be purchased for around $55, and the next step up the line (**) for about $50. And here is a point worth remembering. A well-stocked bar does not mean your guests are going to drink any more, or that the liquor cost per party you give is going to increase. What it does mean however, is that you will be prepared to cater to every whim of your guests. That's one of the trademarks of the perfect host.

While we are on the subject, here are some other points worth remembering. If your guests are of your own choosing, nothing should be too good for them. Don't buy inferior quality liquor and put it in expensive bottles or glass decanters, no matter how beautiful. Display your bottles proudly. There is no more subtle or solid way of telling your friends how highly you regard them. And of course, you know that Seagram's products are recognized for their excellence, so you can always serve them with pride.

THE ALL-IMPORTANT EXTRAS 4

The nicest thing about liquor is that it tastes good, and it combines beautifully with so many other things that are appealing to the palate. Liquor itself comes in a wide variety of tastes and can be combined to provide even more variations. When you add to this all of the extra ingredients that go well with liquor, the possibilities are limitless.

When party planning, again, we repeat — think ahead. Make sure you are well-stocked with those important "extras." The rest of this chapter is devoted to listing these in approximate order of importance, using our * system. You would do well to read the list over and check off those items you think you will need. Perhaps if you have got space in that bartender's tool kit you could put some of the smaller non-perishable items aside strictly for bar use so they won't get used up around the kitchen.

Again, please note the *'s beside each item. They indicate when you are most likely to need each (* for basic drinks, etc.).

Ice — this is the most inexpensive ingredient in the bar and the one that can add the most pleasure to any cold drink. Allow for 15 cubes per person for a three to four hour party. Use it liberally, but make sure it is fresh and always wash it first. The washing part is both practical and aesthetic. Ice left in the refrigerator can pick up other flavours and odors from items stored with it. These can be imparted to the drink. Washing prevents this. Also, washed ice cubes come crystal clear and do not crack and cloud when liquids are added, thus giving your drinks more eye appeal. You'll need —

* *ice cubes* for stirred and shaker drinks.

* *cracked ice* for mists, juleps, etc.

*** *pounded or shaved ice* for frozen daiquiris, frappés.

Note: In the latter two cases, this is where the canvas bag and mallet come in to reduce your ice cubes to the cracked or shaved category.

*** *Frosting or Chilling Glasses.* Always use cold glasses for cold drinks. Don't dilute your hospitality with water from ice cubes overworked from cooling warm ingredients in warm glasses. To chill your cocktail glasses, simply place a cube in the glass and gently swirl the cube with a slight hand motion until it is rotating around the glass. Do this for a few seconds and then tip out the cube and water. This little touch can mean the difference between an excellent and a mediocre drink.

Soft drinks — (You'll need about 4 oz. per highball — that's 7 drinks out of a big bottle.)

* *Club soda*
* *Coke, Pepsi or Tab (for weight watchers).*
* *Ginger ale*
* *Seven-Up, Sprite, Fresca (for weight watchers).*
* *Tonic water, bitter lemon, bitter orange*
* *Collins mix, half and half, etc.*

Hint — Buy large bottles with the screw caps. They are less expensive. Make sure they are cold when you use them, otherwise you'll melt the ice too fast and dilute the drink.

Garnishes — these are the bits and pieces used to top off a drink. Cherries are often used but here are some others:

* *Twists or "zests"* of lemon or orange.

Hint — Don't use huge chunks of peel as so many people mistakenly do. The reason for using the "zest" is to add the flavour of the oil in the outer skin to the drink. A small piece the size of your thumb nail is all that is required. Cut it from the fruit and then take it between the thumb and forefinger of one hand and squeeze it so that the oil sprays over the surface of the drink. Drop the remaining peel in the drink if you wish.

* *Mint leaves* — fresh only

Olives and onions —

* *Olives* — small, with pits, green. Rinse before using. Avoid the larger stuffed ones. The pimento imparts a flavour.
* *Onions* — cocktail size, sour. Rinse before using.

Bitters — and things you add a dash of —

** *Angostura Bitters* — made from an infusion of roots, herbs and botanicals.

** *Worcestershire Sauce*

** *Tabasco Sauce*

*** *Vanilla Extract*

Fruits — use whole chunks that you can spear with colourful toothpicks.

** *Cherries, maraschino,* 1 bottle of red and 1 bottle of green.

** *Orange and lemon slices*

** *Fresh limes*

** *Pineapple chunks*

Juices —

** *Lemon* — the juice from fresh fruit is best but have the concentrate on hand just in case.

** *Prepared Lemon Juice*

You will notice that many of the mixed drink recipes in the following chapter call for "Prepared Lemon Juice." This is a trick of the trade that you should learn now if you do not already know it. You'll find that by using this mixture, your frothy drinks will not separate after they are poured no matter how long you let them stand. Also, your guests will not get that gritty over-sweetness when they get to the bottom of their Collins, Sours, etc., caused by undissolved, granulated sugar. If you make the recipe in advance it will be one less job to do when guests arrive. Here it is:

Prepared Lemon Juice (makes 25 oz.)

1. Squeeze 12 lemons to obtain approximately 15 oz. of juice.
2. Sweeten to taste with Simple Sugar Syrup. (See page 143). Use approximately 2 to 8 oz. of syrup.
3. Add 1 beaten egg to mixture and stir.
4. Keep refrigerated and do not prepare more than you will need for one evening.

** *Lime* — as above.

** *Homogenized tomato juice* (see that it says it is on the label), *V-8 juice, Garden Cocktail.*

** *Orange, grapefruit, and pineapple juice.*

Sweeteners —

** *Grenadine* — this is a bright red syrup made from pomegranates. It is used in many drinks for colour and sweetness

** *Sugar* — use powdered or extra fine, not regular granulated, or better still:

Simple Sugar Syrup — this is another one of those "bartender's friends" that you should know about. It is the perfect answer to the clearness in clear, sweet drinks and solves the problem of undissolved granulated sugar and uneven sweetness. You can make this syrup in advance and keep it for an unlimited time as long as it is tightly capped between uses. Here is the recipe:

> To 16 oz. of cold water, add 1 lb. of powdered fruit sugar. Stir from time to time until a clear syrup is obtained. It is best then to use a funnel and pour it into a clean, empty bottle.

Hint — to frost a glass with sugar, run a wedge of lemon around the rim of the glass and then insert the wet rim in powdered sugar. Let it dry and shake off loose sugar. For drinks with a coffee, chocolate, or mocha base, dip the rim in the liquid and then in a mixture of sugar and instant coffee.

*** *Honey and maple syrup*

Dairy Products

*** *Table cream* (15%)

*** *Eggs* — (to break an egg so that you can separate the yolk from the white, hit the centre of the shell on the edge of the counter, not your mixing glass, and split the shell in two halves. Hold the two halves over your mixing glass and pass the yolk from one half to another, allowing the white to fall into the glass. If you are one of those people that gets more shell into the glass than white, a gadget for separating the white from the yolk is available at hardware and department stores.

*** *Milk*

*** *Butter* — for hot toddies etc.

Sprinklers —

** *Salt and pepper*

*** *Cinnamon and cinnamon sticks*

*** *Nutmeg* — ground

Cocoa ***

Coffee (instant) ***

5

99 - FROM ALEXANDER TO ZOMBIE

Here's the moment we have all been waiting for folks! It's time for you, the perfect host, to step behind the bar and with a flourish, start to concoct all those tantalizing favourites of the mixologist's art that your friends have come to expect from you.

You have the best stocked, best equipped bar in town. The Prepared Lemon Juice (See page 142) and Sugar Syrup (See page 143) are made, the oranges and lemons are sliced and you're ready to go.

So, at this stage, let's get down to brass tacks and discuss the various basic types of drinks, and the appropriate times to serve them

The Thirteen Basic Types Of Drinks

All of the recipes shown on subsequent pages are variations of these thirteen drink types:

** Quick and Easy **

Highballs — are easy to prepare drinks but some of the most satisfying. Any liquor or liqueur served with ice and any effervescent soft drink or water.

On The Rocks — in this case the rocks are ice and it is simply liquor or a liqueur poured over ice cubes, usually in Old Fashioned glasses. Nothing else is added.

Julep — this is an American drink that is not served too often here; cool and refreshing. Uses sprigs of fresh mint, crushed ice and any type of whiskey. Served in a large Old Fashioned or highball glass, with a straw. A **Smash** is a small julep.

Apéritifs — drinks served before a meal, to sharpen the appetite. Usually wine or wine-based, and sweet. Served straight or with ice in sherry. Old Fashioned or cocktail glasses.

Cocktails — (Only a few, such as martinis, Manhattans, Rob Roys, etc. are really * drinks. Most of the others take a little more time to prepare and are ** or *** drinks. See cocktail index on page 169.) Usually served before dinner, always chilled. Generally made with one of the basic liquors in a 1-5 to 1-8 proportion with vermouths, liqueurs, etc. **Daisies** are overgrown cocktails to which soda has been added.

*** A Little More Effort But Worth It ***

Frappés — these are drinks served neat over shaved ice. Usually sweet liqueurs. Served (with straws) after meals as digestives, in Old Fashioned or champagne glasses.

Old Fashioneds — pleasant, refreshing, fruity drinks that can use almost any liquor as a base, with lots of ice, bitters, sugar and an assortment of fruit chunks and slices.

Long Drinks — into this category fall the Collins, Coolers and Rickeys. They are made with almost any type of liquor and often contain some effervescent liquid as a topper. They run from sweet to sour and from exotic (***) to simple (**). Served in 10 to 14-oz. glasses with lots of ice.

Fizzes — mid-afternoon or warm-evening drinks, made with almost any liquor plus fruit juices or fruit syrups; shaken with egg white and then topped with club soda. Served in highball glasses.

Sours — these are in the cocktail family but can be served anytime. Almost any liquor can be used. Usually mixed with lemon juice, ice, sugar, egg white and topped with a cherry. Normally have frothy heads.

**** Earn Your Bartender's Diploma With These ****

Punches — party drinks for winter or summer. Usually made with fruit juices, a block of ice, bitters, sugar and almost any liquor. Served in punch cups.

Flips — frothy drinks, shaken. Usually call for a whole egg; sugar; cracked ice; brandy, sherry, port or any liquor. Topped with nutmeg. Served in sour, wine or Old Fashioned glasses.

Eggnogs — egg, sugar, and milk or cream mixtures in combinations with almost any basic liquor. Usually served in cold weather and at festive occasions, in Old Fashioned glasses or punch cups.

The Order Of Things

Now, let's list the order in which things should be put into the shaker or glass when mixing. Don't think we are getting too ritualistic about this, there are good reasons for this sequence. (You are probably not going to be using all of the ingredients listed below but follow this order with the things you will be using.)

Into your glass or shaker put:

1. ice cubes — this avoids splashing and facilitates chilling.
2. sugar and bitters
3. eggs, milk, cream and/or juice
4. liquor
5. whole fruit slices

6. soft drinks, soda, water, etc.
7. garnishes, cherry topping, nutmeg, cinnamon, etc.

Now For The Recipes

If, up until now, you have confined your talents as a bartender to simply mixing highballs, on the rocks drinks and the occasional martini, because you considered most of the other mixed drinks just too complicated, you are in for a pleasant surprise.

The fact is, all of today's popular drinks are easy to prepare and do not contain any more exotic ingredients than those covered earlier on in this section. Here are 99 of today's "best sellers." They have been carefully selected to include everyone's favourites, from the "in" drinks to the popular old favourites. Although they are listed alphabetically for ready reference, please note that we've used our * system with each name, to help you in deciding what you would like to serve, and starting on page 147 we've listed them all according to our *, **, *** categories, in keeping with the following explanations.

* **Quick and Easy** to prepare, using the basic liquor favourites (V.O., Morgan White Rum, King Arthur Dry Gin, Seagram's 100 Pipers Scotch, Bolshoi Vodka) either by themselves or in combination with Noilly Pratt French Vermouth, Noilly Pratt Italian Vermouth, or the popular mixers such as ginger ale, cola, etc.

** **A Little More Effort but Worth It.** Most of the drinks in this category will call for a combination of more than one liquor or popular liqueur and/or the addition of fruit or vegetable juices. A cocktail shaker will also probably be required.

*** **Earn Your Bartender's Diploma with These.** Here is where your talents really come to the fore. These drinks call for two, three or more liquors and/or liqueurs, and perhaps fruit juices, fruit chunks, eggs, cream, etc. Generally a shaker or blender will be required.

Why did we only pick 99 and not 100? We left the 100th drink for you. It's your "Specialty of the House" — call it what you will.

NOTE: *For all recipes calling for Prepared Lemon Juice, please see page 142, and for recipes calling for Simple Sugar Syrup, please see page 143.*

***

ALEXANDER

1

$^{3}/_{4}$ oz. Chemineaud Brandy
$^{1}/_{4}$ oz. Leroux Crème de Café
$^{1}/_{4}$ oz. Leroux Triple Sec
$^{3}/_{4}$ oz. table cream (15%)

Shake with ice. Strain into chilled cocktail glass. Sprinkle with ground nutmeg.

Note: Alexanders are also prepared with dry gin, rye, rum or Scotch.

***

APRÈS DINER

2

1 oz. Leroux Green Crème de Menthe
$^{1}/_{2}$ oz. Leroux Crème de Café
$^{1}/_{4}$ oz. Leroux Triple Sec
$1^{1}/_{2}$ oz. table cream (15%)

Shake with ice. Strain into chilled cocktail glass.

***

BANANA DAIQUIRI

3

$2^{1}/_{2}$ oz. Trelawny Classic White Estate Rum
1 oz. fresh lemon juice
$^{1}/_{2}$ fresh banana
2 tsp. sugar

Mix in blender with one cup of finely cracked ice. Blend till creamy. Serve in chilled champagne glass.

**

BETWEEN THE SHEETS

4

$^{3}/_{4}$ oz. Chemineaud Brandy
$^{3}/_{4}$ oz. Morgan White Rum
$^{1}/_{2}$ oz. Leroux Triple Sec
$^{3}/_{4}$ oz. Prepared Lemon Juice

Shake with ice. Strain into chilled sour glass. Decorate with a cherry.

**

BLACK RUSSIAN

5

$1^{1}/_{2}$ oz. Bolshoi Vodka
$^{3}/_{4}$ oz. Leroux Crème de Café

Shake with ice. Pour into cocktail glass, or serve on the rocks in an Old Fashioned glass. Decorate with an orange twist.

**

BLOODY MARY

6

Over 3-4 ice cubes in a 10-oz. glass sprinkle salt and pepper to taste before adding other ingredients. Then add:

5-6 drops Worcestershire sauce
3 drops Tabasco sauce
$^{1}/_{2}$ oz. lemon juice
$1^{1}/_{4}$ oz. Bolshoi Vodka

Fill with tomato juice. Stir while pouring.

Note: If you substitute dry gin for the vodka, it's called a **Red Snapper.** One of today's popular variations is a **Bloody Caesar** — exactly as above but with a half and half mixture of clam and tomato juice added. Sometimes called a **Clamdigger** (Vodka).

**

BROWN COW

7

$1^{1}/_{4}$ oz. Captain Morgan Gold Label Rum
$^{1}/_{2}$ oz. Leroux Crème de Café
4 oz. milk
1 Dash Angostura Bitters

Shake thoroughly with ice cubes — strain in 8 oz. glass sprinkle ground nutmeg.

**

BUCK

8 Squeeze juice of 1/2 lime into a 10-oz. glass over ice cubes and drop in rind. Add 11/4 oz. gin, vodka, brandy, rum, or your favourite whisky. Add ginger ale to taste. When you use Boodles British Gin call it a **London Buck.**

**

"BULL SHOT"

9 Into an Old Fashioned glass with ice cubes add salt and pepper to taste, 3-4 drops Worcestershire sauce, 1/4 oz. lemon juice, 11/4 oz. Bolshoi Vodka and cold bouillon (not consommé), as much as you like, and stir gently.

"BULL SHOOTER"

Just like a Bull Shot, except that you finally add bouillon *and* tomato juice in the quantities you perfer:

**

CAFE ROYALE

10 Place two lumps of sugar in a dessert spoon and balance over a demitasse cup of hot coffee. Fill the spoon with Seagram's Crown Royal and when warm, blaze with a lighted match. As flame begins to fade, empty the spoon into the coffee. If preferred, all ingredients can be placed in cup without flaming. Chemineaud Brandy or Captain Morgan Black Label Rum can also be used in place of Crown Royal.

**

CANADA'S PRIDE

11
11/4 oz. Seagram's V.O.
1/8 oz. Leroux Crème de Café
2 oz. Apple juice

Stir with 4 ice cubes, and strain in old fashioned glass.

***

CAPRICE

12
1/2 oz. Bolshoi Vodka
1/2 oz. Leroux Crème de Café
1/2 oz. Leroux Triple Sec
11/2 oz. table cream (15%)

Shake with ice cubes and strain into gimlet glass. Sprinkle chocolate chips.

***

CHAMPAGNE PUNCH

13 *(To be mixed in a punch bowl. Serves 6 persons.)*
Place one cake of ice, or 2 dozen ice cubes, in a punch bowl, then add:

2 oz. Simple Syrup
2 oz. Chemineaud Brandy
2 oz. Leroux Triple Sec
1/2 cup orange cut into thin slices
1/2 cup lemon (as above)
1/2 cup red maraschino cherries (diced)
1 bottle Mumm Cordon Rouge Brut Champagne (cold)

Stir

***

CHERRY DAISY

14
1 oz. Leroux Cherry Brandy
1 oz. Chemineaud Brandy
1/4 oz. grenadine
1 oz. lemon juice
Soda water

Shake with crushed ice and pour into a 12-oz. glass. Top with soda water. Serve with two straws.

***

CHRISTMAS RUM PUNCH

(cold)

15

8 oz. orange juice
4 oz. lemon juice
4 oz. pineapple juice
1 cup diced pineapple
4 oz. Leroux Triple Sec
1/2 cup diced maraschino cherries
1 25-oz. bottle Captain Morgan Gold Label Rum
1 orange and 1 lemon cut into thin 1/2 slices

Place all ingredients in punch bowl and chill for two hours. Add chunk of ice or ice cubes just before serving. Stir and serve in cups (12 to 15 servings).

***

CLOVER CLUB

16

1 1/4 oz. King Arthur Gin
1 1/4 oz. Prepared Lemon Juice
1/4 oz. grenadine
1/4 oz. table cream (15%)

Shake with ice. Strain into chilled sour glass. Decorate with a cherry.

***

CLOVER LEAF

17

1 1/4 oz. Prepared Lemon Juice
1 1/4 oz. King Arthur Gin
1/4 oz. table cream (15%)
1/4 oz. Leroux Green Crème de Menthe

Shake with ice. Strain into a sour glass. Serve with a green cherry.

*

CLUB COCKTAIL

(contains no spirits)

18

1 lump sugar
2 dashes Angostura bitters
1 twist lemon peel
Soda water

Place sugar in Old Fashioned glass and splash with bitters. Add ice cubes and fill with soda water, or lemon soda. Decorate with 1 green and 1 red cherry.

**

COLLINS

19 Fill a 14-oz. highball glass with ice cubes.

Add:

1 1/4 oz. King Arthur Gin
1 1/4 oz. Prepared Lemon Juice

Top with soda water, stirring lightly while pouring.

Note: Collins are also prepared with brandy, rye, rum, Scotch or vodka.

**

DAIQUIRI

20

1 oz. Trelawny Classic White Estate Rum
1 oz. Prepared Lemon Juice

Shake well with ice. Strain into chilled cocktail glass. Decorate with red cherry.
A Pink Daiquiri is tinted with a bar spoonful of grenadine.

**

DEBUTANTE

21

1/2 oz. Leroux Cherry Brandy
3/4 oz. Chemineaud Brandy
3/4 oz. pineapple juice

Shake with ice and strain into a chilled cocktail glass. Decorate with a cherry.

***

EGG NOG

22

1 1/4 oz. Chemineaud Brandy
1 1/2 oz. Simple Syrup
5 oz. milk
1 whole egg
5 or 6 drops vanilla extract

Shake with ice. Strain into a 12-oz. glass. Sprinkle ground nutmeg on top.

Note: Can also be prepared with rye, rum, or port wine.

**

ENGLISH ROSE

23

1 1/4 oz. King Arthur Gin
1/2 oz. Leroux Cherry Brandy

Stir well with ice. Strain into chilled cocktail glass. Top with a red cherry.

**

FAVOURITE

24

1 oz. Seagram's Extra Dry Gin
1 oz. Noilly Pratt French Vermouth
1/2 oz. Leroux Apricot Brandy
1/2 oz. lemon juice

Stir well with ice. Strain into sour glass. Serve with a cherry.

**

FIZZ

25

1 1/4 oz. of your favourite liquor
1 1/4 oz. Prepared Lemon Juice

Shake thoroughly with 4 ice cubes. Pour unstrained (ice and all) into 10-oz. glass. Fill with chilled soda.

***

FLIP

26

1 1/4 oz. Morgan White Rum
1 whole egg
1/2 oz. Simple Syrup
4-5 drops Angostura bitters

Shake with ice and strain into an Old Fashioned glass. Sprinkle ground nutmeg on top. Flips can also be made with brandy, rye, Scotch, sherry or port wine.

*

FLOAT

27 Into an 8-oz. wineglass, pour 5 oz. chilled Vichy water. Float 1 1/4 oz. Chemineaud Brandy on top.

Note: No ice should be used.

***

FRENCH "75"

28

1 1/4 Seagram's Extra Dry Gin
1 1/4 oz. Prepared Lemon Juice
1/2 oz. Leroux Triple Sec
Mumm Champagne

Pour first three ingredients over ice cubes into 14-oz. glass. Then stir while pouring champagne. Garnish with two red cherries.

*

GIBSON

29 See "Extra Dry Martini" (No. 53).

**

GIMLET

30
1¼ oz. King Arthur Gin
½ oz. Leroux Triple Sec
1¼ oz. Prepared Lemon Juice

Shake with ice. Strain into chilled champagne glass. Serve with a green and a red cherry.

*

GIN AND "IT"

31
1¼ oz. Seagram's Extra Dry Gin
1¼ oz. Noilly Pratt Italian Sweet Vermouth

Chill. Serve in chilled cocktail glass.

**

GIN AND SIN

32
1¼ oz. Seagram's Extra Dry Gin
¼ oz. orange juice
¼ oz. lemon juice
1 dash grenadine

Shake well with ice. Strain into cocktail glass.

*

GIN AND TONIC

33 See "Highball' (No. 40).

***

GLUEHWEIN

(an après-ski favourite)

34 In an earthenware jug, or heat-resistant glass or ceramic pot, add one glass (per person) of B&G Prince Noir or B&G Côtes de Luberon. (Never use a fortified wine.) Add (again, on a per person basis) about 3 inches of cinnamon stick, 1 clove, 3 lumps of sugar, 1 slice of orange peel, and 1 slice of lemon peel. If a quantity is made, it is better to allow the pot to stand on a slow fire and bring to near the boiling point slowly. Serve in earthenware mugs with the fruit slices floating on top.

***

GRASSHOPPER

35
½ oz. Leroux Crème de Café
¾ oz. Leroux Green Crème de Menthe
¾ oz. table cream (15%)

Shake with ice. Strain and serve in a cocktail glass. Garnish with a green cherry.

***

GREEN LADY

36
¾ oz. Leroux Green Crème de Menthe
½ oz. Leroux Cherry Brandy
¾ oz. table cream (15%)

Shake with ice. Strain into a chilled cocktail glass. Decorate with a green cherry.

**

HABITANT

37
1½ oz. Seagram's V.O.
½ oz. fresh lemon juice
¼ oz. maple syrup

Shake with ice. Strain into cocktail glass. Garnish with red cherry.

**

HARRY'S WALLBANGER

38

$1^1/_4$ oz. Bolshoi Vodka
$^1/_4$ oz. Leroux Apricot Brandy

In a 12 oz. glass with 4 ice cubes pour Apricot Brandy and Vodka, stir gently while adding fresh orange juice to taste.

**

HAWAIIAN BREEZE

39

1 oz. Trelaway White Rum
$^1/_4$ oz. Leroux Triple Sec
$^1/_4$ oz. grenadine
$1^1/_2$ oz. unsweetened pineapple juice

Shake with ice cubes and strain into chilled sour glass. Decorate with chunk of pineapple and a red cherry.

*

HIGHBALL

40 $1^1/_4$ oz. of any whisky, gin, brandy, vodka or rum, served in a 10 to 14-oz. glass with ice cubes and club soda, ginger ale or other soft drink — is called a highball. People who prefer their liquor with ice and water will order it as "100 Pipers Scotch and Water," "V.O. and Water," etc. Always put the mixer down in front of the guest, beside the glass containing the liquor and ice. Ask the guest if he'd like you to mix it. Many people prefer to do it themselves.

*

HORSE'S NECK

(contains no spirits)

41

Rind of lemon peel in a spiral
Ginger ale

Arrange spiral of lemon rind so that one end curls over edge of a highball glass. Add ice cubes. Fill with ginger ale.

***

HOT BUTTERED RUM

42

$1^1/_2$ oz. Captain Morgan Gold Label Rum
$^1/_3$ oz. lemon juice
1 tsp. honey
1 tsp. butter
Ground cinnamon (to taste)

Rinse an Old Fashioned glass, a mug, or pewter tankard with boiling water to heat it thoroughly. Put in butter, honey, cinnamon and lemon. Pour in rum, then fill with boiling water while stirring.

Note: Morgan White Rum is sometimes substituted for Gold Label. Brown sugar or maple syrup can be substituted for honey. Should be served with a small silver spoon.

**

IRISH COFFEE

43

$1^1/_4$ oz. "Old Bushmills" Irish Whiskey
1 tsp. brown sugar
Strong black coffee (very hot)
Whipped or heavy cream

Pre-heat large, stemmed goblet. Place sugar in bottom of "frosted" glass (see page 143). Pour in whiskey and stir. Fill $^3/_4$ of glass with boiling coffee. Top with a large spoonful of whipped cream.

**

IRISH ROSE

44

1½ oz. "Old Bushmills" Irish Whiskey
¾ oz. fresh lemon juice
½ oz. grenadine

Shake with ice cubes and strain into chilled sour glass. Decorate with a red cherry.

**

JAMAICAN COLLINS

45

1¼ oz. lemon
1 tablespoon honey
1¼ oz. Captain Morgan Gold Label Rum

Stir with ice cubes and pour without straining into a 12 oz. glass. Fill with soda water while stirring.

*

KING'S APPLE

46

1½ oz. King Arthur Gin
1½ oz. apple juice

Pour into Old Fashioned glass with 3 to 4 ice cubes. Add a zest of orange.

***

LONDONDERRY AIR

47

1 oz. "Old Bushmills" Irish Whiskey
½ oz. Leroux Crème de Café
3 oz. milk

Shake with ice cubes and pour into Old Fashioned glass. Sprinkle with ground nutmeg.

**

MAIDEN'S PRAYER

48

1 oz. King Arthur Gin
½ oz. Leroux Triple Sec
¼ oz. lemon juice
¼ oz. orange juice

Stir well with ice. Strain into cocktail glass. Top with red cherry.

***

MAI TAI

49

2 oz. Morgan White Rum
1 oz. Captain Morgan Gold Label Rum
1 packet powdered "Party Tyme" Mai-Tai pre-mix (or liquid pre-mix)

Shake with ice. Pour into double sized Old Fashioned glass half full of crushed ice. Mix gently. Decorate with a sprig of mint, pineapple spear and maraschino cherry.

*

MANHATTAN

50

1¼ oz. Seagram's V.O.
½ oz. Noilly Pratt Italian Sweet Vermouth
1 dash of Angostura bitters

Stir with ice. Strain into a chilled cocktail glass. Serve with a cherry.

Note: A **Rob Roy** is simply a Scotch Manhattan.

**

MARGUARITA

51

1 oz. fresh Lime juice
½ oz. Leroux Triple Sec
1 oz. Tequila (Olmeca)

Shake thoroughly with ice cubes and strain in gimlet glass. Float thin slice fresh lime. Prior to straining wet rim of glass with a wedge of lime and dip into coarse salt.

***

MARINER'S GROG

52

1½ oz. Captain Morgan Black Label Rum
1½ oz. Captain Morgan Gold Label Rum
1½ oz. lemon juice
½ oz. grenadine
1 oz. orange juice

Shake with ice cubes. Mound a handful of crushed ice into a cone by packing the ice into a small funnel. Place funnel with ice in bottom of a double Old Fashioned glass. Strain drink into glass around funnel. Agitate funnel gently to free cone of ice and remove it slowly, leaving the ice, cone-shaped, in the glass.
Serve with straw that has been pushed through 2 maraschino cherries.

Note: This drink can be served with ice cubes instead of the cone of crushed ice.

*

MARTINI (Regular)

53

1¼ oz. Boodles British Gin or Seagram's King Arthur Gin
½ oz. Noilly Pratt French Vermouth

Stir with ice. Strain into a chilled cocktail glass. Serve with an olive. Can also be made with vodka, or for a new twist, try Trelawny Classic White Estate Rum instead of gin and garnish with a black olive.

If you prefer a **VODKA MARTINI,** substitute Bolshoi Vodka for the gin.

MARTINI (Extra Dry)

2 oz. Boodles British Gin or Seagram's Extra Dry Gin
10 drops Noilly Pratt French Vermouth

Serve with a zest of lemon. An **EXTRA DRY ROB ROY** is exactly the same but Black Watch Scotch replaces the gin. Add a dash of Angostura bitters. A **GIBSON** is an Extra Dry Martini served with a small pearl onion.

***

MILK PUNCH

54

1¼ oz. Captain Morgan Black Label Rum
½ oz. Chemineaud Brandy
½ oz. Leroux Triple Sec
2 dashes Angostura bitters
5 oz. milk

Shake with ice cubes. Strain into a 12-oz. highball glass. Top with grated nutmeg.

*

MIST

55

1¼ oz. of your favourite liquor

Fill an Old Fashioned glass ¾ full of shaved or finely crushed ice. Pour in liquor. Top with a twist of lemon peel. Serve with straws.

***

MOONLIGHT

56

1 oz. Boodles British Gin
¼ oz. Leroux Cherry Brandy
½ oz. Noilly Pratt Italian Vermouth

Stir with ice. Strain into chilled cocktail glass. Serve with a zest of orange.

***

MORGAN MY LOVE

57

1 1/4 oz. Morgan White Rum
1/4 oz. Leroux Triple Sec
3/4 oz. pineapple juice
3/4 oz. orange juice

Shake with ice cubes and strain in sour glass. Garnish with red cherry and a small pineapple chunk.

***

MORGAN PUNCH

58 Fill a 14-oz. glass with ice cubes, and pour in 1/2 oz. each of the following ingredients:

grenadine
lemon juice
pineapple juice
orange juice
grapefruit juice

Then add:

1 1/4 oz. Captain Morgan Black Label Rum
1/2 oz. Morgan White Rum
1/4 oz. Leroux Cherry Brandy

Try not to mix ingredients as you pour. Tilt glass and pour on inside edge of glass. Decorate with fruit chunks and slices. Serve with a long handled spoon and straws. Raise straws between sips, replace and drink in layers.

***

MORGAN RUM COOLER

59

2 oz. Captain Morgan Gold Label Rum
1/2 oz. Leroux Triple Sec
1/2 oz. grenadine
3 oz. pineapple juice
2 oz. orange juice
1 oz. lemon juice

Shake with cracked ice and pour without straining into a tall slim glass — garnish with 1/2 slice of orange & lemon.

*

MOSCOW MULE

60

2 oz. Bolshoi Vodka
1 ginger beer
Juice of 1/2 lime

Put several ice cubes in a 10-oz. glass or copper mug. Add lime juice and drop in lime rind. Add vodka. Fill with ginger beer. Stir gently and serve. A thin strip of cucumber may be added as a garnish.

**

OLD FASHIONED

61 Over a cube of sugar, in an Old Fashioned glass, pour 3 drops of Angostura bitters. Muddle sugar with 1 oz. of soda water. Add ice cubes and 1 1/4 oz. Seagram's V.O. Decorate with fruit and serve with a cocktail pick.

Note: You can also use Scotch, brandy or rum.

*

ON THE ROCKS

62 In an Old Fashioned glass, pour over ice cubes 1¼ oz. of any liquor, liqueur or apéritif wine. A zest of lemon may be added.

***

PARADISE

63
1 oz. King Arthur Gin
½ oz. Leroux Apricot Brandy
½ oz. orange or lemon juice

Shake well with ice. Strain into sour glass. Decorate with a cherry.

**

PERFECT

64
¾ oz. Seagram's Extra Dry Gin
¾ oz. Noilly Pratt French Vermouth
¾ oz. Noilly Pratt Italian Vermouth
1 dash Angostura bitters

Stir with ice. Strain into a cocktail glass. Add a zest of lemon.

***

PINA COLADA

65
1½ oz. Captain Morgan Gold Label Rum
½ oz. Leroux Apricot Brandy
½ oz. coconut milk
1 oz. orange juice (fresh)
2 oz. pineapple juice (canned)

Shake thoroughly with (6) ice cubes and pour without straining into a 12 oz. glass. Garnish with ½ slice of orange, red cherry and pineapple chunk on a party pick. Crushed ice can be used instead of cubes when using an electric blender.
Or, if you prefer use Party Tyme Pina Colada powdered mix following the instructions on the box.

*

PINK GIN

66
2 oz. Boodles British Gin
1 dash Angostura bitters

Tint cocktail glass with Angostura by rolling it around edge. Add gin and then cold water to taste.
Do not add ice.

**

PINK LADY

67
1¼ oz. King Arthur Gin
½ oz. grenadine
1¼ oz. Prepared Lemon Juice

Shake well with ice. Strain into sour glass. Decorate with a cherry.

**

PINK SANDS

68
1¼ oz. Morgan White Rum
1 oz. grenadine
4 oz. milk

Shake with ice cubes. Strain into 8 oz. glass. Decorate with 2 red cherries on a party pick.

***

PLANTER'S PUNCH

69 See "Morgan Punch" (No. 58).

***

POUSSE CAFE

70

1/6 oz. grenadine (red)
1/6 oz. Leroux Green Crème de Menthe
1/6 oz. Leroux Cherry Brandy (Red)
1/6 oz. Leroux Crème de Café (brown)
1/6 oz. Leroux Triple Sec (white)
1/6 oz. Chemineaud Brandy (amber)

Pour, in the order named, very carefully and slowly into a cordial or pony glass so that they form layers and do not mix. This may be best accomplished by tilting the glass and pouring the different liquers slowly down the inner edge.

***

PRAIRIE OYSTER

71

1 1/4 oz. Chemineaud Brandy
1 egg yolk
2 oz. tomato juice
1 dash Worcestershire sauce
1 dash lemon juice
Salt and pepper to taste

Carefully break the egg and separate the yolk from the white, being careful not to break the yolk. Place yolk in the bottom of an Old Fashioned glass. Add lemon, salt and pepper, and Worcestershire sauce. Then brandy, and finally tomato juice to taste. Do not stir.

**

RED SNAPPER

72

See "Bloody Mary" (No. 6).

*

RICKEY

73

1 1/4 oz. King Arthur Gin
1/2 fresh lime

Squeeze the half lime over ice cubes in a 10 or 12-oz. highball glass. Toss in lime rind. Add soda water to taste. Stir gently.

Note: 1/2 oz. of lime juice concentrate may be substituted if the whole fresh fruit is unavailable.

*

ROB ROY

74

See "Manhattan" (No. 50).

**

ROSE'S GIN

75

1 1/4 oz. Seagram's Extra Dry Gin
1/4 oz. Leroux Cherry Brandy

Pour into Old Fashioned glass filled with crushed ice. Add a zest of orange.

***

RUM COW

76

1 1/2 oz. Morgan White Rum
4 drops vanilla extract
1 pinch ground nutmeg
1 dash Angostura Bitters
4 oz. milk
1 oz. simple syrup

Shake thoroughly with ice cubes and strain into a 10 oz. glass.

**

RUM'N CHERRY FIZZ

77

1 1/4 oz. Trelawny Classic White Estate Rum
1/2 oz. Leroux Cherry Brandy
1 oz. lemon juice

Shake with 5 ice cubes. Pour without straining into a 12 oz. glass. Stir with soda water while pouring.

***

RUM SWIZZLE

78

2 oz. Morgan White Rum
1 oz. lemon juice
1 oz. orange juice
1 tsp. Simple Syrup
2 dashes Angostura bitters
Soda water

Put juices, sugar and a couple of ounces of soda water in 12-oz. Collins glass. Fill with cracked ice and stir thoroughly with swizzle stick. Then add bitters and rum. Fill to top with soda water. Serve with the swizzle stick in glass.

**

RUSTY NAIL

79

1 1/2 oz. Black Watch Scotch
1/2 oz. Lochan Ora

Pour over ice cubes in an Old Fashioned glass. May be served with a zest of lemon.

**

SALTY DOG

80

1 1/2 oz. Seagram's Extra Dry Gin or Bolshoi Vodka
Dash grenadine
Grapefruit juice

Pour grenadine, then liquor over ice in a 10-oz. highball glass. Add grapefruit juice to taste. Stir. Do not garnish. You can, if you wish, frost the rim of the glass with coarse salt.

***

SANGRIA

81

1 bottle dry red wine (B&G Prince Noir)
1/2 lemon
1/2 orange, cut into 1/4 inch slices
1/2 large apple, cut in half lengthwise, cored, and cut into thin wedges
1/4 to 1/2 cup superfine sugar
Club Soda, chilled (1 large bottle)
Ice Cubes (optional)

Combine the lemon, orange, apple and 1/4 cup sugar in a large pitcher. Pour in the wine and stir with a long-handled spoon until well mixed. Add more sugar to taste. Refrigerate until thoroughly chilled. Just before serving, pour in chilled club soda to taste, adding up to 24 oz. Stir again, and serve in chilled wine-glasses. Or the glasses may be filled with ice cubes before adding the sangria.

*

SCREWDRIVER

82

1 1/4 oz. Bolshoi Vodka
Orange juice

Fill an 8-oz. glass with ice cubes. Pour in vodka, Add orange juice to taste. Stir.

**

SIDECAR

83

3/4 oz. Chemineaud Brandy
1/2 oz. Leroux Triple Sec
3/4 oz. Prepared Lemon Juice

Shake with ice. Strain and serve in a chilled cocktail glass. Top with a cherry.

***

SINGAPORE SLING

84 Fill a 14-oz. Zombie glass with cracked ice and pour down the side of glass 1/2 oz. each of the following ingredients.

grenadine
lemon juice
pineapple juice
orange juice

Then in the same fashion add:

1 1/4 oz. King Arthur Gin
1/2 oz. Leroux Cherry Brandy
1/4 oz. Leroux Triple Sec

Decorate with fruit and serve with a spoon and straw.

**

SOMBRERO

85
1 oz. Captain Morgan Black Label Rum
1 oz. Leroux Crème de Café
3 oz. milk

Shake rum, crème de café and milk with ice and pour, ice and all, into a tall glass. Serve with a straw.

**

SOUR

86
1 1/4 oz. Seagram's V.O.
1 1/2 oz. Prepared Lemon Juice

Shake with ice and strain into a chilled sour glass. Serve with a cherry.

Note: Sours are also prepared with dry gin, vodka, rum or Scotch.

***

SPANISH COFFEE

87
1 oz. Chemineaud Brandy
1/2 oz. Leroux Triple Sec
1 tsp. brown sugar
Strong black coffee (very hot)
Whipped or heavy cream

Preheat a large stemmed goblet. Place sugar in bottom after "Frosting" the glass. (see p. 143). Pour in triple sec and brandy. Stir. Fill 3/4 of glass with boiling coffee. Top off with a large spoonful of whipped cream & a red cherry.

**

STINGER

88
1 1/2 oz. Chemineaud Brandy
3/4 oz. Leroux White Crème de Menthe

Shake or stir with cracked ice. Strain into chilled cocktail glass and serve. Sometimes served with a pair of short straws and finely crushed ice (see "Mist" No. 55.). Can also be served on the rocks in an Old Fashioned glass.

**

TEATOTALER

89
8 oz. Trelawny Classic White Estate Rum
1/4 - 1/2 cup instant ice tea mix powder

Mix ice tea powder with 20 oz. of water in a one quart pitcher. Add rum and ice. Stir and garnish with lemon or orange slices. Serve in tall 8 oz. glasses.

**

TEQUILA SUNRISE

90

1 oz. Tequila (Olmeca)
1 oz. orange juice
1/4 oz. grenadine

Pour grenadine into bottom of a cocktail glass. Separately stir tequila and orange juice with crushed ice. Then strain and pour gently into cocktail glass so as not to disturb the grenadine. For an **Orange Blossom,** use exactly the same recipe substituting King Arthur Gin for the tequila. Then, skaking all of the ingredients together, strain & pour into cocktail glasses.

***

TODDY

91

2 oz. Chemineaud Brandy, Captain Morgan Gold Label Rum, or your favourite whisky
1/2 tsp. Simple Syrup
2 to 5 cloves
Pieces of cinnamon stick
1 lemon twist

Using a silver spoon, mix liquor with syrup, honey or maple syrup in a heated glass, mug or Old Fashioned glass. Leave spoon in glass and then add boiling water. Add lemon twist, cloves and cinnamon. Stir. Serve with spoon.

***

TOM & JERRY

92

1 1/2 oz. Captain Morgan Gold Label Rum
1 tsp. Simple Syrup
1 egg
Pinch of allspice

Separate yolk and white of egg and beat yolk. Separately beat white until fairly stiff, then add sugar and beat again until very stiff. Combine yolk, white and add allspice by swirling lightly together. Put the mixture into a scalded Tom and Jerry or coffee mug. Add rum, then fill with boiling water or hot milk. Stir well.

***

V.O. CHRISTMAS PUNCH

(20 persons,
2 3-oz. Glasses each)

93

20 oz. Seagram's V.O. Canadian Whisky
5 oz. Leroux Triple Sec
5 oz. Leroux Cherry Brandy
20 oz. orange juice
20 oz. pineapple juice
20 oz. grapefruit juice

Bland all ingredients in large earthenware or glass container and keep in refrigerator until ready to serve. Pour in punch bowl 1/2 filled with ice cubes, add slices of orange, pieces of pineapple and red cherries — serve in gimlet or punch glasses.

***

V.O. PUNCH

(20 persons, 2 servings each, 3 oz. glass)

94

35 oz. Seagram's V.O. Canadian Whisky
5 oz. Crème de Café Leroux
5 oz. Triple Sec Leroux
20 oz. pineapple juice
20 oz. grapefruit juice
20 oz. apple juice
10 oz. orange juice

Please follow the same instructions as for V.O. Christmas Punch.

*

VILLENEUVE SPECIAL

95 In a 10-oz. glass containing 3 or 4 ice cubes, pour $1^1/_4$ oz. Seagram's Extra Dry Gin and fill with equal parts of tonic water and 7-Up. Add a zest of lemon.

**

WARD "8"

96

$1^1/_4$ oz. Seagram's V.O.
$^1/_2$ oz. Prepared Lemon Juice
$^1/_2$ oz. orange juice
$^1/_8$ oz. grenadine

Shake with ice. Strain into chilled sour glass. Serve with a cherry.

**

WHITE COW

97

$1^1/_4$ oz. Morgan White Rum
$^1/_2$ oz. Leroux Triple Sec
4 oz. milk
4 drops vanilla extract

Shake thoroughly with ice cubes. Strain into 8 oz. glass. Sprinkle with ground cinnamon.

**

WHITE LADY

98

$1^1/_4$ oz. King Arthur Gin
$1^1/_4$ oz. Prepared Lemon Juice
$^1/_4$ oz. Leroux Triple Sec

Shake well with ice cubes. Strain into a sour glass. Decorate with red cherry.

***

ZOMBIE

99

2 oz. Captain Morgan Black Label Rum
1 oz. Morgan White Rum
1 oz. Captain Morgan Gold Label Rum
$^1/_2$ oz. Leroux Triple Sec
$^1/_2$ oz. Leroux Apricot Brandy
$^1/_2$ oz. grenadine
$^1/_2$ oz. Prepared Lemon Juice
$^1/_2$ oz. pineapple juice
$^1/_2$ oz. grapefruit juice
$^1/_2$ oz. orange juice

Shake well with cracked ice all ingredients except Black Label Rum. Pour unstrained into 16-oz. Zombie glass half full of cracked ice. Decorate with a pineapple spear and a cherry. Top with Black Label Rum, being careful to pour so that it floats on the surface. Serve with a straw.

* Quick & Easy *

	Recipe No.
Club Cocktail (contains no spirits)	18
Extra Dry Rob Roy (Scotch, French Vermouth)	74
Float (Brandy)	27
Gibson (Dry Gin, French Vermouth)	29
Gin & "It" (Dry Gin, Italian Vermouth)	31
Gin & Tonic (Dry Gin)	33
Highball (any Liquor)	40
Horse's Neck (contains no spirits)	41
King's Apple (Dry Gin)	46
Manhattan (V.O., Italian Vermouth)	50
Martini (Dry Gin, French Vermouth)	53
Mist (any Liquor)	55
Moscow Mule (Vodka)	60
On The Rocks (any Liquor)	62
Pink Gin (Dry Gin)	66
Rickey (Dry Gin, or any Liquor)	73
Rob Roy (Scotch, Italian Vermouth)	74
Screwdriver (Vodka)	82
Villeneuve Special (Dry Gin)	95

** A Little More Effort, But Worth It **

	Recipe No.
Between the Sheets (Brandy, White Rum, Triple Sec)	4
Black Russian (Vodka, Crème de Café)	5
Bloody Mary (Vodka)	6
Brown Cow (Rum, Crème de Café)	7
Buck (any Liquor or Liqueur)	8
Bull Shooter (Vodka)	9
Bull Shot (Vodka)	9
Café Royale (either Brandy, Rum or Crown Royal)	10
Canada's Pride (V.O. Crème de Café)	11
Collins (any Liquor or Liqueur)	19
Cuban (Brandy, Apricot Brandy)	20
Daiquiri (Rum)	20
Débutante (Brandy, Cherry Brandy)	21
English Rose (Dry Gin, Cherry Brandy)	23
Favourite (Dry Gin, French Vermouth, Apricot Brandy)	24
Fizz (any Liquor)	25
Gimlet (Dry Gin, Triple Sec)	30
Gin & Sin (Dry Gin)	32
Habitant (V.O.)	37
Harry's Wallbanger (Vodka, Apricot Brandy)	38
Hawaiian Breeze (White Rum, Triple Sec)	39
Irish Coffee (Irish Whiskey)	43
Irish Rose (Irish Whiskey)	44
Jamaican Collins (Rum)	45
Maiden's Prayer (Dry Gin, Triple Sec)	48
Marguarita (Tequila, Triple Sec)	51
Old Fashioned (either V.O., Scotch, Brandy or Rum)	61
Orange Blossom (Dry Gin)	90
Perfect (Dry Gin, Italian or French Vermouth)	66
Pink Lady (Dry Gin)	67
Pink Sands (Rum)	68
Red Snapper (Dry Gin)	72
Rose's Gin (Gin, Cherry Brandy)	75
Rum'n Cherry Fizz (Rum, Cherry Brandy)	77
Rusty Nail (Scotch, Lochan Ora)	79
Salty Dog (Vodka)	80
Sidecar (Brandy, Triple Sec)	83
Sombrero (Rum, Crème de Café)	85

(The liquors and liqueurs in brackets after the names of the drinks are the spirits you will require in preparation.)

	Recipe No.
Sour (any Liquor)	86
Stinger (Brandy, White Crème de Menthe)	88
Teatotaler (Rum)	89
Ward "8" (V.O.)	96
White Cow (Rum, Triple Sec)	97
White Lady (Dry Gin, Triple Sec)	98

*** Earn Your Bartender's Diploma *** With These

	Recipe No.
Alexander (Brandy, Crème de Café, Triple Sec)	1
Apres Diner (Crème de Café, Triple Sec, Crème de Menthe)	2
Banana Daiquiri (White Rum)	3
Caprice (Vodka, Crème de Café, Triple Sec)	12
Champagne Punch (Brandy Triple Sec, Champagne)	13
Cherry Daisy (Brandy, Cherry Brandy)	14
Christmas Rum Punch (Rum, Triple Sec)	15
Clover Club (Dry Gin)	16
Clover Leaf (Dry Gin, Crème de Menthe)	17
Egg Nog (either Brandy, Rum, V.O. or Port Wine)	22
Flip (either Scotch, V.O., Rum, Brandy, Sherry or Port Wine)	26
French "75" (Dry Gin, Triple Sec, Champagne)	28
Gluehwein (Red Wine)	34
Grasshopper (Crème de Café, Green Crème de Menthe)	35
Green Lady (Green Crème de Menthe, Cherry Brandy)	36
Hot Buttered Rum (Rum)	42
Londonderry Air (Irish Whiskey, Crème de Café)	47
Mai Tai (2 different Rums)	49
Mariner's Grog (2 different Rums)	52
Milk Punch (Rum, Brandy, Triple Sec)	54
Moonlight (Dry Gin, Cherry Brandy, Italian Vermouth)	56
Morgan My Love (Rum, Triple Sec)	57
Morgan Punch (2 different Rums, Cherry Brandy)	58
Morgan Rum Cooler (Rum, Triple Sec)	59
Paradise (Dry Gin, Apricot Brandy)	63
Pina Colada (Rum)	65
Planter's Punch (2 different Rums, Cherry Brandy)	69
Pousse Café (Brandy, 4 Liqueurs)	70
Prairie Oyster (Brandy)	71
Rum Cow (Rum)	76
Rum Swizzle (White Rum)	78
Sangria (Red Wine)	81
Singapore Sling (Dry Gin, Cherry Brandy, Triple Sec)	84
Toddy (either Brandy, Rum or V.O.)	91
Tom & Jerry (Rum)	92
V.O. Christmas Punch (V.O., Triple Sec, Cherry Brandy)	93
V.O. Punch (V.O., Triple Sec, Crème de Café)	94
Zombie (3 different Rums, Triple Sec, Apricot Brandy)	99

Brandy Or Cognac-Based Drinks

Chemineaud Brandy, Bisquit Cognac, Bisquit V.S.O.P. Cognac

	Recipe No.
Alexander (Crème de Café, Triple Sec)	1
Between the Sheets (White Rum, Triple Sec)	4

(The liquors and liqueurs in brackets after the names of the drinks are the other spirits you will require in preparation.)

	Recipe No.
Brandy Buck	8
Café Royale	10
Champagne Punch (Champagne, Triple Sec)	13
Cherry Daisy (Cherry Brandy)	14
Collins	19
Débutante (Cherry Brandy)	21
Egg Nog	22
Fizz	25
Flip	26
Float	27
Highball	40
Milk Punch (Rum, Triple Sec)	54
Mist	55
Old Fashioned	61
On the Rocks	62
Pousse Café (4 Liqueurs)	70
Prairie Oyster	71
Sidecar (Triple Sec)	83
Sour	86
Spanish Coffee (Triple Sec)	87
Stinger (White Crème de Menthe	88
Toddy	91

Canadian Whisky-Based Drinks

Seagram's Crown Royal, Seagram's V.O., Seagram's 83, Seagram's Five Star

	Recipe No.
Alexander (Crème de Café, Triple Sec)	1
Buck	8
Café Royale	10
Canada's Pride (Crème de Café)	11
Collins	19
Egg Nog	22
Fizz	25
Flip	26
Habitant	37
Highball	40
Manhattan (Italian Vermouth)	50
Mist	55
Old Fashioned	61
On the Rocks	62
Sour	86
Toddy	91
V.O. Christmas Punch (Triple Sec, Cherry Brandy)	93
V.O. Punch (Crème de Café, Triple Sec)	94
Ward "8"	96

Gin-Based Drinks

Boodles British Gin, Seagram's King Arthur London Dry Gin, Seagram's Extra Dry Gin

	Recipe No.
Alexander (Crème de Café, Triple Sec)	1
Bloody Caesar	6
Buck	8
Clover Club	16
Clover Leaf (Crème de Menthe)	17
Collins	19
English Rose (Cherry Brandy)	23
Favourite (French Vermouth, Apricot Brandy)	24
Fizz	25
Flip	28
French "75" (Champagne, Triple Sec)	28
Gibson (French Vermouth)	29
Gimlet (Triple Sec)	30
Gin & "It" (Italian Vermouth)	31
Gin & Sin	32
Gin & Tonic	33
Highball	40
King's Apple	46
London Buck	8
Maiden's Prayer (Triple Sec)	48

(The liquors and liqueurs in brackets after the names of the drinks are the other spirits you will require in preparation.)

	Recipe No.
Martini (French Vermouth)	53
Mist	55
Moonlight (Italian Vermouth, Cherry Brandy)	56
Old Fashioned	61
On the Rocks	62
Orange Blossom	90
Paradise (Apricot Brandy)	63
Perfect (Italian Vermouth, French Vermouth)	64
Pink Gin	66
Pink Lady	67
Red Snapper	72
Rickey	73
Rose's Gin (Cherry Brandy)	75
Salty Dog	80
Singapore Sling (Cherry Brandy, Triple Sec)	84
Sour	86
Villeneuve Special	95
White Lady (Triple Sec)	98

Liqueur-Based Drinks

	Recipe No.
Leroux Apricot Brandy	
Favourite (Dry Gin, French Vermouth)	24
Harry's Wallbanger (Vodka)	38
Highball	40
On the Rocks	62
Paradise (Dry Gin)	63
Pina Colada (Rum)	65
Zombie (3 different Rums)	99
Leroux Cherry Brandy	
Cherry Daisy (Brandy)	14
Débutante (Brandy)	21
English Rose (Dry Gin)	23
Green Lady (Green Crème de Menthe)	36
Highball	40
Mist	55
Moonlight (Dry Gin, Italian Vermouth)	56
Morgan Punch (2 different Rums)	58
On the Rocks	62
Planter's Punch (2 different Rums)	58
Pousse Café (3 Liqueurs, Brandy)	70
Rose's Gin (Dry Gin)	75
Rum'n Cherry Fizz (Rum)	77
Singapore Sling (Dry Gin, Triple Sec)	84
V.O. Christmas Punch (V.O., Triple Sec)	93
Leroux Crème de Café	
Alexander (any Liquor, Triple Sec)	1
Apres Diner (Triple Sec, Crème de Menthe)	2
Black Russian (Vodka)	5
Canada's Pride (V.O.)	11
Caprice (Triple Sec, Vodka)	12
Clover Leaf (Gin)	17
Grasshopper (Green Crème de Menthe)	35
Londonderry Air (Irish Whiskey)	47
On the Rocks	62
Pousse Café (3 Liqueurs, Brandy)	70
Sombrero (Rum)	85
V.O. Punch (V.O., Triple Sec)	94
Leroux Green Crème de Menthe	
Clover Leaf (Dry Gin)	17
Grasshopper (Crème de Café)	35
Green Lady (Cherry Brandy)	36
Highball	40
On the Rocks	62
Pousse Café (3 Liqueurs, Brandy)	70
Leroux White Crème de Menthe	
Apres Diner (Crème de Café, Triple Sec)	2
Highball	40
Mist	55
On the Rocks	62
Stinger (Brandy or Vodka)	88
Lochan Ora	
On the Rocks	62
Mist	55
Rusty Nail (Scotch)	79

(The liquors and liqueurs in brackets after the names of the drinks are the other spirits you will require in preparation.)

Leroux Triple Sec

	Recipe No.
Alexander (any Liquor, Crème de Café)	1
Apres Diner (Crème de Café, Crème de Menthe)	2
Between the Sheets (Brandy, White Rum)	4
Caprice (Rum, Crème de Café)	12
Champagne Punch (Champagne, Brandy)	13
Christmas Rum Punch (Rum)	15
French "75" (Dry Gin, Champagne)	28
Gimlet (Dry Gin)	30
Hawaiian Breeze (White Rum)	39
Highball	40
Maiden's Prayer (Dry Gin)	48
Margarita (Tequila)	51
Milk Punch (Rum, Brandy)	54
Mist	55
Morgan My Love (Rum)	57
Morgan Rum Cooler (Rum)	59
On the Rocks	62
Pousse Café (3 Liqueurs, Brandy)	70
Sidecar (Brandy)	83
Singapore Sling (Dry Gin, Cherry Brandy)	84
Spanish Coffee (Brandy)	87
V.O. Christmas Punch (V.O., Cherry Brandy)	93
V.O. Punch (V.O., Crème de Café)	94
White Cow (Rum)	97
White Lady (Dry Gin)	98
Zombie (3 different Rums, Apricot Brandy)	99

Drinks Containing No Spirits

	Recipe No.
Club Cocktail	18
Horse's Neck	41

Irish Whiskey-Based Drinks

"Old Bushmills"

	Recipe No.
Irish Coffee	43
Irish Rose	44
Londonderry Air (Crème de Café)	47
On the Rocks	62

Rum-Based Drinks

Captain Morgan Black Label, Captain Morgan Gold Label, Morgan White, Trelawny Classic White Estate

	Recipe No.
Alexander (Crème de Café, Triple Sec)	1
Banana Daiquiri	3
Between the Sheets (Brandy, Triple Sec)	4
Brown Cow (Crème de Café)	7
Buck	8
Café Royale	10
Christmas Rum Punch (Triple Sec)	15
Collins	19
Daiquiri	20
Egg Nog	22
Fizz	25
Flip	28
Hawaiian Breeze (Triple Sec)	39
Highball	40
Hot Buttered Rum	42
Jamaican Collins	45

(The liquors and liqueurs in brackets after the names of the drinks are the other spirits you will require in preparation.)

	Recipe No.
Mai Tai	49
Mariner's Grog	52
Milk Punch (Brandy, Triple Sec)	54
Mist	55
Morgan My Love (Triple Sec)	57
Morgan Punch (Cherry Brandy)	58
Morgan Rum Cooler (Triple Sec)	59
Old Fashioned	61
Pina Colada (Apricot Brandy)	65
Pink Sands	68
Planter's Punch (Cherry Brandy)	69
Rum Cow	76
Rum'm Cherry Fizz (Cherry Brandy)	77
Rum Swizzle	78
Sombrero (Crème de Café)	85
Sour	86
Teatotaler	89
Toddy	91
Tom & Jerry	92
White Cow (Triple Sec)	97
Zombie (Apricot Brandy, Triple Sec)	99

Scotch Whisky-Based Drinks

Seagram's 100 Pipers, Black Watch

	Recipe No.
Alexander (Crème de Café, Triple Sec)	1
Buck	8
Collins	19
Extra Dry Rob Roy (French Vermouth)	74
Fizz	25
Flip	26
Highball	40
Mist	55
Old Fashioned	61
On the Rocks	62
Rob Roy (Italian Vermouth)	74
Rusty Nail (Lochan Ora)	79
Sour	86
Toddy	91

Vodka-Based Drinks

Bolshoi Vodka

	Recipe No.
Black Russian (Crème de Café)	5
Bloody Mary	6
Bloody Caesar	6
Buck	8
Bull Shooter	9
Bull Shot	9
Caprice (Crème de Café, Triple Sec)	12
Clamdigger	6
Collins	19
Fizz	25
Harry's Wallbanger (Apricot Brandy)	38
Highball	40
Martini (French Vermouth)	53
Mist	55
Moscow Mule	60
Old Fashioned	61
On the Rocks	62
Rickey	73
Salty Dog	80
Screwdriver	82
Sour	86
Stinger (White Crème de Menthe)	88

(The liquors and liqueurs in brackets after the names of the drinks are the other spirits you will require in preparation.)

Wine-Based Drinks

	Recipe No.
Champagne (Mumm)	
Champagne Punch (Brandy, Triple Sec)	13
French "75" (Dry Gin, Triple Sec)	28
Port Wine	
Egg Nog	22
Flip	26
Sherry	
Flip	26
Red Table Wine (Dry) (B&G Prince Noir)	
Gluehwein	34
Sangria	81
Vermouth	
French (Noilly Pratt)	
Extra Dry Rob Roy (Scotch)	74
Favourite (Dry Gin, Apricot Brandy)	24
Gibson (Dry Gin or Vodka)	53
Martini (Dry Gin or Vodka)	53
On the Rocks	62
Perfect (Italian Vermouth, Dry Gin)	64
Italian (Noilly Pratt)	
Gin & "It" (Dry Gin)	31
Manhattan (V.O.)	50
Moonlight (Dry Gin, Triple Sec)	56
On the Rocks	62
Perfect (French Vermouth, Dry Gin)	64
Rob Roy (Scotch)	74

After-Dinner Drinks

	Recipe No.
Apres Diner (Crème de Menthe, Crème de Café, Triple Sec)	2
Brown Cow (Rum, Crème de Café)	7
Café Royal (either Brandy, Rum or V.O.)	10
Float (Brandy)	27
Irish Coffee (Irish Whiskey)	43
Pousse Café (Brandy, 4 Liqueurs)	70
Rum Cow (Rum)	76
Rusty Nail (Scotch, Lochan Ora)	79
White Cow (Rum, Triple Sec)	97

(And, of course, any one of the fine Leroux Liqueurs.)

Cocktails

	Recipe No.
Black Russian (Vodka, Crème de Café)	5
Canada's Pride (V.O. Crème de Café)	11
Caprice (Vodka, Crème de Café, Triple Sec)	12
Club Cocktail (contains no spirits)	18

(The liquors and liqueurs in brackets after the names of the drinks are the other spirits you will require in preparation.)

	Recipe No.
English Rose (Dry Gin, Cherry Brandy)	23
Extra Dry Rob Roy (Scotch, French Vermouth)	74
Favourite (Dry Gin, Apricot Brandy, French Vermouth)	24
Gibson (Dry Gin, French Vermouth)	53
Gin & "It" (Dry Gin, Italian Vermouth)	31
Hawaiian Breeze (White Rum, Triple Sec)	39
Irish Rose (Irish Whiskey)	44
King's Apple (Dry Gin)	46
Maiden's Prayer (Dry Gin, Triple Sec)	48
Manhattan (V.O., Italian Vermouth)	50
Marguarita (Tequila, Triple Sec)	51
Martini (Dry Gin, Franch Vermouth)	53
Mist (any Liquor)	55
Moonlight (Dry Gin, Cherry Brandy, Italian Vermouth)	56
Morgan My Love (Rum, Triple Sec	57
On The Rocks (any Liquor or Liqueur)	62
Paradise (Dry Gin, Apricot Brandy)	63
Perfect (Dry Gin, French and Italian Vermouth)	64
Pink Gin (Dry Gin)	66
Rob Roy (Scotch, Italian Vermouth)	74
Rose's Gin (Dry Gin, Cherry Brandy)	75
Rum'n Cherry Fizz (Rum, Cherry Brandy)	77
Rusty Nail (Scotch, Lochan Ora)	79
Stinger (Brandy, White Crème de Menthe)	88
Trelawny Martini (Rum)	53

Creamy Drinks

	Recipe No.
Alexander (Brandy or Rum, Crème de Café)	1
Brown Cow (Rum, Crème de Café)	7
Caprice (Vodka, Crème de Café, Triple Sec)	12
Egg Nog (almost any Liquor)	22
Flip (almost any Liquor)	26
Grasshopper (Crème de Café, Green Crème de Menthe)	35
Green Lady (Green Crème de Menthe, Cherry Brandy)	36
Irish Coffee (Irish Whiskey)	43
Londonderry Air (Irish Whiskey, Crème de Café)	47
Milk Punch (Brandy or Rum)	54
Pina Colada (Rum, Apricot Brandy)	65
Pink Sands (Rum)	68
Rum Cow (Rum)	76
Sombrero (Rum, Crème de Café)	85
White Cow (Rum, Triple Sec)	97

Fruit Drinks

	Recipe No.
Collins (almost any Liquor)	19
Debutante (Cherry Brandy, Brandy)	21
Fizz (almost any Liquor)	25
Harry's Wallbanger (Vodka, Apricot Brandy)	38
Hawaiian Breeze (White Rum, Triple Sec)	39
Jamaican Collins (Rum)	45
Mai Tai (2 different Rums)	49
Mariner's Grog (2 different Rums)	52

(The liquors and liqueurs in brackets after the names of the drinks are the spirits you will require in preparation.)

	Recipe No.
Morgan Punch (2 different Rums, Cherry Brandy)	58
Morgan Rum Cooler (Rum, Triple Sec)	59
Old Fashioned (almost any Liquor)	61
Pina Colada (Rum, Apricot Brandy)	65
Planter's Punch (2 different Rums, Cherry Brandy)	69
Rickey (either Gin, Vodka or Rum)	73
Rum Swizzle (Rum)	78
Salty Dog (Gin or Vodka)	80
Sangria (Red Wine)	81
Screwdriver (Vodka)	82
Singapore Sling (Dry Gin, Cherry Brandy, Triple Sec)	84
V.O. Christmas Punch (V.O. Triple Sec, Cherry Brandy)	93
V.O. Punch (V.O. Crème de Café, Triple Sec)	94
Zombie (3 different Rums, Apricot Brandy)	99

Hot Drinks

	Recipe No.
Café Royale (Crown Royal, Brandy or Rum)	10
Gluehwein (Red Wine)	34
Hot Buttered Rum (Rum)	42
Irish Coffee (Irish Whiskey)	43
Spanish Coffee (Brandy, Triple Sec)	87
Toddy (either Brandy, Rum or Whisky)	91
Tom & Jerry (Rum)	92

Long Drinks

	Recipe No.
Bloody Caesar (Gin)	6
Bloody Mary (Vodka)	6
Bull Shooter (Vodka)	9
Buck (any Liquor)	9
Collins (any Liquor)	19
Clamdigger (Vodka)	6
Fizz (any Liquor)	25
Float (Brandy)	27
French "75" (Dry Gin, Champagne)	28
Gin & Tonic (Dry Gin)	33
Harry's Wallbanger (Vodka, Apricot Brandy)	38
Highball (any Liquor)	40
Horse's Neck	41
Jamaican Collins (Rum)	45
Mariner's Grog (2 different Rums)	52
Milk Punch (any Liquor)	54
Morgan Punch (2 different Rums, Cherry Brandy)	58
Morgan Rum Cooler (Rum, Triple Sec)	59
Moscow Mule (Vodka)	60
Pina Colada (Rum, Apricot Brandy)	65
Planter's Punch (2 different Rums, Cherry Brandy)	69
Red Snapper (Gin)	72
Rickey (either Gin, Rum or Vodka)	73
Rum Swizzle (Rum)	78
Salty Dog (Vodka)	80
Sangria (Red Wine)	81
Screwdriver (Vodka)	82
Singapore Sling (Gin, Triple Sec)	84
Teatotaler (Rum)	89
Villeneuve Special (Gin)	95
Zombie (3 different Rums, Apricot Brandy)	99

(The liquors and liqueurs in brackets after the names of the drinks are the spirits you require in preparation.)

Pick-Me-Ups

	Recipe No.
Bloody Caesar (Gin	6
Bloody Mary (Vodka)	6
Bull Shooter (Vodka)	9
Bull Shot (Vodka)	9
Clamdigger (Vodka)	6
Prairie Oyster (Brandy)	71
Red Snapper (Gin)	6

Punches

	Recipe No.
Champagne Punch (Brandy, Champagne, Triple Sec)	13
Christmas Rum Punch (Rum, Triple Sec)	15
Sangria (Red Wine)	81
V.O. Christmas Punch (V.O., Triple Sec, Cherry Brandy)	93
V.O. Punch (V.O. Crème de Café, Triple Sec)	94

Sours

	Recipe No.
Frothy:	
Banana Daiquiri (Rum)	3
Between the Sheets (Brandy, Rum, Triple Sec)	4
Clover Club (Gin)	16
Clover Leaf (Gin, Crème de Menthe)	17
Gimlet (Gin or Vodka)	30
Pink Lady (Gin)	67
Rum'n Cherry Fizz (Rum, Cherry Brandy)	77
Sidecar (Brandy, Triple Sec)	83
Sour (any Liquor)	86
Ward "8" (V.O.)	96
White Lady (Gin, Triple Sec)	98
Plain:	
Daiquiri (White Rum)	20
Gin & Sin (Dry Gin)	32
Habitant (V.O.)	37
Margarita (Tequila, Triple Sec)	51

(The liquors and liqueurs in brackets after the names of the drinks are the spirits you will require in preparation.)

BARTENDING TIPS FROM THE EXPERTS 6

Throughout this section we have been discussing many of the tricks of the trade that can help turn you into a real pro behind the bar. Such things as Prepared Lemon Juice, Simple Sugar Syrup, the order in which ingredients go into the drink etc. are examples, but there are many others that you might want to add to your list. So here they are in random fashion.

How Much For How Many?

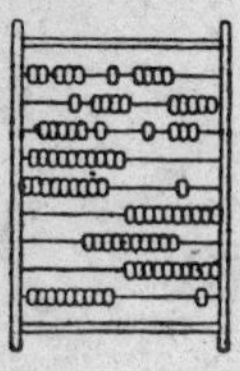

Soon after you've decided to entertain, this is probably the first question that comes to mind.

The chart below will give you an idea of the average number of drinks each guest will consume during the types of parties indicated.

TYPE OF PARTY	AVERAGE NO. OF DRINKS PER PERSON REQUIRED (Reduce these figures by ⅓ for the ladies.)				
	1st hr.	2nd hr.	3rd hr.	4th hr.	add'l hrs.
BRUNCH — usually pick-me-ups and long, refreshing drinks.	2	1	1	—	—
AFTERNOON — lawn parties, TV sports, etc.	3	2	1	1	½
COCKTAILS • 5 to 7 — usually short drinks and some highballs.	2-3	1	½	—	—

TYPE OF PARTY	AVERAGE NO. OF DRINKS PER PERSON REQUIRED (Reduce these figures by ⅓ for the ladies.)				
	1st hr.	2nd hr.	3rd hr.	4th hr.	add'l hrs.
• 7 to 9 — perhaps cocktails to start, but trend will switch to longer drinks. Don't expect people to leave at 9. Some will want to make an evening of it.	**3**	**1**	**1**	**1**	**½**
COCKTAILS & DINNER — assuming invitations are for 1 hour prior to dinner. 2nd hr. is mealtime and wine, 3rd is liqueurs or brandy. After that your guests will probably want highballs.	**2-3**	**—**	**1½**	**1**	**½**
EVENING (8:30 on) — usually highballs or long drinks.	**2-3**	**1**	**1**	**1**	**1**
BEFORE & AFTER (the game, skating, hay ride, etc.) — 2nd and 3rd hr. is the activity itself. Highballs or hot drinks, depending on the season.	**2**	**—**	**—**	**2**	**1**

Once you have determined the drinks-per-person figure, multiply it by the number of guests attending.

Now you have an estimate of the total number of drinks to plan for. Then —

- If you are using 25-oz. bottles, you'll get 20 $1\frac{1}{4}$-oz. drinks from each.
- If you are using 40-oz. bottles, you'll get 32 $1\frac{1}{4}$-oz. drinks from each.

Some Special Cases

- Apéritif drinks such as sherry, port, etc. are usually served 2 oz. at a time. Therefore you will get 13 drinks from a standard 26-oz. bottle.
- When ordering wine to serve with a meal, allow one bottle for every three people.
- If you are serving champagne, for dessert, or as a toast plan on one bottle for every six people. (one glass each)

What About Mixers?

- Carbonated drinks used in highballs are available in a variety of sizes (6, 10, 26 and 30 oz. etc.). Allow for approximately 4 oz. per $1\frac{1}{4}$-oz. drink.
- As for other ingredients you might use, check the recipe and multiply by the number of drinks you plan on serving, to get the total quantities you will require.

Measuring Drinks

Always measure and be sure you follow your drink recipe exactly. We recommend that you pour $1\frac{1}{4}$-oz drinks. If people want more they can always come back. If they like their highballs strong they can always add less soda. It is a mistake to be too generous. You are not being nice to your friends by pouring them strong drinks. You are not being nice to your party either.

Remember too, that generally speaking, women drink less than men.

Here's a Table of Measures that will be useful to you.

1 dash = 3 to 5 drops *Generally the measure called for when adding highly flavoured ingredients. Using more than indicated can spoil a drink.*

1 teaspoon = $\frac{1}{6}$ oz.

1 pony	= 1 oz.	
$1^1/_4$ oz.	= standard measure for a drink	
1 jigger	= $1^1/_2$ oz.	*It is also the name of the thing you use to measure drinks in.*
1 "fifth"	= $26^2/_3$ Imperial oz.	*This is a U.S. measure and is equivalent to $^1/_5$ of the U.S. gallon.*

Mixing Drinks For A Large Party

If you are entertaining 20 or 30 people, things are inclined to stay pretty busy around the bar. So, if you are acting as bartender, or have hired one for the evening, don't try to mix the gamut of exotic cocktails. Stick to two standard cocktails, such as Martinis, Manhattans, Old Fashioneds, etc. Also, pick one additional cocktail that's a little more decorative, such as a Sour, Flip, etc. Also have one teetotaler's drink available, plenty of highball mixers, and the full range of liquors to go with them.

Of course, if it's an informal evening, your best bet is to lead each male guest to the bar, mix the first drink for him and his partner, show him where everything is and then let him serve himself from there on in. Most people enjoy this and it lets you enjoy the rest of the evening in relaxed fashion.

Save your talents as dipenser of exotic libations for smaller gatherings when there's more time and the fruits of your labour can be fully appreciated.

Using The Professional Cocktail Shaker — It does by far the best job and is the mark of a real bartending pro. You don't have to go through unusual contortions and gyrations to do it properly. Experiment a few times after you get your shaker yourself, using water and some ice cubes. When the big day comes and you go into your performance in public, as one real bartending expert says, "While you're shaking, keep your feet together and SMILE." This helps create a pleasant mood of anticipation.

Pouring Drinks From A Shaker — There is no special way to do this. Just make sure that the strainer is firmly in place so that it does the job it is intended to do.

If you have mixed up a batch of several drinks and wish to pour them quickly, place the glasses in a row rim-to-rim, pour each glass half full all the way down the line and then return to the first glass and repeat the process, completing the job. This way you get a uniform distribution of the liquid, and all drinks will have equal body and head.

Practice Makes Perfect — Don't try mixing exotic new drinks for the first time with your guest already seated and waiting in anticipation. He, and you, might be disappointed. It is possible to make mistakes. Practice quietly one evening so that (by the time the guests arrive), you have become an expert.

Flaming Drinks

Many drinks topped with brandy and rum are improved if they are flamed. It's also a spectacular addition to your list of bartending feats. Here's how.

Preheat a teaspoon of the liquor over an open flame, light it and then slowly pour it over the rest of the liquid. (See drink recipe No. 11, Café Royale.)

Floating Drinks — such as a Brandy Floater (Recipe No. 29) and Pousse Café (Recipe No. 76) require that you "layer" liquids one on top of the other so that they do not mix. To do this —

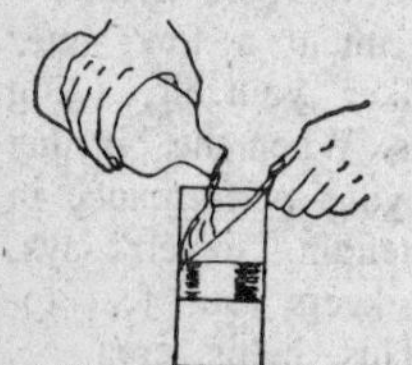

1. tilt the glass slightly
2. insert a teaspoon bottom side up so that the point of the spoon is just touching the liquid
3. pour the liquor slowly over the rounded side of the spoon

Be sure that you are familiar with the specific density of the liquids so that one will float on top of the other. But even if you make a mistake, particularly when making Pousse Café, you'll find that if you use the above technique the liquids will seek their own level and remain separated.

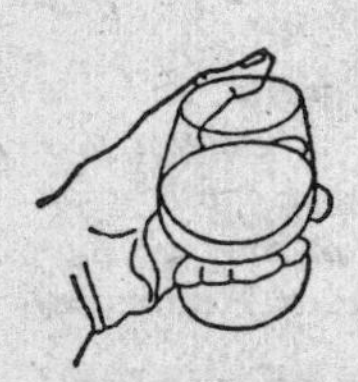

Serving Brandy — If you have a brandy snifter use it, but don't heat the glass before or after the brandy has been poured.

Connoisseurs advise that the best way to truly enjoy the bouquet and flavour of good brandy or cognac is simply to keep it at room temperature, pour it into a snifter (also at room temperature) and then palm the glass to that your hands warm it slowly, while you bask in the aroma.

Serving Liqueurs — The so-called pony, cordial, and liqueur glasses might make your after-dinner drinks look pretty but they don't do very much for a liqueur. Try instead using a 4-oz. tulip-shaped wineglass or even a brandy snifter. Many liqueurs have a fine aroma and it is wasted in small glasses.

Pre-Mixes — The Pros And Cons — Today there are many pre-mixed drinks available on the market both in liquid and powdered form.

When it is so easy to make such things as Sours, Gimlets, Manhattans, etc., it seems pointless to use pre-mixes. But when it comes to such exotic drinks as Mai Tais, Piña Coladas, etc., we suggest you try them. You might be pleasantly surprised. In many cases the taste is excellent and also, surprisingly enough, they can cost far less than the fresh ingredients and are certainly more convenient. On the whole, the powdered ones seem to be best because they are more precise. Try a few.

Food For Thought

Whenever you are serving drinks and entertaining for a half hour or more be sure to put out something for nibbling such as peanuts, chips, etc. They improve the taste of the drinks, enhance conversation, and add to your guests' general feeling of well-being.

PART V

THE ART THAT ISN'T — ENJOYING WINE!

"Wine is one of the most civilized things in the world, and one of the natural things that has been brought to the greatest perfection. It offers a greater range of enjoyment and appreciation than possibly any other purely sensory thing that may be purchased."

— **Ernest Hemingway**

So often we hear the phrase, "the art of enjoying wine," that one is inclined to have the feeling there is an aura of mystery and ritual surrounding its pleasures that is difficult to master. The truth is, there is no secret at all. Simply drink what you like, when you like it, and you will discover that enjoying wine is **not** an art . . . it's a pleasure.

Your taste is the only consideration. To those who really know, the simple golden rule is, "If wine tastes good — it is good."

Variety Is The Spice Of Life

One of wine's great virtues is that its infinite variety and myriad tastes make it just right for so many different occasions. And don't be deceived into thinking that the only good wine is expensive. The subtle differences that make one particular vintage a rare delight to the connoisseur, also can raise its price beyond the reach of most of us. But there are literally hundreds of excellent, reasonably priced wines, both domestic and imported, to choose from.

While we are on the subject of good wines at reasonable prices, it's worth noting that one Canadian Company, La Maison Secrestat Ltée, is taking the lead in creating a new family of wines that we believe will become very popular.

As you are no doubt aware, because of our climate, wine-producing grapes cannot really be considered one of our national products. So, La Maison Secrestat Ltée is now importing grape "musts" (unfermented grape concentrate) selected from the best crops around the world, and making its own distinctive wines here. These are then blended with the best cask-imported wines available. The net result is excellent quality and taste at near domestic prices (see page 188 under the heading "Canada" for a more complete description).

THE WINES OF FRANCE, GERMANY AND ITALY

1

As we have said before, your own taste is the only consideration in making a choice of wines, but as there is a great variety to choose from, it will certainly add to your enjoyment if you know in advance a little about what tastes and characteristics to expect from the different wines available.

Following are charts describing wines from France, Germany and Italy. These three countries are the acknowledged leaders in producing the best of the grape, and vintners from many other countries often use the same descriptive names for their own products with similar characteristics.

FRENCH WINES

GROWING AREA (type)	APPELLATION (Sub-Region)	SUGGESTED BRANDS*	CHARACTERISTICS	DELICIOUS WITH
BORDEAUX **Red** Usually described as Claret in England, from the French Clairet. Serve at room temperature.	Appellation Bordeaux Supérieur	B&G Château Cantegrive	An elegant, well-balanced chateau wine.	Roasts, chops (not pork, veal), liver, steak, and cheese.
	Appellation Bordeaux Contrôlée	B&G Prince Noir	A consistent, well-blended wine.	
	Médoc	B&G Médoc	Dry, medium-bodied, very flavoursome.	
	St. Emilion	B&G Roi Chevalier	Richer, dry, more fragrant.	
White Serve chilled (45° to 50°F) The sweeter the wine, the more chilled it should be served.	Appellation Bordeaux Contrôlée	B&G Prince Blanc	A blend. Dry, natural fruity flavour.	Fish, cold poultry.
	Graves	B&G Graves	Very dry, full-bodied, flavour-some.	
	Sauternes		Sweet, rich flavour.	Baked ham, creamed lobster, desserts or as an apéritif.

BURGUNDY **Red** Serve at room temperature.	Beaujolais (Can be served slightly chilled)	B&G Beaujolais St. Louis	Light, dry, fruity. Best when young.	Same as for red Bordeaux. Also with duck, venison, cheese, hot poultry.
	Mâcon	B&G Mâcon Rouge	Fine deep colour, full bouquet flavourfull, assertive.	
	Côte de Nuits	B&G Côte de Nuits-Villages	Light, young, aromatic.	
	Gevrey Chambertin	B&G Gevrey Chambertin	Full-bodied. Rich style.	
White Serve chilled.	Mâcon	B&G Mâcon Blanc	Fresh, light, dry.	Fish, oysters, seafood, ham, white meats, chicken.
	Pouilly Fuissé	B&G Pouilly-Fuissé	Crisp, medium bodied, well balanced.	
	Chablis	B&G Chablis	Crisply dry, light, fruity. Pale yellow colour.	
LOIRE VALLEY Best when young. **White**	Nantes	B&G Muscadet	Very dry, crisp, fragrant.	Fish, poultry, rich or spicy foods, all seafoods.
	Vouvray	B&G Vouvray	Fruity, dry, light and lovely.	

Rosé	Anjou	Nectarosé Still	Delicate, medium-dry.	Hors d'oeuvres (as an appetizer), ham, pork salmon.
ALSACE **White** Best when young.	Riesling		Fresh, crisp, dry. Good bouquet.	Pork, poultry, chèese, salads, fish, ham, veal. Brunches.
	Traminer		Medium-dry. Full flavour.	
	Sylvaner		Light, fresh, slightly fruity.	
	Gewurtztaminer		Medium bodied, clean, spicy taste.	
RHONE VALLEY **Red**	Côtes du Rhône	B&G Domaine de la Meynarde	Full, rich, firm. Deep in colour.	Roasts, stews, all highly spiced meat dishes, cheese.
	Châteauneuf Du Pape	B&G Châteauneuf du Pape		
	Hermitage		Rich, fruity.	
	Côte Rotie		Heavy, robust.	

Rosé Serve chilled.	Côtes du Rhône	B&G Domaine de la Meynarde	Flinty, dry. Fruity flavour.	As an apéritif, or with fish, meats in light sauces, ham.
PROVENCE **Red**	Côtes de Provence		Ruby colour. Full-bodied. Delicate and subtle bouquet.	Beef, lamb, veal, pork, game, spaghetti and spiced dishes.
Rosé	Côtes de Provence		Flinty, dry. Light bouquet and body.	Hors d'œuvres, fish, poultry, veal.

GROWING AREA	SUGGESTED BRANDS*	DEGREE OF SWEETNESS	SERVING SUGGESTIONS
CHAMPAGNE	Cuvée René Lalou (vintage) Perrier Jouet Brut Mumm's Cordon Rouge Brut Mumm's Extra Dry	0 to 1/2% 0 to 1/2% 0 to 1/2% 1% to 2%	As an aperitif and excellent with all food.

MAY WE ALSO SUGGEST

V.D.Q.S. WINES — These are excellent, reasonably priced, blended wines which are just a grade below the Appellation Contrôlée wines, (see glossary). Sometimes they will come from a specific growing area but not necessarily.

Red	B&G Côtes de Luberon	Dry. Young, earthy, sturdy.
	B&G Costières du Gard	Dry. Fine bouquet, strong body, slightly fruity.
	B&G Corbières	Young, medium-heavy. Ruby colour. Good bouquet.

GERMAN WINES

GROWING AREA (type)	GROWING REGION	SUGGESTED BRANDS*	CHARACTERISTICS	DELICIOUS WITH
RHINE VALLEY	Rheingau		Full-bodied, fruity, dry.	
(Also known as "Hock.")	Oppenheim		A blend. Light, medium-dry. Good bouquet.	Game, ham, veal, cheese, salads, seafood, fish.
White	Nierstein		Full-bodied. Rich bouquet.	
Serve well chilled.	Liebfraumilch a blended Rhine wine, especially fromRheinhessen.		A blend. Full, flowery, medium-sweet. Rich bouquet.	

MOSELLE VALLEY **White** Serve well chilled. Best when young.	Bernkastel		Fruity, medium-sweet, well balanced.	
	Graach		Rich. Fruity bouquet.	Alone or with fish, game, ham, veal, mild cheese, trout, pork, Brunches.
	Zell		Pleasant, medium-sweet. fruity.	
	Zeltingen		Soft. Steely dry taste, summery bouquet.	

ITALIAN WINES

TYPE	GROWING REGION	SUGGESTED BRANDS*	CHARACTERISTICS	DELICIOUS WITH
Red	Tuscany	Brolio Riserva	Pungent bouquet, full-bodied. Ages well.	Red meat, pastas.
		Brolio Chianti Classico	Robust, well balanced. Good bouquet, Ages well.	
	Piedmont	Bersano Barolo	Strong, flowery bouquet. Ruby colour. Well balanced body. Dry.	
	Veneto	Ricasoli Valpolicella	Light, fruity, soft, fragrant.	

TYPE	CROWING REGION	SUGGESTED BRANDS*	CHARACTERISTICS	DELICIOUS WITH
Red (Cont.)	Veneto	Ricasoli Bardolino	Dark, full-bodied.	Red meat and pastas.
White	Orvieto		Dry or sweet.	Fowl, ham, seafood.
	Soave		Dry.	
	Piedmont		Dry, fresh. Best when young.	

Note: If you wish to become a real expert in selecting wines, the glossary section of this book, entitled, "I Didn't Know That!", describes in detail many of the descriptive fine points found on bottle labels — particularly French wines. (See headings, "Nomenclature of Wines," "Grapes," "A.O.C.," "V.D.Q.S.," "Vintage," etc.)

**Suggested brands may not be available in all provinces.*

2

WINES FROM OTHER COUNTRIES

The previous chapter dealt exclusively with wines from France, Germany and Italy, but this does not mean that these three countries have cornered the market in producing fine wines. Far from it. Many other parts of the world are ideal for grape growing, and whether you have just discovered the pleasures of good wine or consider yourself a connoisseur, you owe it to yourself to try some of the wines discussed on the following pages. Many of them have characteristics similar to the products of France, Germany and Italy. Still others have distinctive qualities all their own that are well worth exploring.

Here then, in alphabetical order, are some brief commentaries on wines from 14 other countries that are available, in varying supply, across Canada.

Algeria

This country, along with other North African countries, in the past has had a somewhat bad name in wine export circles because of the large, unclassifiable quantities produced. The climate for winegrowing is very good though, and the wine is actually considered uniformly average. Much Algerian wine was consumed in France where it was looked upon as a good coarse "vin ordinaire."

Argentina

A prolific wine producer. The industry was started by the large Italian population which emigrated there. Some very creditable wines are produced, several of which are now available in Canada. Mendoza is the best Argentinean winegrowing region.

WE RECOMMEND:*

White — Chablis Valentin Bianchi

Red — Nuestro Margaux V. Bianchi
Bianchi Borgogna
**Not available in all provinces.*

Australia

Australia produces some reliable, standard quality, full-bodied table wines. It also produces some port and sherry type wines.

Austria

Austrian wines closely resemble the German Rhine and Moselle wines but are not considered quite as good. Some of the better known names are Grinzinger and Kremser. These wines are almost always white, and have a light, fruity taste.

Canada

Canada is not normally considered a wine-producing country in the strictest sense of the word. Although there are several vineyard regions, the grapes produced are ordinarily not well suited to dry or medium-dry red and white table wines. However, the specialty wines made from these grapes are quite popular for domestic use. Canadian sweet ports and sherries are quite good, as are the currently popular fortified and flavoured "pop" wines. It is to be noted that Canadian, especially Ontario wines, are being produced with more attention to quality.

La Maison Secrestat

As previously noted. La Maison Secrestat Ltée. is now producing a variety of excellent table and specialty wines at reasonable prices to meet the rapidly increasing demands of Canadian wine-lovers. These are not "Canadian wines" in the truest sense, since they are a blend of good quality imported wines from many countries, and the "musts" of imported grapes fermented in the Secrestat winery near Montreal. Here is a sampling of some of the wines it is now producing. They warrant your serious consideration.

Still Table Wines*

Red — Moulin Mouton
— Chambord

White — Papillon
— Chantilly

Crackling Wines*

Rosé — Portugese type — Pica Rosé
White — Portugese type — Pica
— a blend of red and white wines — crackling Cold Duck

Specialty Wines*

Vermouth	— Italian	— San Mareno
Sherry	— Golden colour, medium sweet.	— Grenada
Sangria	— A fruit-flavoured red wine named after its popular Spanish counterpart.	— La Maison Secrestat

**Some of these wines may not be available in all provinces.*

Chile

An excellent winegrowing country with some fine reds and whites made with Bordeaux and Burgundy grapes but with their own characteristics. As these are becoming more popular in Canada, it is perhaps wise to know the four age classifications shown on Chilean wine label:
Courant — *1 year old,* Specia — *2 years old,* Reserva — *4 years old,* Gran Vino — *6 years old.*

Greece

Greece produces some excellent wines (white, red and rosé). But, a word of advice: only buy those wines with the word "Aretsina" on the label. The Greeks also produce another group of wines, labelled "Retsina," which contain sandarac and pine resins. They impart a unique flavour that can be unpleasant unless you have acquired a taste for them.

Hungary

Hungary is famous for a rich, white dessert wine called Tokay (mainly sweet). Some good, dry, white or red table wines are also available, such as —

Red	— Egri Bikaver (Bull's Blood)
White	— from the Lake Balaton area

Portugal

Portuguese wine is usually made with the stems and stalks of the grapes as well as the fruit itself. Much Portuguese wine is sold while it is still too young.. But one young variety, "Vinhos Verdes," is bottled while it is still fermenting and is therefore slightly sparkling and very enjoyable. It comes in red, white and rosé. The best Portuguese wines are labelled "Reserva" or "Garraferra." Portuguese sparkling white and rosé wines are pleasant.

South Africa

South Africa produces Burgundy and Rhine type wines that can be very good, as are its fortified wines. The latter have a distinctive taste quite different from Spanish sherries or Portuguese ports.

Spain

Spanish wines can be unpredictable but the quality is rapidly improving. The best Spanish wines have "Guarantia De Oriden" on the label. This indicates that the wines are bottled under government regulation. More and more Spanish wine is now being bottled under such controls. Available in red (Tinto), white (Blanco), and rosé. The best known winegrowing region is Rioja. Specially aged wines are also labelled "Reserva" and carry a date.

WE RECOMMEND:*

Red	— Sin Rival	— B. Franco - Españolas
	Claret	— B. Franco - Españolas
	Royal	— B. Franco - Españolas
White	— Diamante	— B. Franco - Españolas

**Not available in all provinces.*

Switzerland

Switzerland produces both red and white wines that are crisp and spritely. The best are the whites and these are usually the only ones exported.

Look for: Fendant de Sion and Neuchatel.

United States

The northern part of California has many of the finest vineyards in the world and several vintners in this region produce excellent red and white table wines. Wines sold under the name of the grape are known as varietals.

WE RECOMMEND:*

Red	— Bordeaux type	— Paul Masson Cabernet Sauvignon
	— Burgundy type	— Paul Masson Gamay Beaujolais
White	— Loire type	— Paul Masson Chemin Blanc
Rosé		— Paul Masson Pink

**Not available in all provinces.*

Another U.S. wine-producing area is upper New York State, but the quality of table wines from this region is not as good or reliable as that of their California counterparts. It does produce some good sweet fortified and "pop" wines.

Yugoslavia

Produces some good white wines with characteristics of Rhine and Moselle wines. They are named after the type of grape. There are also some good, robust, full-bodied reds such as Pinot Noir and Cabernet Beda. Look also for a delicious dessert wine called Tiger Milk.

3

SPECIALTY WINES

All wines fall into either the "table" or apéritif "specialty" category. Table wines almost invariably are an unaltered product of the grape with nothing added, and as the name implies, are usually consumed as an accompaniment to food.

Specialty wines on the other hand, are usually either fortified with other distilled spirits, or are made "aromatic" through the addition of herbs, spices and special flavourings. And unlike table wines, they are most often considered as wines to be consumed by themselves or with rather specific types of dishes. These wines usually owe their origin to one specific country or part of the world, but today, counterparts of the originals are produced in almost every country that grows grapes. Here, in chart from, is a description of five of the traditional types of specialty wines.

Recently, a varied new group of specialty wines has made an appearance. For want of a better name they are generally described as "pop" wines, and as the name implies, some of them are becoming very popular.

To try to classify them is almost impossible, because the differing tastes and combinations are limited only by the ingenuity of the vintners. They can either be still or sparkling, but most are sweet to medium-sweet and the wine taste can either be quite apparent or almost non-existent.

Two of the most popular varieties are Cold Duck and Sangria.

THE MORE POPULAR SPECIALTY WINES

NAME	TYPE	SUGGESTED BRANDS*	TASTE	DELICIOUS WITH
SHERRY *(Spanish origin)* Blended wine fortified with brandy. Dry sherries should be served well chilled. Produced in the Jerez de La Frontera region.	Manzanilla		Extremely dry.	Alone, as an apéritif, or in the afternoon.
	Amontillado		Very dry. Nutty flavour.	
	Fino		Dry. Golden colour.	
	Amorosa		Fuller, sweeter.	Soup, fish, coffee.
	Oloroso		Dark, sewwtest.	Pastries, fruit, desserts, cheese, cake, coffee.
PORT *(Portuguese origin)* Fortified wine. Heavy and sweet. Usually well-aged, often blended. Serve at room temperature. Can now be purchased in "dry" forms.	Vintage (unblended)		Mellow, fruity, heavily crusted.	Before or after dinner; with cheese, nuts, fruit.
	Tawny (blended)		Rich, lighter coloured.	
	Ruby (younger, deep purple)		Sweeter.	

Not available in all provinces.

NAME	TYPE	SUGGESTED BRANDS*	TASTE	DELICIOUS WITH
VERMOUTH Aromatic (herbs), fortified wine.	Italian	Noilly Pratt	Deep red, sweet, slightly bitter.	As an apéritif, on the rocks, mixed with V.O. or Scotch.
	French	Noilly Pratt Dry	Light golden colour, dry, slightly bitter.	As a mixer with gin, on the rocks.
MADEIRA *(Spanish origin)* Fortified with brandy. Serve slightly chilled.	Sercial		Light, dry. Pale or golden colour.	As an apéritif; with soup.
	Verdelho		Medium-dry. Amber colour.	With desserts, coffee.
	Bual		Medium-sweet, full-flavoured. Russet colour.	As an apéritif; with soup.
	Malmsy		Very sweet, full-bodied. Deep brown colour.	After dinner and between meals.
MARSALA Fortified dessert wine. Serve at room temp.	Italian		Sweet. Similar to port.	Fruit, cheese, nuts, desserts.

**Not available in all provinces*

THE FINER POINTS OF WINEMANSHIP

4

This chapter title might sound like a contradiction of our earlier statement that, "there are no rules to follow in enjoying wine other than the dictates of your own palate." But, like any other pleasure there are some procedures, that if followed, will help enhance any good wine. Here then, are some of these procedures, discussed in Question and Answer form.

Q. How should wine be stored?

A. It should always be stored away from sunlight in a well-ventilated, dry place with a temperature that does not go below 45° or over 70°F. It is most important to try and maintain a constant temperature. Screw top bottles and fortified wines can be stored standing upright. Corked bottles should be kept on their sides so that the cork will remain moist and airtight. If you buy wine by the gallon, it is best to decant it into smaller bottles and cork each tightly to prevent spoilage. If left in the larger bottle and constantly exposed to air each time it is used, it can turn to vinegar.

Q. What are the best serving temperatures for various wines?

A. White, sparkling and rosé wines and dry sherries should be chilled. "Chilling" does not mean freezing to the marrow. The ideal temperature is between 45° and 50°F. Place the bottle in the refrigerator an hour before serving or in water and ice filled busket 15 to 20 minutes before serving.

Red wines, ports and sweet sherries should be served at room temperature but never at more than 70°F. The lower quality red wines can be slightly chilled. Always open red table wines an hour before serving to allow the wines to "breathe." The younger the wine the longer it should be left to breathe.

Q. What is the best type of glass to use with table wines?

A. Today the large 8-oz. tulip-shaped glass is very popular. It should only be half filled. The larger bowl allows you to sniff the aroma and bouquet. Always pick a good clear glass, not patterned or couloured, so that replacement is easier in the event of breakage.

Q. Is there any special way to open a wine bottle?

A. Yes. With red wine, or older wines that might develop a sediment — let the bottle stand for three or four hours before opening so that the sediment has a chance to settle, and try not to agitate the bottle while opening. White wines do not require this special treatment. With all wines, wipe the top of the bottle with a damp cloth after the foil or plastic covering has been removed. Extract the cork with a good substantial corkscrew, and then wipe the mouth of the bottle again.

Q. Is there any particular way to pour wine?

A. No. The only recommendation is that red wines in particular be poured gently so that any sediment in the bottle is not agitated. Do not fill the glasses too full; half full is sufficient. Your guests can always come back for more.

Q. There seems to be quite a ritual involved in the serving of wine. What is it? Is it important?

A. Wine has been enjoyed for so long that it is only natural some traditions and etiquette have evolved around its serving on formal occasions. It's not a life-and-death situation if you don't follow these rules, but if you wish to be correct, there is a procedure to follow.

After the host has opened the bottle, he smells the cork, to check for possibly bad smell. Next he pours a little of the wine into his own glass to see that there are no cork particles floating on top, and to sample the quality, taste, appearance and bouquet. Once he is satisfied that it is up to the standard he wishes, he pours for his guests, serving himself last.

In a restaurant, the waiter or sommelier will usually present the unopened bottle to the "host" so that he may read the label to be sure he is getting what he ordered. Then after opening the bottle, he will sniff the cork himself and place it beside the host. He will next pour a little of the wine in the host's glass for him to sample. After it has received the host's approval it will be served to the guests.

It is these nice touches that seem to add even more to the taste of a good wine.

Q. In tasting a wine what should be looked for?

A. There is so much enjoyment in a glass of wine — colour, aroma, bouquet, sweetness and flavour — that it should be well-savoured. In judging wine, use your sense of sight, smell and taste.

Esperienced wine tasters use this procedure:

1. Pour about one ounce into a stemmed glass, raise it to the light and examine the colour and clarity.
2. Twirl the wine in the glass and sniff the bouquet.
3. Sip the wine, rolling it around on the tongue. Note the tartness or richness. Sip again, noting in turn the degree of sweetness or dryness, the body and the flavour.
4. Swallow and enjoy the after-taste.
5. It is best to clear the palate between tasting different types of wine with a piece of cheese, or a cracker.
6. Taste dry wines before sweet wines and not too many wines at one time. Taste white wines before red wines, young before old.

Q. After a bottle has been opened can it be stored?

A. Yes. Recork the bottle tightly and store it on its side in a cool place. Most red and white table wines should be restored for a short time only. Like all foods, wine is perishable. Dessert wines can be kept longer or can be decanted.

Q. Are there any foods to avoid with wine?

A. Wine goes well with almost everything, but there are a few exceptions to prove the rule.

Curries and some highly spiced foods are not well suited to wine. Don't serve wine with food that will be accompanied by a mint sauce or cocktail sauces — they will overwhelm the taste of the wine.

Chocolate and dessert wines do not go well together, egg dishes sometimes give wine and odd taste, and salads and antipastos can make wine taste a bit vinegary.

5

THE SMALL WINE CELLAR

It's probably safe to say that most people who enjoy wine buy it a few hours before they are ready to use it, and only buy what is required for a specific occasion. But this is not necessarily the best idea. Most retail outlets keep their wines under the worst of conditions. Bottles are kept in an upright position and usually exposed to light or in areas that are overly warm. Therefore, after they are purchased, they should be allowed a period of storage under proper conditions so that they can recover before being used.

The ideal is to have your own wine cellar. This probably won't be a "cellar" in the literal sense of the word but rather just a collection of bottles. Wine need not be kept underground. In fact, many old cellars are not the best places to keep it. They are often damp, and dampness is the enemy of wine storage because it rots the cork.

If you decide you'd like to start a wine cellar, try to select an area that is dark, ventilated, vibration-free and with a temperature that does not go below 45° or over 70°F.

Here are some suggested locations:

A cabinet under the stairs, a pantry cupboard, a closet in an unused room that receives less than full heat in the winter, or a cool location in a dry basement.

Arranging The Wines In Your Cellar

Try to store bottles in their own individual compartments so that when you remove one, the remainder are not disturbed. For these individual compartments you might use the heavily divided cardboard boxes that wine or distilled spirits are shipped in, or a wooden soft drink crate. Cement pipes with four-inch interior diameters stacked one on top of the other are also excellent. Or, you might consider the new plastic modular wine racks now available.

White wines need the coolest place and should be kept nearest the floor. Red Bordeaux type wines should be placed next and the Burgundies on top. All should be laid on their sides.

A Wine Rack In The Dining Room?

The trouble with most of the fancy wine racks is that they are made for people to look at rather than for wine to slumber in comfortably. They're often kept in the dining room, which is a great place for them to be seen but is not the best place for something that shuns light and loves moderate, even temperatures. Take that rack back to the cellar.

Now, What Goes Into The Wine Cellar?

Here are three groups of suggestions for cellars of different sizes. We have listed types of wines only, without mentioning specific brand names. It is always wise to choose from names you are familiar with and from vintners with a reputation for quality. In Chapters 1, 2 and 3, we have made brand name suggestions. They are well worth remembering.

12-Bottle Cellar

2 Red Bordeaux type
2 Red Burgundy type
1 White Burgundy type
1 White Bordeaux type
1 Red Côte du Rhône
1 Chianti Classico
1 Imported "Must" (red)
1 Imported "Must" (white)
1 Champagne or Sparkling Burgundy
1 Sparkling Rosé

24-Bottle Cellar

2 Red Bordeaux (no specific region)
2 Red Bordeaux (appellation contrôlée)
2 White Bordeaux (no specific region)
1 White Bordeaux (appellation contrôlée)
2 Red Burgundy (no specific region)
2 Red Burgundy (appellation contrôlée)
1 White Burgundy (no specific region)
1 White Burgundy (appellation contrôlée)
1 German Rhine or Moselle (white)
1 Loire or Rhone Valley (white)
2 Imported "Must" (red)
2 Imported "Must" (white)
2 Chianti Classico
1 Champagne or Sparkling Burgundy
2 Sparkling Rosé

48-Bottle Cellar

2 Rhine or Moselle (white)
1 Loire Valley (white)
1 Rhone Valley (white)
2 Red Bordeaux (no specific region)
2 Red Bordeaux (appellation contrôlée)
1 Red Bordeaux (Château)
2 White Bordeaux (no specific region)
2 White Bordeaux (appellation contrôlée)
1 White Bordeaux (Château)
2 Red Burgundy (no specific region)
2 Red Burgundy (appellation contrôlée)
1 Red Burgundy (Château)
2 White Burgundy (no specific region)
2 White Burgundy (appellation contrôlée)
1 White Burgundy (Château)
1 Chianti Classico
1 Chianti Riserva
2 Italian (red)
2 Italian (white)
2 Argentine or Chilean (red)
2 Argentine or Chilean (white)
4 Imported "Must" (red)
4 Imported "Must" (white)
1 Spanish (red)
1 Spanish (white)
1 Champagne (Brut or Extra Dry)
1 Anjou Sparkling Rosé
1 Portuguese Sparkling Rosé
1 Portuguese Sparkling White

Of course, these three cellars are suggestions only and you probably have ideas of your own for wines that you would like to add to or substitute for the selections we have made. That's the fun of wines and the hobby of keeping your own cellar. In Canada, we are fortunate in having an almost unlimited array of fine wines to choose from and the list is growing daily. Try experimenting — you'll be in for some pleasant surprizes.

If there are any specific points you would like to have clarified, or if you simply wish to have more information generally about wines, direct your inquiries to:

INTERNATIONAL WINES & SPIRITS LTD.

1430 Peel St.
Montreal, Que.
H3A 1S9

They will be happy to be of service to you.

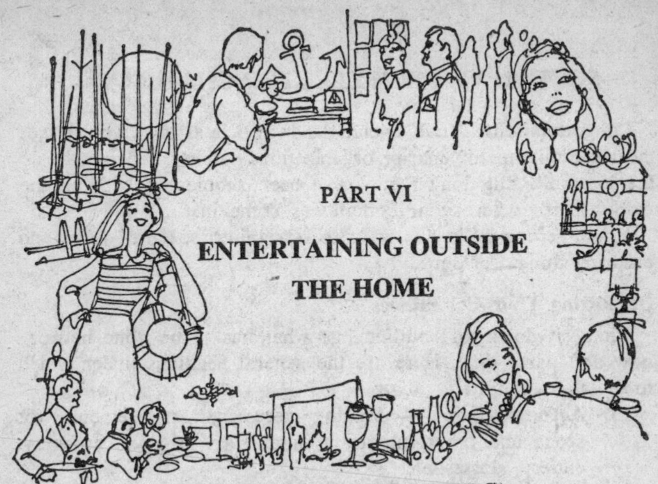

PART VI

ENTERTAINING OUTSIDE THE HOME

— FOR FUN AND FOR FUNDS —

Many of the most entertaining events you may attend during the year are those held elsewhere than in a home. They might be part of the social program of a club of which you are a member or simply a "let's have a party" decision made by a group of mutual friends.

There is one important element that makes these occasions different from the entertaining you do yourself:

> *They are always organized and run by a group of people working as a team, with one person acting as the chairman.*

Although many aspects of such functions are similar to "at home" entertaining, there are enough important differences of which you should be aware, that we have set aside this section to discuss them.

There are two different categories that these parties fall into: 1) for fun, and 2) for funds.

For the strictly fun party, your objective (besides having a good time) is to break even financially. If you want to raise funds however, either for your own group's benefit, or your favourite charity, the important thing is to clear costs *and* make a profit. Money is raised through subscriptions, ticket sales, donations, collections, etc. Hopefully, the fun aspect will also have top priority!

Two parties with two different purposes, yet the basic organization is much the same. For both kinds of events, the secret is to work by *committee.*

SO, YOU'VE BEEN ELECTED CHAIRMAN! 1

Congratulations! Your friends and associates feel you've got the right mixture of charm, organizational ability and tact to do the job well. But don't feel you've been shouldered with all the work. That's where your committees come in.

Your responsibility rests with assigning specific jobs and ensuring things get done.

Organizing Your Committees

First, sit down and outline just what has to be done between now and party time. Here are the general headings under which most jobs will fall:

1. **Accommodation** — Making necessary arrangements for space and other important items such as staff, crockery, cutlery, glasses, etc.
2. **Clean-Up** — Either cleaning up, or making arrangements to have it done.
3. **Decorations** — The buying, renting, or borrowing of decorations. Their installation and removal.
4. **Communications** — "Bird dogging" meetings, recording minutes, keeping account of who's doing what and reminding them of deadlines.
5. **Music and Entertainment** — Contacting and booking entertainment, and obtaining necessary props, equipment, etc. Entertainment includes speakers.
6. **Food and Liquor** — The type and quantity to be served. The budgeting for, and ordering of it.
7. **Prizes and Donations** — Obtaining prizes, arranging drawings, etc.
8. **Publicity** — Contacting newspapers, radio or TV stations. Handling posters, mailings, etc.
9. **Tickets and Sales** — All aspects of sales and solicitation.
10. **Treasurer** — Supervising the budget.

These may be the names of your individual committees. You might find there are also other jobs in your particular project that are not mentioned here. If so, and the task warrants it, set up another committee to handle it.

If your group is small, several of these jobs might be undertaken by one or two hard-working individuals, including yourself. Make those you appoint entirely responsible for work assigned to them. Don't let them think for one minute you will pick up the pieces if they fall down on the job. That's the secret of delegating.

Choosing Committee Members

Use tact and common sense in picking people. Someone with a flair for art should be in charge of decorations. Someone good at figures can be treasurer, etc.

Don't pick friends just because they are friends. Make sure they are prepared to pitch in and help. Look for talent, ability and past experience.

Get Going . . . Now!

An early start is essential. Good planning makes for a successful event. Set up a budget right at the start, pick your committee and assign tasks. Delegate work *evenly, fairly* and *separately*. Then you will have better control over who is doing what. Once you've assigned your workload, don't interfere.

There's that secret word again . . . DELEGATION.

What About Meetings?

Hold regular meetings so you know just where you stand. Meetings are not the be-all and end-all of your committee's activities, but they do keep everyone on their toes. A get-together over a cup of coffee will often suffice.

Here are some basic rules that should cover all such get-togethers regardless of size.

- Start on time, with a definite agenda.
- State the purpose of the meeting at the outset.
- Take minutes.
- Keep things moving.
- Speak clearly, to the group, not to individuals.
- Insist on control to prevent hubbub, but invite criticism and even disagreement. Clarify issues by obtaining majority support and ride with the majority.
- Don't squelch a troublemaker yourself. Let the meeting handle it. Rise above internal politics.
- The chairman is *always* neutral. Don't argue.
- At the end of meetings, check to see everything has been properly covered.
- The chairman votes only in the case of a deadlock.
- Establish the time and date of the next meeting before adjournment.

How often you meet and how early you start meeting will depend on the size and type of party. For formal banquets and dances, six months ahead is not too early. As the event approaches, your meetings can be scheduled closer together. Plan meetings at a time and place convenient to your workers.

2 NOW, WE'RE ALL SET TO GO

Let's Give It A Name!

Always work with a "theme" in mind. It is a key factor in choosing decor, music, food, entertainment and the general program of the event itself.

The following questions will probably affect your choice of theme:

- Is there a special date, season, or holiday connected with the event?
- Is it being run in conjunction with another activity?
- What facilities have you access to? Will it be held outdoors or in?
- Is it strictly an "inside" affair, or are guests or the general public invited?
- Will those who attend be children, young adults, middle-aged, over forty, married, single, or families?
- Will there be as many men as women, or women as men?
- How many will attend?
- Will it be held in the afternoon? At dinner time? At night?
- Have you studied the flops and successes of the past?

Tailor the theme to create maximum appeal to those who will attend.

Now, give your party an intriguing name. Don't stick an ordinary label like "Costume Ball" onto that Hallowe'en affair — call it a "Spooks 'n Spirits Soiree." Creates a little more atmosphere, doesn't it?

When Should It Be Held?

Remember, large numbers of people are often away or heavily committed over Christmas, Easter, long weekends, etc. Once you have set the date, announce it as soon as possible so guests can put you on their schedule.

If it's a fund-raising event, you would be wise to determine when other groups are holding theirs so that you don't compete.

What Facilities Have You Access To?

In your enthusiasm to do something original, be sure the local recreation hall you've rented has facilities to serve charcoal broiled steaks for your Western Barbecue. Or, if you plan a dinner-dance for 50, don't book a hall that will accommodate 150. All that bare space will make for a cold atmosphere. It is vital to match space and facilities to the size and theme of your event.

These are the things to watch for:

- Are there enough tables and chairs?
- How many people can be safely accommodated in the space? (Check fire regulations.)
- Is there sufficient china, glass and silverware? Or must these items be rented? What about tablecloths and napkins?
- Is the kitchen and refrigerating space and equipment adequate? Who does the preparation?
- Are there adequate washroom and checkroom facilities?
- Is smoking permitted?
- What decorating is permitted? Can lighting be altered in any way? Are candles allowed? How far ahead of time can decorating be done?
- Is there a stage or platform for entertainment or speakers? Microphone(s), lecturns, curtains, etc.?
- Does the building owner have insurance or do you have to make these arrangements?

Don't Overlook The Law

Know, for sure, what kind of licences and/or permits are required in connection with your event.

First, let's deal with liquor. You'll find there are laws governing whether, when and how you can serve liquor. These laws vary from municipality to municipality and province to province. This is one area where Seagram's Reception Service can be of real assistance (please see the Foreword to this book for more details). These are some of the things on which this excellent service can help set you straight.

- What are your province's laws governing the serving of liquor in a rented hall or hotel?
- Are there special closing hours for halls or hotels?
- If you've booked a hotel or catering hall, may you provide the liquor or must the establishment? If you provide it, how much will it cost you in addition to the cost of the liquor itself? Many hotels charge an additional "corkage" fee.

- How do you order liquor in bulk and have it delivered?
- If your city is normally "dry," can you and how do you apply for special permission to serve liquor?
- If everyone brings their own liquor into a rented public hall, do you need a permit*?
- Is it permissible to serve liquor out of doors in your area? Is a permit* required?
- If your club or group now has a permit to sell liquor on their own premises to their own members, do you need a special permit* to sell to "outsiders"?

***Most of these permits must be applied for in writing well ahead of time. Most permits involve paying a nominal fee.**

Municipal Laws To Watch Out For

Don't forget to check local city regulations. For your Beach Party Cookout you'll most likely require a fire permit, or if you're planning to have booths for an outdoor carnival or bazaar, you might need a concessions or selling permit. You'd like to have a parade? Better consult the local laws here too. The same goes for street dances. Don't forget too, to check on local laws governing games of chance if you are planning a Monte Carlo night or carnival.

Some Provincial Laws That Might Affect You

If you are providing entertainment and charging admission, better check to see if Amusement Taxes are applicable. If it's a bazaar, fair, tombola, rummage sale, auction, etc. and you are selling things, you'd better do some probing into whether or not you should collect Auction and Retail Sales Taxes.

3 THE FOUR ESSENTIALS OF A GREAT PARTY!

- Good music and entertainment
- Good atmosphere
- Good food and drink
- Good company

Up tlll now, we've been talking about the all-important behind-the-scenes activities that must be done first to make any event run smoothly. But now, let's get on with those elements that are the visible signs of all your hard work — the ones people will remember.

Make It Or Break It With Music

Choose your music to relate to the theme. It can be relaxing, vivacious, subdued or loud, depending on the preferences of people who will attend. Remember — their tastes have priority over your own.

Sign On The Dotted Line

If you hire live talent, it is normal procedure to draw up and have both parties sign a contract, for your protection as well as theirs. Make sure the contract states clearly the time, date, place, and number of hours they will work, and the fee agreed upon. Often a deposit is required. If so, be sure the amount is stipulated in the contract. A word of caution: audition entertainers **before** signing. Be sure both parties are clear on who provides and installs props, equipment, etc. and who pays for it.

Creating An Atmosphere

Who ever heard of a Hallowe'en Party without at least one jack-o'-lantern on display, or a Mexican Fiesta without sombreros, serapes and maracas? A few simple decorative touches can transform a school gym into a South Seas paradise or a Dixieland jazz emporium.

It requires imagination. Sure! And a little work. Certainly! But the end result can put people in a party mood the minute they set foot inside the room. So, isn't it worth the effort?

On pages 58 to 78 we've listed several entertaining ideas

along with some decorating hints for most of them. Even though these hints are tailored to suit smaller home parties, many can be used even for the largest gala affair. If you want to go further with your decorating plans, here are some more suggestions to help set the stage for the best party ever.

Tips From The Pros

According to professional display artists and stage-set designers, there are five invaluable rules to follow, a few basic tools to have at your disposal, and a few tricks to know, to make party decorating easy.

Here are the five rules —

1. If ceilings are high, "drop" them. (How, will be explained shortly.)
2. Resist the small, dainty, time-consuming decorations.
3. To keep budgets down, always try to make, rent or borrow any expensive items you'll need.
4. Make use of so-called obstacles such as pillars, basketball nets, storage bins, etc., by making them part of your decor.
5. If you have neither the time nor the budget to completely decorate your whole party area, pick the focal point of the room, decorate it to the hilt and gradually taper off as you move away. Illuminate the decorated area and let the rest slide into obscurity with subdued lighting.

Here Are The Tools You'll Need

- ladders (at least two)
- large staple gun
- razor blaze knives
- scissors
- a screwdriver
- paint brushes
- finishing hammers
- pliers
- clean-up rags
- a bucket
- a small saw

. . . And The Basic Materials You Might Want To Use

- finishing nails
- mini screw eyes
- thumbtacks
- straight pins
- push pins
- crêpe paper
- poster paper

- construction paper (coloured)
- invisible wiring (fine, light-weight, strong.)
- tissue paper (coloured)
- wallpaper paste
- rubber cement
- paste
- masking tape
- cellulose tape
- poster or spray paint
- foil
- pine 1″ x 2″'s, in 8′ lengths
- heavy cardboard sheets
- corrugated cardboard
- string
- latex house paint

Make Your Own Ceiling!

If you are faced with a room with a high ceiling, and you want an intimate atmosphere, try "dropping" it to the height you wish, by criss-crossing invisible wire at the desired level. Then, place hanging decorations on the wire. This creates an effective false ceiling. It also serves to soften bright overhead lights if you can't turn them out altogether. The wire can be affixed to the walls with screw eyes, or, if this is not permitted, with masking tape. Don't worry, it's capable of holding fairly heavy weights, providing the wall is clean, dry and dust-free where you stick it.

For decorations on these wires, you can use crêpe paper streamers, paper lanterns, balloon clusters, ribbons, silver icicles, snowflakes, stars, etc.

Walls and Obstacles

Use posters on the walls and pillars, or create your own drawings. They can be simple but bold. Use felt pens, poster or latex paint and poster paper (preferably coloured). Big, coloured paper cut-outs can also be effective, especially with the proper lighting.

As for those "obstacles," they are merely new shapes to play with. Thread vines around them, turn them into mock people, stick artificial fruit or flowers on them. You'll soon find a hundred and one ideas when you confront the situation.

Crêpe Paper, The Party Decorator's Best Friend

The decorating possibilities with this versatile material are almost endless. Dennison Mfg. Co. of Canada Ltd. have produced many excellent booklets on how to transform the myriad colours of their crêpe paper products into almost every conceivable kind of decoration. Write to them % Dennison, "Fun With Crêpe Service," P.O. Box 460, Drummondville, Quebec.

For other decorating ideas using other materials, write:

Reynolds Aluminum Co. of Canada Ltd.
1420 Sherbrooke St. West,
Montreal, Quebec.
(Aluminum Foil)

Lighting

Lighting can be the most important part of your decor. Variations can range from simply putting coloured lights in existing outlets and using colourful candle holders on tables, to intricate lighting systems, involving ultraviolet "black lights" and flashing strobe lights. Basically the lighting effects you use fall into two categories: 1) spotlighting, which highlights one specific area or object, and 2) indirect lighting, which is used to create an aura over the whole room.

Be careful about the colours and intensities you use. Pinks or reds provide the most flattering effect on people, yellow creates somewhat of a pallor. Blues and greens make whites whiter, and create a cool, eerie feeling. If you use the "black light" tubes, be sure they are shielded from people and directed only on the subjects that you want to glow in spectacular fashion. Looking directly into these lights can be damaging to the eyes, and the lighting itself can cause some extremely unpleasant effects in how people look. Similarly, strobe lights have all the candlepower of flash bulbs and the same blinding effects if they go off directly in people's eyes. Also, make sure you do not place inflammable objects too close to light bulbs, or cut them off from a free circulation of air, especially if these bulbs are any stronger than 25 watts.

4

IT PAYS TO ADVERTISE

If your party is strictly for your own group, outside publicity will not be important. A telephone committee or word of mouth is probably all that is required. But if your affair is a big one, or falls into the fund-raising category, then advertising is one of the keys to success. If you are lucky, you can corral someone for your committee who is in advertising. But let's assume your publicity chairman is new to the game. Here are some useful tips:

The Press Release

This is the "news article" type story concerning social events you so often see on the social or entertainment pages of newspapers, or hear on radio social calendar segments. It's most valuable because it gets widely read or listened to as a news item, and because it's **free.** But it is also the most difficult type of advertising to obtain. Most editors are besieged with such an unending stream of dull, poorly prepared material, they become callous about it, and are only attracted to something that catches their eye. Even when the item interests them, often it's so poorly written it requires re-writing — that takes time and most editors have little of it to spare. So, if you want your press release to be published or read, follow these rules:

1. Start by typing the name of your organization, the name of the publicity chairman and his phone number, and the date you would like the release to run, in the upper right hand corner of an 8½" x 11" sheet of paper.
2. Next, all in capital letters, write the headline right across the page. Make it short, sharp, to the point, and above all, eye-catching.
3. Then comes the story itself, typed out double-spaced and in short, punchy, paragraph form. Get the most interesting and pertinent details up as close to the beginning of the story as possible. Stick to the facts: don't express opinions. Keep it lean and interesting. One-page releases stand a better chance than longer ones. If you have to use more than one page, staple them firmly together.

Do you have your release written? Phone to get the name of the Society or Entertainment Editor (newspaper), or the News Director (radio and TV), and address your envelope directly to him (or her).

Lots of luck!

A Word About Photographs

If you want to send a photo out with your press release, or are having one taken at the event as part of the press coverage, there are a few rules to follow:

- Newspapers usually use 8″ x 10″ glossy black and whites.
- Don't mark or type names on the back of a photograph. Put this information on a sheet of paper and paste it to the back of the picture so that it can be seen below the photo.
- Never send the same photo to two different newspapers.

Try not to send a photograph that shows a row of people doing absolutely nothing. Be creative. Have them doing interesting things. This improves the chance of having it published.

Press Coverage

Because this takes place on the day of the event itself, it doesn't sell any tickets, but it can do wonders for future activities, and the egos of those who worked so hard to make this one a success.

Have a table set aside for the Press and seat your Publicity Chairman with them. If the event features a speaker, and copies of his speech are available, hand each reporter an advance copy when he arrives.

Poster Power!

Advertising on a small scale? Use posters. Hang them on church, supermarket or school bulletin boards, or in store windows. They can be printed commercially, but if the budget is limited or only a few are required, do them by hand. You might Xerox one original, and then fill in the Xerox copies with coloured felt pens. Kids love to do this. Make sure the time, place and price of admission are included on your poster.

Use The Mail

Have flyers printed and mailed to your own membership, and possibly the membership lists of other groups you think might be interested. If it's strictly printed or duplicated material, you can fold and staple it and send it out without an envelope. Or if you have to use an envelope, buy "Pennysavers" (envelopes with a flap which can be opened for postal inspection; used for 3rd class mail) and save on postage. Ask your local envelope company or stationer about them.

Telephone Committees

If each member phones a friend, who in turn phones a friend, you might very well increase attendance. But this method is advisable only as a final follow-up to your other advertising, as the chain can easily be broken.

Travelling Loudspeakers

If you are staging an event open to the public, you could use a loudspeaker-equipped truck to travel up and down streets, announcing to one and all the marvels of your group's coming attraction. It's noisy, but can be effective (in suburban areas only), and it's relatively inexpensive. (Check permit requirements.)

Tickets

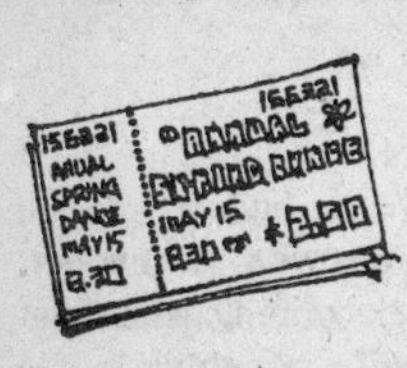

Go to a small, local printer to have your tickets made. Tell him the size you want, and print out clearly for him what is to go on the ticket. He will be able to show you samples of paper, type sizes and style, and suggest colours. If you are having a raffle or drawing, the ticket should have a perforated tear-off section, and the ticket number should be printed on both portions.

Don't give too many tickets to each person to sell (five is a good figure.) **Never** accept credit for tickets sold. You'll end up collecting long after the event is over — if ever.

Prizes

Lucky draws for prizes always add excitement and interest to any occasion. Good prizes can also be promotional features for your publicity campaign.

For big fund-raising events, ask local merchants and companies to donate prizes. If you can assure them they will be well-publicized, chances are they are likely to give you a prize in return for the advertising.

After the drawing, be sure to write and thank donors for their support.

5 FEEDING THE MULTITUDES

When you are faced with feeding a large group of people — and that means 30 or more — there are several factors to be considered.

The obvious method is to have the affair catered in a hall using outside help, or in a hotel. But let's assume this is going to be a do-it-yourself project.

On succeeding pages there are some suggestions on how to go about feeding 30, 50 or even 200 people under somewhat difficult circumstances.

Take Stock First

Draw up a list in advance of all of the kitchen, cooking and serving items you will need and use this as a checklist when you visit the kitchen you have rented. Turn back to page 205 for another look at the questions to ask yourself when doing this stocktaking.

The Menu

Don't decide on the menu before you have had a chance to look over the available facilities, because along with the budget, they constitute the most important factor in determining what you will be able to serve. At this point you will probably decide whether you will serve a hot meal or a cold one. Even if a hot meal appears feasible, perhaps you had best consider the old stand-by of hot casseroles and scalloped potatoes that can be brought in, pre-prepared and simply kept warm.

Now, let's consider these points before coming to a firm decision on the menu.

- When is the party being held? A luncheon? A dinner? A late night buffet?
- Who will attend? All women? A mixed group? Families? Boys and girls?
- What foods are in season?
- Is this party being held in conjunction with a festive occasion where the menu is almost determined by tradition?
- What is the theme of your party? Does it have any bearing on your menu choice?

- Do you want to consider certain specific regional or national dishes in your menu planning?
- Are there dietary laws to consider?

Now, let's get down to the specifics. Your recipes should be simple and your planned quantities should allow for generous servings.

If it is a sit-down meal you are probably going to want a soup and/or salad dish, a main dish consisting of meat or fish, a starch vegetable such as potatoes or rice, and one other vegetable of contrasting colour, plus a dessert and beverage.

When making the selection of food, always bear in mind that it will probably have to stand around for quite a while before being served. Choose foods that will not deteriorate and lose their appeal during the wait. Also be sure not to pick items that are questionable when it comes to general approval. For instance, many people don't like fresh spinach and it doesn't stand up well over long waiting periods. Some people don't like or are allergic to some types of seafood or shellfish. Foods that require fast frying, such as steaks, lose all of their appeal if they are kept warm for half an hour or so. Elaborate aspics, moulded desserts, etc. will wilt rapidly on a 90° July day.

Remember too, that it is not only the fact that you can keep things hot in the kitchen that counts, but also how long it will take to serve things. Serving time will take at least ½ to ¾ minute per course, per person, per server. This means that if you have a hundred people to serve and five waitresses, it is going to take 10 to 15 minutes between the time the first and the last person is served. This rule of thumb applies to each course. So, the late starters might still be getting their soup when those who were served first are ready for the main course. It is proper to wait until everyone has finished one course before removing dishes and serving the next.

This is probably a good time to consider the pros and cons of a served meal vs. a buffet. Obviously the buffet has many advantages when it comes to serving large numbers and allowing your guests much more freedom. But then again, if this is to be a banquet involving such formalities as a head table, guests of honour, speakers, etc., the sit-down dinner is really the only appropriate way.

The Food Budget

Remember the last time you entertained eight people at home and bought all the food you thought you needed, only to discover there were some last-minute items you had forgotten that added up to a few extra dollars?

The same thing can happen when you are catering to large groups, only now those forgotten extras are not just a few dollars. They represent 20% of your initial estimated cost. This could well be the difference between a profit and a loss.

It is essential to consider in detail every single item that will go into the meal preparation. The list should also include many things you would consider incidental or "non-cost" items in home entertaining — such as napkins, rental glasses and cutlery, table decorations, washing supplies — even salt and pepper.

How Much For How Many?

Now is the time to practice portion control. Here are a few guide lines to follow, when calculating the food budget and quantities required.

The following table is prepared to indicate quantities required to serve 50 people. Divide or multiply it to suit your planned attendance.

Please see notes and tables for metric equivalents on page 126.

FOOD TYPE	QUANTITY FOR 50 PEOPLE
MEAT	
1.Boneless meat (ground, stew, variety meats, cold cuts, etc.)	11 lbs.
2.Cuts with little bone (beef round or center cuts; beef, pork, lamb or veal cutlets)	15 lbs.
3.Cuts with medium amount of bone (whole or end cuts of beef round, veal leg shoulder, leg of lamb, bone-in ham; loin, rump, rib or chuck roasts; steaks and chops)	21 lbs.

FOOD TYPE	QUANTITY FOR 50 PEOPLE
MEAT (Cont)	
4. Cuts with much bone (shank, ham hock, brisket, plate, shortribs, spareribs, breast of veal or lamb)	38 lbs.
POULTRY	
1. Roast turkey (drawn)	40 lbs.
2. Roast chicken (drawn)	30 lbs.
3. Fried chicken	12-13 lbs.
4. Cooked and cubed chicken	Each 5-lb. chicken yields about 4 cups cut up meat and 3-4 cups stock.
— Chicken à la King	4 5-lb. chickens
5. Note:	
— Poultry stuffing	6-7 qts. (for 1/2-cup servings)
— Cranberry sauce	4 qts.
FISH	
1. Fish fillets	17 lbs.
2. Whole stuffed fish	29 lbs.
3. Fish steaks	25 lbs.
SOUP OR BOUILLON	12 qts.
VEGETABLES	
1. Potatoes:	
mashed	13 lbs. potatoes, 30 oz. milk, 1/2 lb. butter or margarine, 5 tsp. salt
scalloped	13 lbs. potatoes, 3 qts. white sauce (3/4 lb. butter, 3/4 cup flour, 2 1/2 qts. milk, 5 tsp. salt, 1 tsp. pepper)
French fried	13 lbs. potatoes (pre-cut)
potato chips (dry)	6 lbs.
potato salad	12 lbs. potatoes (diced), 6 cups mayonnaise
2. Peas, Beans, Carrots, Beets, etc. (canned)	200 oz. (less than 1/2-cup servings)

(See page 126 for metric equivalents)

FOOD TYPE	QUANTITY FOR 50 PEOPLE
VEGETABLES (Cont)	
3.Carrots, Turnips, Parsnips, Beets (fresh)	10 lbs.
4.Rice	8 cups uncooked (If using pre-cooked instant rice, read package directions to determine how much to use to get 25 cups of cooked rice.)
SANDWICHES (one per person)	
Bread	4 - 5 loaves
Butter or Margarine	$2^1/_2$ lbs.
Filling or Spread	12 cups
SALAD	
1.Lettuce for the base	12 firm heads
Tomatoes, celery, cucumbers	50 oz. of each (weight)
Dressing	40 oz. (liquid)
2.Fruit salad	280 oz. (7 qts)
3.Chicken Salad	8 qts. (20 lbs. chicken, 4 qts. celery, 1 cup French dressing, 4 cups mayonnaise)
4.Coleslaw	6 lbs. cabbage, $1^1/_2$ lbs. grated carrots, 1 qt. mayonnaise, $1^1/_2$ cups chopped green peppers, 2 tbsp. sugar, 2 tbsp. salt
OLIVES (3 per person)	96 oz.
CELERY	7 - 8 bunches
DESSERTS	
1.Ice Cream & Sherbet	9 qts.
2.Pie	9 10″-pies
3.Cake	5 large 2-layer cakes
4.Fruit Cocktail	5 qts. (200 oz.)
5.Whipped Cream Topping	1 qt. whipping cream (35%) yields 2 tbsp. whipped cream per person
BEVERAGES	
1.Coffee	$1^1/_4$ lbs.
2.Tea	25 tea bags
3.Cream for coffee	1 qt.
4.Sugar (cubed)	$1^1/_2$ lbs.

(See page 126 for metric equivalents)

Some Menu Suggestions

Here are six that contain all of the elements required for easy feeding of a large group.

1. Celery and olives, cream of tomato soup, Swedish meat balls*, pickled beets, mashed potatoes, rolls and butter, fruit cocktail, coffee or tea.
2. Beef bouillion, ham rolls au gratin*, lettuce and tomato salad, potato chips (dry crispy kind), bread and butter, apple pie with cheese, coffee or tea.
3. Scotch broth, baked beans, mustard pickles, brown bread and butter, lemon pie, coffee or tea.
4. Fresh fruit cup, chili con carne*, coleslaw, rolls or buns and butter, ice cream with butterscotch sauce, coffee or tea.
5. Split pea soup, baked ham, pickles or relish, mustard, potato salad, finger rolls and butter, chilled fruit cocktail, coffee or tea.
6. Tomato juice, roast turkey, cranberry sauce, scalloped potatoes, hot rolls and butter, string beans, cherry pie à la mode, coffee or tea.

*(See Part III, page 79, for these recipes.)

Other main dishes that might be considered because of their easy preparation are: Individual chicken-pot pies. Scalloped salmon, tuna or other fish. Eggs à la king. Boneless meats such as smoked beef brisket (corned beef), which can be served with cabbage and boiled potatoes. Any boneless rolled beef roast either roasted or cooked pot roast style. And of course, the pasta stand-bys of spaghetti with meat sauce, lasagna, ravioli, etc. Meat loaf with tomato sauce. Stuffed cabbage or vine leaf rolls.

Who Buys The Food?

One person should do the buying. Place orders at least a week in advance to be sure of delivery and check all purchases as they are delivered to make sure nothing has been forgotten.

If you are buying food in advance, there are some steps that should be taken to assure its freshness when it will be served.

Fish and Seafood

If fresh fish is to be kept for more than one day, it should be frozen solid. Frozen fish should not be allowed to thaw and then refreeze but rather kept in its frozen state until ready for use. Smoked fish will keep for a reasonable time refrigerated and does not need to be frozen. Many shellfish are purchased live, as in the case of oysters, mussels and clams. You can be sure they are alive if the shells are tightly closed. If the shells have opened even slightly do not take a chance — get rid of them. Whether cooked or live, all shellfish should be kept on ice or at least at 40°F until ready for use.

Fresh Meats and Poultry . . .

especially hamburger, should be kept frozen until ready to use. It is not necessary to thaw the meat before you commence cooking, just allow sufficient extra time in preparation. By using a meat thermometer, you can tell exactly when the meat is done. If you are planning to serve turkey, remember that the giblets and innards are often packed in bags inside the body cavity. If the bird is frozen the innards are almost impossible to remove so make allowances for this.

Fresh Vegetables

Keep at 40°F. Do not freeze.

Bread and Rolls . . .

can be frozen and thawed quickly.

Cakes and Pies . . .

can be kept for not more than a day unfrozen or can be purchased in a frozen state. Do not attempt to freeze them yourself and thaw them later.

The storing of food until preparation time should be the responsibility of the person designated to make the purchases.

Everyone Chips In

If food is being contributed by members of your group, make sure it arrives in time for any advance preparation required. Also, discretely check to see that members are capable of producing the food item alloted to them. If this food is being delivered in a glass baking dish or casserole, make sure the container is clearly marked with the owner's name so that it can be returned. Try to have the donors take their utensils home after the party. This saves a lot of post-party delivery by someone.

Enough Room For Everyone

When planning seating and serving arrangements, allow at least four feet between tables, and a few main aisles should be wider. This will allow servers 18″ between chair-backs for servings. Each guest needs 20″ to 25″ of table space.

Have service tables spotted at convenient places around the room. These are used to hold cutlery, water, butter, coffee, etc. Recepticals for used dishes can be placed underneath. A copy of the menu should be placed in strategic spots so that each server will know what is being served, and in what order.

The Clean-Up Patrol

After it's all over somebody has got to clean up the mess. If it's been a long evening, some of your committee members will think seriously about just sliding quietly out the door. So make sure your "clean-up patrol" is appointed in advance and that one person is in charge of operations.

You might consider the use of disposable plastic or paper utensils. They can save a lot of problems, but could conceivably add 15¢ to 20¢ per person to the cost of the meal itself.

6 THE WRAP-UP

This is the time when you, as chairman, should sit back, relax, and take stock of how things went. It is the time to put the finishing touches to the diary you have been writing and to make a complete report for your group's executive. Bear in mind that this report can also serve as a pattern for events in the future. So be sure to cover the problems, pitfalls and your recommendations honestly and in detail.

Don't leave this chore too long. It's amazing how quickly one forgets the inconveniences or the highlights of an evening.

You will also want to tally up the cost and draw up your Profit and Loss Statement. Earlier we mentioned that tickets should be sold only for cash, and that money and purchase receipts should be turned in as quickly as possible. It's now that you realize how important this is. If ticket money is still outstanding, or if you are not completely sure of all your purchase costs, it is almost impossible to complete this statement. Straightening up loose ends can eventually be more time consuming than the actual preparation for the party itself.

But being the kind of planner you are, this probably has not been the case. Chances are by now you are looking back on a most successful event.

Congratulations!

PART VII

COMBINING BUSINESS WITH PLEASURE

The pace of today's business can become pretty hectic, and the constant interruptions of office routine are often not conducive to the type of relaxed, constructive discussion that is so necessary in arriving at many decisions. That is why business entertaining can play such a key role in the give and take of much meaningful business activity.

Sales meetings and conventions conducted over a meal or in convivial surroundings foster a spirit of camaraderie and a feeling of "let's get on with the job," that just can't be duplicated between nine and five in the company board room.

Whether you are sometimes responsible for the organization of press parties, business meetings, etc., or if the limit of your business entertaining is to take clients out for lunch, this section is for you.

There is one important phase of business entertaining that this section does **not** cover however, and that is conventions. This subject almost requires a book in itself. If you have ever had the task of organizing a major company or industry-wide function, you will know that it requires all the skills of a master planner who has the knack of split-second timing and the ability to delegate to an efficient, well-co-ordinated committee. Because of the general nature of this book, we decided not to delve into the intricacies of convention-planning here. But here's a tip! Perhaps you weren't aware of it, but Seagram's has a Convention Department made up of experts in this field. They know all of the ins and outs of big party-planning. If you've got a large sales meeting, plant tour program or convention coming up, give your Seagram's representative a call. He'll put you in touch with a great back-up team.

COMPANY ENTERTAINING WITH A PURPOSE 1

Most companies who are aware of their public relations image know that formal entertaining with a specific purpose in mind can be worth its weight in gold. Four of the most frequent reasons for these parties are discussed on the following pages. Each type should be well co-ordinated and carefully planned to achieve the desired results. Give them the same time and effort you would an elaborate sales presentation and you can't go wrong.

Launchings

It's a poor ship that doesn't get a champagne christening before it slides down the slipway into the sea. Likewise, it's an opportunity missed not to hold a public party when your company has something to celebrate, such as the Grand Opening of a new office or plant.

Launchings are good business. News of your prosperity and success gets around, to those people who matter the most — your carefully chosen guests.

The secret is to pull no punches. Install a canopy across the sidewalk from the road to your main entrance, and lay down a red carpet. Provide a doorman uniformed like a full-dress field marshal. Rented, of course. You can still do this even if yours is but one office in a multi-storey complex. Even the passers-by will be impressed. And of course, don't forget to let them know what it's all about — just outside the door, place a sign on an easel proclaiming, "Grand Opening. XYZ Widget Co. Oshawa Office." You'll find suppliers for all the trappings you'll need listed in the Yellow Pages. Use showmanship. Remember, your aim is to get yourself talked about. And while we're on the subject, be sure to invite members of the local press, particularly the trade publications.

Once they are inside your sparkling new premises, treat your guests to a superb cocktail party with all the trimmings — the drinks ice cold, the hors d'oeuvres scalding hot.

Then, perhaps with drinks in hand, guests can be conducted,

in groups, on a tour of the new layout. (See next section, "The Plant Tour.") This is your opportunity to start reaping returns on your party investment. It's the chance your salesmen have been looking for to quietly corral their "special" clients and show them that new widget they've been talking about.

In about an hour and a half, your cocktail party will have reached its height and many guests will be looking around for more hearty fare than hors d'oeuvres. Some will perhaps be planning on leaving with friends to go out for a bite to eat, or simply heading home for dinner. Your party can end here if you wish, and it will be a success. But to this point it will have been just like a million and one other similar affairs.

Here's a bit of a twist that could make your opening the standout event of the season. It's going to cost a fair amount more, but if impact is what you are after, this could do the trick.

As soon as the first signs appear that your guests are making for the exits, have your hostesses start distributing menus you have picked up earlier from a restaurant that will now become the venue for the rest of the evening's activities. As they hand out these magnificient documents with heavy gold covers and silver cords, they will tell the guests that there are limousines (rented) awaiting outside to whisk them off to dine in luxury. And, of course, it's all on the XYZ Widget Company.

By the time your guests are settled at their restaurant tables, your reputation as a spare-no-expense host has soared into the stratosphere. The inside story is, however, that this is a far less expensive way to feed such a group than the extravagance of a catered buffet. If you compare prices you'll see that even the most lavish table d'hote selections in a restaurant will not cost more than the simplest catered buffet. It can also be a lot easier on your new rugs and desks.

Your guests can leave the cocktail part of the evening as they wish, using either the limousine shuttle service or their own cars. They can eat in groups of their own choosing, and stay in the restaurant as long as they want.

When everyone has arrived, you can then do some table-hopping in the restaurant on an informal, friendly, no-business basis.

You can bet this type of evening will be a real hit. Your guests will praise your hospitality — especially the fact that the corporate message was not forced down their throats. But you can be sure the theme of the whole evening — "You are the type of people we'd like to do businss with." — will come through loud and clear.

The Plant Tour

Strange, how often companies take a very casual approach to plant tours, for they can play a very important part, not only in gaining extra business, but also in improving your company's community relations.

Some corporations fully realize this and maintain a special staff to conduct tours of visiting businessmen or local schools and clubs. For you, this may not be economically feasible or practical, but one form or another of the tour ideas outlined below might be worth considering. No great expenditure is involved in following the program set out below.

The Individual V.I.P.

He should, of course, be met and driven to your plant. After normal offers of refreshment, his tour begins — *in your office.*

Before he sets foot in the plant however, give him a good idea of its layout and operations. If you have an audio-visual presentation that does this job, now's the time to use it.

Now he is ready to visit the plant itself. If it is going to be noisy and if these tours are a regular occurrence, you might want to consider investing in a pre-recorded "Plant Tour" tape, and mini-tape players fitted out with earphones. Then, instead of half-hearing explanations shouted above the din, he listens comfortably to the recorder, which politely directs him from place to place and at specified locations gives him all the information he needs on the operations around him. These taped "tours" are becoming increasingly popular, and most good audio-visual producers can prepare them for you. The tape players themselves are equipped with a beep mechanism that turns them on and off at various locations throughout your plant. If you have multilingual groups taking these tours, this system can solve a lot of problems.

We've taken for granted, naturally, that all safety precautions have been observed — glasses, hard hats and footwear are being worn as prescribed. We're not taking it for granted however, that your visitor is walking, particularly if yours is one of those huge single-storey layouts that covers acres of floor or yard space. Why not conduct the tour seated in an electric golf-cart (which can be easily rented from your local club)?

After the plant visit, it's back to your office or reception room for the usual hospitality — drinks, hors d'oeuvres, and perhaps an informal question and answer period. Then the trip back to town, where you might top off the whole affair with dinner in a good restaurant.

With such V.I.P. treatment, there's no question that you will have cemented the good relations you were trying to establish.

General Group Tours

Many companies, particularly in the consumer products field, find these tours an excellent way of building community acceptance and a hard core of enthusiastic customers who in turn do a great word-of-mouth selling job, for not only the products manufactured, but also the company itself.

This goodwill can pay off in creating enlightened shareholders, prospective employees who think your company is an ideal employer, and an easier road to follow in municipal councils when new permits and other considerations are required.

If your company is big enough, perhaps you might want to establish a staff to do this sort of thing on a full time basis. Or you might consider it as a student summer employment program.

The usual procedure is to arrange for the visiting group to meet at a set time in your reception room or lobby, and then break it up into smaller groups (5 to 7 people), with a guide for each. This helps to create as little disruption as possible in the plant itself and eliminates stragglers. Also, with small groups like this, your guide will not have to shout to be heard. As much as possible, try to avoid lengthy question and answer periods during the tour itself. Ask people to save their questions for later — they can upset the schedule and small groups start to merge if one is held up.

After the actual tour, it's back to the reception room, perhaps for coffee and doughnuts, and the question and answer period. Wrap up this part of the proceedings in under half an hour, and send everybody on their way with some company sales literature and, if possible, a sample of your company's product. They'll be delighted.

Perhaps yours is a company where such tours are just not possible, for any one of many reasons (danger, secrecy, nothing really visibly interesting, etc.). If so, and yet you'd still like the advantage of such occasions, consider a modified tour, consisting of a motion picture or slide presentation, a question and answer period and plenty of descriptive literature. This can often work out just as well as an actual tour.

V.I.P. Group Tours

Essentially, the format for this type of tour follows the same pattern as the individual V.I.P. tour, but on an expanded basis. If you really want to go all out, combine this with those ideas discussed under the heading, "Launchings," and you've got all of the elements for a plant tour no one who attends will ever forget.

The Press Party

Our launching party was designed to make the maximum possible impression on the invited guests, almost all of whom were customers or suppliers of the company. True, some representatives of the media were present, but any news coverage of the event, however welcome, was a secondary consideration.

It's a different situation where a press party is concerned. Success here is measured solely by the amount of exposure you achieve in newspaper, magazines, on radio and television. Public relations, not customer relations, is the main aim. The yardstick of achievement is the number of lines published.

First of all, be sure you have something really newsworthy to announce before you decide to even hold the party. Simply creating goodwill is not a good enough reason. Press people are professionals with a job to do, deadlines to meet and an editor to satisfy. Mutual respect demands that your invitation offers not only hospitality, but also the valid opportunity of gathering news that's truly newsworthy.

Uppermost in the reporter's mind is what will interest his readers, listeners or viewers. You may be fascinated by the fact that your new plant means widget production can be increased by 36.24%. Congratulations! But don't expect, after the party, to find that kind of news spread all over the early editions. Such figures are of real interest only to you, your employees and perhaps your shareholders. The general public couldn't care less.

When you have got a story to tell, look at it from the reader's point of view. So you've opened a new plant? Fine. How many new jobs will this mean in the community? You've signed a big contract? Jobs again. You're installing anti-pollution equipment? The story is cleaner air and cleaner water for the neighbourhood.

Provide an *event*. Make it *easy*. Make it *enjoyable*. These are the three rules for a successful press party.

Now For The Mechanics

First, make it easy for members of the press to attend. Claims on their time are many and varied, and being only human, they will choose those that are most convenient. Select a central rendezvous, perhaps a downtown hotel, the city press club itself or, if an out-of-the-way location is absolutely essential, provide transportation — a bus, limousines or chauffeur-driven cars, depending on the budget.

The rendezvous chosen, issue written or printed invitations to individuals, and follow up with phone calls. Make it easy for them to remember.

The day you choose for your press party is crucial. Be sure it does not clash with other possibly more important events. Also avoid the day of the Big Game! The hour you hold the party matters far less; any time during the working day is acceptable. All other things being equal, 11 A.M. is not too early, not too late, and leaves you, as organizer, free for the afternoon.

The standard entertainment offered at a press party is bar and buffet, catered by the hotel or an outside caterer. Nothing more elaborate is needed; it is, essentially, a casual, drop-in affair.

But far from casual for you, the organizer.

The Press Kit

Make sure every guest takes away with him a carefully-prepared press kit, containing all the information you can supply on your story, in compact editorialized style that will involve as little re-writing as possible. And don't forget the old adage about a picture being worth a thousand words. Good, interesting "action" pictures will often succeed where wordy releases fail. Provide a typewritten caption with each photo that identifies everyone (name, title, etc.). Check to see that all details are precisely correct ("Limited" or "Ltd."?)

Don't, as sometimes happens, just leave these press kits lying about waiting to be picked up. They're far too important. Instead, make sure a receptionist greets each guest as he arrives to give him the kit (but only after his coat has been checked, or else that's where the kit will end up, instead of with the reporter in the interview). It's a good idea to make kits pocket-sized, unless 8″ x 10″ photographs are essential.

Ask your receptionist to check off guests' names, as they arrive, from your master list. Then later you can make a telephone follow-up, to be sure they got all the information they required.

Once guests have arrived, and have a drink in hand, it's time to make your announcement. Ask everyone to sit down and close down the bar — but make it clear it will open again.

You step to the microphone (in good light, to simplify the job of the photographers) and deliver your address, word for word according to the copy in the press kits. Then, be ready to answer questions. You might also want to display additional information on posters, or with an audio-visual presentation.

It's a good idea too, particularly for radio and TV purposes, to have one or two personable key people available for on-the-spot interviews.

Then it's back to the bar and the buffet — and on to tomorrow's headlines.

This kind of press party is well suited to the needs of most industrial organizations. However, companies in more glamorous businesses — fashion, cosmetics, travel — habitually make far more use of showmanship. These are normally handled by a professional public relations staff which looks after all of the details involved — arranging lighting, music, entertainment; booking models; safeguarding expensive dresses and furs, etc.

A Party For Suppliers

Here is an idea that is catching on and makes a great deal of good sense — the annual "thank you" party for suppliers.

Let's face it. If it weren't for the excellent service and quality products of the companies you buy from, chances are your company would not be as successful as it is. Naturally, these suppliers value your business and you expect that they are going to bend over backwards to give you what you need. But there's more to the give-and-take of the customer-supplier relationship than that. These firms are your corporate friends in the truest sense of the word, and their representatives have probably, in many instances, become personal friends of some of your staff members as a result of their business dealings.

Here is the format for one such successful party we know of. Perhaps it could serve as a guide in your planning.

Well in advance of the party date selected, each department head who purchases supplies or services used in your business is asked to submit a list of those suppliers' representatives he would like to attend. With this request, it is made clear that the criterion for selection should be to pick only those representatives who have been of genuine service to the company over the year.

Once the list has been decided on, printed invitations are sent out. The wording should be such that there is no doubt in the recipient's mind that this is a special invitation and is your company's way of thanking him for his assistance.

Now for the event itself, in quick order:

- 6 - 7 p.m. — Reception of guests in your company's receiving room, at which time a pretty receptionist takes their coats, gives them their own name badges and perhaps a red carnation. They are then escorted to the cocktail bar for a drink and introductions all round (preferably by the person who invited them). There should be present as many as possible of the company's key people — certainly the top men of the departments dealing with the suppliers — all wearing name badges and all acting as hosts.
- 7 p.m. — The announcement is made that dinner will be served in fifteen minutes and that now's the time to refill glasses and find a seat. The "dining room" in this particular case is the company cafeteria, which has been specially set up and decorated for the occasion.
- 7:15 - 8:30 p.m. — The banquet. Note: if you haven't got a cafeteria kitchen staff, or you have doubts about their capabilities, call in a good outside caterer and let him handle things.
- 8:30 - 8:45 p.m. — A very short speech by the top man present or company spokesman, thanking his guests for attending and perhaps giving them some "insiders'" knowledge of the success of the company, its future plans, and how each guest has contributed to that success.

If yours is a consumer products company, make up a substantial gift hamper of your company's line for each guest to take home. (You've then got a supplier's wife who thinks you're the greatest as well.) If these hampers are heavy, as a final gracious touch, make arrangements to have them deposited in your guests' trunks as they drive away from the front door. Or, if they are carless, have them delivered to their homes the following day.

As you can well appreciate, this is not an inexpensive evening, and the expenditure will never show up on your sales chart. But companies who have entertained in this fashion say the rewards in future supplier co-operation make it a real bargain. And if you talk to sales representatives who have attended one of these parties, you will know that they would jump through hoops to give that company the best service they know how. After all, they want to get an invitation next year!

ENTERTAINING IN A RESTAURANT

2

It Can Be Quite A Business

As always, when entertaining, the rule is: consider the guest(s) first, and your own particular tastes second.

When planning a lunch or dinner in a restaurant for a business associate, ask yourself, "Where would he like to go?"

If you're located in a smallish town, where the selection of first-class restaurants is limited to one, your problem is solved.

But if you live in a city, the array of restaurants can be staggering. You are probably familiar with at least a handful of good ones.

Make a short list of choices from these. Don't be tempted to try a new restaurant, no matter how highly others speak of it. Stay on familiar ground.

Now, give a thought to your guest and his possible preferences. Is he a "meat and potatoes" man or a sophisticated gourmet? And, most important, what kind of mood is he likely to be in — raring to go, or craving rest and relaxation after a 400-mile drive?

At once, your choice narrows. An out-of-towner in a get-up-and-go mood will probably go for your city's most palatial rendez vous, with all the trimmings. A long-distance traveller from another big city is likely hoping for somewhere with soft lights where the service is deft and the music, if any, is low.

It's best, as we've mentioned, to select a restaurant you know, and also where you're known. Especially if you can make a quick call to the maître d'hôtel to ask him to arrange a little V.I.P. treatment. It might cost you a substantial extra tip, but it's all in a good cause. The difference this "extra" brings in the way of service can, in some restaurants, be amazing. But be warned, giving tips to maître d's is an art — it must be done with quiet poise, so that it is a secret between the two of you.

Getting There Should Be Half The Fun

It's odd, but many a host will thoughtessly leave an out-of-towner to find his own way to a strange restaurant. The rule is — go and fetch him from his hotel or motel and see him back again at the end of the evening.

Obviously, a visit to a favourite bar for an apéritif on your way to the restaurant breaks the ice for the evening ahead and adds an extra touch of festivity.

"The Wine, Sir?"

Soon after you've arrived at the restaurant of your choice, have perhaps ordered another drink and made your selection from the menu, the waiter or sommelier will ask this important question, and will probably proffer you the "Carte de Vin."

Earlier on, we've discussed wines and their whys and wherefores. But perhaps you don't see a familiar name on the list, or perhaps you just can't decide what to order. In that case, ask the waiter to make some suggestions. If he's worth his salt, he knows what is expected of him. After he is aware of what you have ordered, he will probably make two or three suggestions in various price ranges, and give you an idea of what to expect from each. Now, the choice is yours.

Now, For A Nightcap

Before you know it, after a sumptuous repast, your guest is saying, "We're all having such a good time, why don't we go somewhere else?" By now your evening will have taken charge of itself, and you can play it by ear from here on in.

A Tip About Tipping

The rules are pretty simple. Standard practice today is to tip between 10% and 15% of the total bill — before taxes. Whether you decide it will be closer to the 10 or the 15 is entirely up to you. It depends on the calibre of the restaurant and the quality of the service. If you ask for cigarettes while dining, they will probably be delivered by the busboy, or the now almost extinct cigarette girl. Pay and tip for these when they arrive.

3 OFFICE PARTIES FOR THE "INSIDERS"

The parties that companies throw for their own employees fall into two categories — formal and informal. Let's have a look at each.

The Formal Office Party . . .

is usually held to make an announcement or to mark an occasion. It may celebrate the birthday of the company or the signing of an important contract, or pay tribute to a retiring employee. It is usually strictly an "inside" affair, with no "outside" guests.

It involves people who have lived with the ups and downs of the company, seen many of its birthdays, participated in changing fortunes and prospects, and perhaps have worked for decades with the employee being honoured, and have shared many of his problems and triumphs.

It is fitting, therefore, that such an occasion should take place in the atmosphere of the office if the space and facilities are available. Most fitting of all, it should be held in the board room or the office of the chairman of the company, to lend it status and dignity. If yours is a smaller company, where no such space is available, or if it is a very large company and only one or two departments are involved, it's best to rent a suite in a nearby, convenient hotel.

The proceedings should also be short — no longer perhaps, than an hour. The reason is that the party most likely pivots on a moment of emotion — a sense of achievement as an award is presented, sentimentality as the cake is cut, pleasure at the receipt of a parting gift.

Such moments cannot be stretched out — their value dims the longer they last.

Question: what's the best time to begin? Answer: four o'clock. Because this is an occasion when the office should feel like a family. The company should give up its own time to celebrate its achievements or its people. Forcing staff to stay late is a sure way to lower, rather than raise, morale.

And starting at four, that magic 60 minutes is up at the normal going-home time — there's then an automatic tendency for celebrations to come to an end before that "emotional moment" begins to stale.

Organization of the "in-the-office" party is quite simple. A bar in the chairman's office, with a hired white-coated barman. For food, hors d'oeuvres. (Catered, not prepared by the female office staff — that takes the fun out of the event for them.)

Simple enough, so far — but one odd psychological quirk must be dealt with. There always seems to be a reluctance to begin any office festivity. Maybe it's because of the leap to be made from attention to facts and figures to sheer frivolity, or because nobody wants to seem too eager to drop duty for gaiety. Whatever the reason, an internal phone call at four p.m. should summon everyone to the chairman's office. The switchboard should then be shut down. Phones ringing during proceedings can foul things up. Especially if they're answered.

Allow time for a drink all around and a sampling of the hors d'oeuvres to break the ice. Then the speeches. (Try to keep them short, terse and to the point.) Then a toast to mark the occasion — and after an interval to shake a hand or two, the party's over. (Or, if plans have been laid to make a night of it, the celebration's just begun.)

Just a note or two more. Even such a brief affair as our formal office party requires forethought. For example, a cake with candles is a natural at any company birthday party, but who should cut it? Why not the youngest employee, that newly-joined secretary — to signify that while your thoughts are with the past, your concern is with the future?

And when you present the farewell gift to that retiring employee, chances are it won't be the once-traditional gold watch. The trend now seems to favour colour television sets. But this could create a problem. There's this enormous box that could be a great, stumbling effort to undo (and wrap). And worse still, how are you going to get it from the chairman's office to the happy recipient's home in the suburbs?

It's far better to present your honoured guest with a toy TV set as a token and have the real one delivered to his home. Human nature being what it is, he'll probably still treasure the toy years from now — long after he's traded in the TV for a much later model.

And, don't forget the photographer!

Informal Parties

'Tis The Season To Be Merry . . . Christmas At The Office

Traditionally, Christmas is the time for the informal office party. In the spirit of the season, good fellowship reigns supreme and office rank is forgotten.

But before we get into the whys and wherefores of how to plan for this year's get-together, let's talk about the controversy surrounding this annual event. As you know there are schools of thought for and against, and far be it from us to get too involved in the debate on either side.

If you are in a position to decide whether your company will have a party or not, let's just say there are rules of party etiquette that should be followed. If they are adhered to, chances are everyone will have a pleasant time, and all will agree that your company's Christmas party was a great success.

The first thing to bear in mind is that the party should be started and wound up during company hours. People like to get home to their families on Christmas Eve, even a little on the early side if possible.

Secondly, leave it to the girls to organize the party. Appoint a chairwoman, give her a budget and have her form a committee, and then keep out of the way. The balance of this section is directed to your appointee.

Quench any enthusiasm on the part of your committee for cooking or elaborate food preparation. Use your budget to either cater the party or make full use of the Seagram Reception Service. Simplicity should be the key-note.

You'll find several other sections of this book invaluable in your decorating, food planning, etc. And here are some further hints about office entertaining worth knowing.

People like to keep on the move. A word with Charlie, a chat with Joan; a chance for the girls in accounting to get a really good look at the handsome new salesman (and vice versa); an opportunity for company executives to stroll around and chat . . . these are the mobile patterns that people enjoy.

So while it may be tempting to set out candles on the cafeteria tables, it's much better to set up a service and seating pattern that avoids freezing the party into foursomes. (Candles anyway, are out — take no chance with fire hazards. Be wary too, about damage — don't hold the party in the computer room!) A recommended choice is the buffet and the bar with a professional barman. Let people stand around, cocktail party style.

Should wives (or hubands) be invited? The opinion of your committee, without doubt, is "No!" And they're right. An office party is an annual private affair, to give people who work together 364 days a year a chance to meet each other in holiday, rather than business, mood.

What About Dancing?

Your committee might go for it, but we're not 100% in favour. First of all, getting an adequate sound system in can be a problem. Secondly, it tends to polarize people into two dancing and non-dancing groups and cuts down on the chances for pleasant chit chat and the exchange of season's greetings. And finally, it can cause embarrassements. Some people just plain don't like to dance, or they might not want to dance with the person who asks them. If they say no when asked, for either reason, it's unpleasant. If they agree in the spirit of the season, it's still not the best of arrangements. But, we know of many office parties where most of the participants would feel it just wasn't a party without dancing — so you be the judge.

Moderation, a Key Word

This is an occasion for a good-natured "spirited" exchange of best wishes. It is one of those rare occasions when people of all ages and salary groups will get together. Some party members will try to play the situation up to the hilt. It is your responsibility to keep things on a low key and make sure the party ends when it should. This is where your professional bartender can be your strong right arm — he's an expert in saying no tactfully.

Here's some final advice to the company executives: when you've spoken to as many people as possible and wished them all a Merry Christmas, when the party's well under way — then slip quietly off and leave the rest of the staff to enjoy their fun. And a last word: see to it that those on the office cleaning staff get a bonus for their extra work.

I DIDN'T KNOW THAT!

(Here is a descriptive glossary of many of the terms often used in discussing distilled spirits and wine.)

Ageing — The "ripening" period during which most distilled spirits and wines are brought to maturity, usually in white oak casks. The casks may be of new wood, or charred or seasoned by previous use, depending on the spirit or wine being produced. In the case of whisky, although ageing helps develop character, it is the skill in blending of the whisky which determines fine taste and quality. (See Blending.)

Anisette — Mild, clear, colourless liqueur flavoured with aniseed (licorice flavour).

A.O.C. — "Appellation d'Origine Contrôlée" (Controlled Name of Origin.) Refers to French wines that come from a specific region. If you see these initials on the bottle, you can be assured it comes from the region indicated. Usually referred to as simply "Appellation Contrôlée."

Apéritif — A "before-the-meal" drink to improve and whet the appetite. Most of the fortified wines that also contain herbs and botanicals are considered as apéritifs (eg. Vermouth). Strictly speaking, fortified wines without additives, such as sherry and port, are not apéritifs, but the dry versions are often served as such. Cocktails and some medium-dry table wines also fall into the apéritif category.

Appellation Contrôlée — See A.O.C.

Apricot Brandy — Apricot-flavoured liqueur **(Leroux Apricot Brandy).**

Aroma — The characteristic scent that distinguishes the various types of liquors and wines.

Bitters — An infusion of aromatics for flavouring cocktails and other drinks. Used in very small quantities only.

Blending — Samuel Bronfman, founder of Distillers Corporation — Seagrams Limited, himself a highly skilled blender, defined blending as:

> the art of successfully combining a large number of meticulously selected, mature, high-quality whiskies, each with its own flavour and other

desirable characteristics, in such a skillful and judicious manner that the whole is better than the sum of its parts and that each makes its own significant contribution to the finished blend without any one, however good, predominating.

To enable its blenders to create and maintain the distinctive taste and character of each of its brands, Seagram has an inventory of over 1,200 different single whiskies from which to draw. Seagram's V.O., for example, is a blend of more than 70 separate whiskies.

Scotch, rum, brandy and many wines are also products of blending.

Body — The degree of fullness on the palate of a distilled spirit or wine.

Bordeaux — A light, dry, red or white table wine from the Bordeaux region of France. "Bordeaux type" wines using the same grapes are also made in many other countries. (See Wine Selection Chart.)

Bottled in Bond — A term meaning that the distiller agrees under law to store his spirits in bonded warehouses without paying the excise duty until he is ready to withdraw the spirits from the warehouse.

Bouquet — The degree of pleasantness combined with distinctiveness of fragrance in liquors and wines.

Bourbon — A straight whiskey of American origin, made from a mash that is at least 51% corn.

Brandy — A dry spirit distilled from fruit, usually grapes. Cognac and Armagnac are types of brandies from specific areas. Many types of fruit brandies are available, made from the juice or mash of fresh fruit, such as plums, cherries, apples, apricots, peaches, and berries. Fruit brandies are so identified by the label; if the bottle is simply labelled brandy, the contents have been distilled from grapes.

Breathing — When spirits and wines are aged in oak casks, there is a constant exchange of air between the liquor and the outside through the pores in the wood. This process is called breathing, and is essential to the proper ageing of spirits and wine.

The term breathing is also used in reference to the uncorking of a bottle of wine an hour or so before serving, to release its bouquet and flavour.

Brut — The term used for the driest of the champagnes.

Burgundy — A hearty, dry, red or white table wine, either still or sparkling, from the Burgundy region of France. There are also many "Burgundy type" wines from other parts of the world that use the same grape strains. (See Wine Selection Chart.)

Canadian Whisky — A unique Canadian product enjoyed around the world. It is a light, blended whisky made from corn, rye and malted barley, that owes its distinctive character to Canadian grain, clear Canadian water and the Canadian weather. It is aged and mellowed in charred oak casks, then a number of these mature whiskies of varying taste, body and aroma are "married" to create a blend with a uniquely Canadian flavour.
The House of Seagram is justifiably proud of the reputation earned by the quality and character of its Canadian whiskies. Seagram's Five Star enjoys greater sales than any other brand of distilled spirits in Canada. And Seagram's V.O. is the largest selling Canadian whisky in the world. In fact, it outsells *any* whisky exported from *any* country (including Scotland and the U.S.).

Champagne — A highly effervescent wine, white or pink, originally from the Champagne region of France. Today however, sparkling wines from many regions of the world are called "Champagne." (See Wine Selection Chart.)

Château — The French brand name for a wine for which the grapes are grown, fermented and bottled on a particular estate or "Château." The name of the Château, along with the region and vintage year, is your ultimate assurance of a specific taste characteristic in the wine you choose.

Cherry Brandy — A cherry-flavoured liqueur **(Leroux Cherry Brandy).**

Cherry Whisky — Cherry-flavoured whisky. Served as a liqueur. **(Leroux Cherry Whisky.)**

Cocktail — A short, mixed drink, usually served before meals, and very popular in North America. There is a wide choice of cocktails to suit every taste — almost endless when you take into account the variations and personal touches of the individual bartender.

Cocktails are usually made with a liquor base — gin, vodka, rum or whisky — mixed with vermouth, bitters, fruit juice or liqueurs, and often garnished with a cherry, olive, pickled onion, fruit or a twist of lemon peel. You'll find all your favourites in the list of cocktail recipes on page 169 — and probably a few more you'd like to try or add to your repertoire.

Cognac — Is the finest grape brandy made. This name is only given to brandy coming from the Charente region of France. The following is the label coding system used to indicate age:

V.O. — very old. *V.E. — very extra.*
(These two indicate cognac is from 5 to 12 years old.)
V.S.O. — very special old (12 to 18 years).
V.S.O.P. — very special old pale (18 to 25 years).
V.V.S.O.P. — very very special old pale (more than 25 years).
(All of these ages refer to time in the cask, since there is no improvement after bottling.)

Cordials — See liqueurs.

Crème de Café — Coffee liqueur **(Leroux Crème de Café).**

Crème de Menthe — Mint-flavoured liqueur. Available in both white and green colours. (Ask for **Leroux White or Green Crème de Menthe.)**

Decanting — Pouring wine from the original bottle into another container before serving. Recommended with red wine and port, to remove the natural sediment that occurs in red wine after six or seven years in the bottle, and to improve both the smell and taste of young red wine. Prior to decanting, wine should be kept upright in the bottle for at least two hours (preferably a day), to let sediment settle. White wine does not need decanting. It is not necessary to decant distilled spirits or liqueurs.

Dessert Wine — A general description for all sweet or partially sweet fortified wines, such as port and sweet sherry.

Distillation — Distillation is the process of extracting and strengthening the natural alcohols in liquids and fermented mashes. It is an exacting science requiring heating of the liquid or mash until the alcohol boils and vaporizes. Then these vapours are cooled so that the alcohol condenses again into liquid form. This process is performed in a variety of stills, the exact selection of still depending on the strength, clarity or flavour development required of the alcohol.

D.O.C. — "Denominazione di Origine Controllata" (Controlled Name of Origin). Refers to Italian wines that come from a specific region.

Dry — Little or no sweetness.

Eau de Vie — A brandy first produced by the Arabs in the 7th Century and the "original" of today's brandies and cognacs.

Fermentation — Fermentation is the process by which the sugars in grain mash, malt barley, molasses or fruit are converted to alcohol. It is a natural process produced by the action of carefully selected yeasts on these sugars. This action is typified by the energetic bubbling and frothing of the grain mash in enormous fermentation vats and kettles. Of course, in the case of distilled spirits, the "liquor" resulting from this fermentation is then carefully distilled and subsequently aged in the various methods characteristic to each type of spirit.

Fining — The process of clarifying wine by carrying the sediment to the bottom of the cask with an albumen-wine mixture that is mixed in with the wine and then allowed to settle.

Fortified Wine — A wine in which the alcohol content has been increased by the addition of grape brandy or similar spirits (sherry, port, Madeira, etc.).

Fortifying — The process of adding distilled grape spirit or brandy to wines.

Gin — A distilled spirit made by the redistillation of grain spirits flavoured with juniper berries and a variety of other flavourings called botanicals. This type of gin is called London Dry Gin, and is very popular in mixed drinks and cocktails.

The flavour characteristics of gin depend upon the skill of the distiller. In the case of Seagram's Extra Dry Gin, traces of angelica root, orange peel, and other ingredients enhance the juniper flavour. It is aged in oak casks before bottling to acquire its faint amber colour and excellent smoothness. It is this smoothness which makes Seagram's Extra Dry Gin an ideal choice for an extra dry martini, or by itself on the rocks.

Geneva or Holland Gin has a malted flavour in addition to the juniper, and is a heavier, more pungent gin. It can be either redistilled or blended, the latter process being more common. Often called "Le Gros Gin" in Quebec, it is usually taken neat, slightly chilled, or with hot or cold water.

Grapes — Red wines and rosés are made from dark coloured grapes; their skins are what give the colour to the wine. White wine may be made from either dark or white grapes. If dark grapes are used, the skins are removed before the juices can begin to ferment. Both white and dark grapes may produce sweet or dry wine.

Grenadine — A red, pomegranate flavoured syrup for sweetening, containing no spirits.

Grog — A name for rum derived from the nick name of Admiral Edward Vernon, the English naval officer after whom George Washington's estate was named. The Admiral was known as "Old Grog" because he wore a shabby coat made out of "grogram," a coarse fabric woven from silk and wool. He insisted his men take a daily drink of rum and water as a caution against scurvy. (See also Rum.)

Liqueur — A liquor made with spirits and a variety of flavours with a high (10% to 30%) sugar content, very popular as a digestif after meals. Liqueurs generally have a lower alcohol content than other distilled spirits.

Liqueurs have a long history. The Chinese distilled a liqueur from rice wine as early as 800 B.C. The Greek physician, Hippocrates, wrote of a cinnamon, wine and honey liqueur. Many liqueurs that originated with monks in medieval monasteries for medicinal purposes are still popular today. The famous French chef, Escoffier, advocated the use of liqueurs and brandies in gourmet cooking.

The Leroux family of fine liqueurs — made from natural ingredients in seven mellow fruit, herb and coffee flavours (Apricot Brandy, Cherry Brandy, Cherry Whisky, Triple Sec, Green Crème de

Menthe, White Crème de Menthe, Crème de Café,. Kummel) — can be enjoyed after dinner in small liqueur glasses or as frappées with crushed ice. They also play their part among the ingredients of many popular mixed drinks and cocktails — and imaginative cooks use them frequently in desserts and flambéed dishes.

Each Leroux liqueur has its own specific gravity, so together they can be successfully floated or layered in the spectacular, multi-coloured Pousse Café.

Lochan Ora (T.M.) — A fine, distinctive Scotch-based liqueur. Sweet, lightly aromatic.

Malt — Grain that has been steeped in water and allowed to germinate. See also "Mash."

Mash — The mixture of grain and grain malt that is cooked in water to convert the soluble starches into sugar prior to fermentation.

Maturity — That stage in the ageing of beverage alcohols when they have developed to full perfection. Whiskies are fully matured before blending and bottling, but many wines, particularly the reds, continue to age in the bottle.

Nomenclature in Wine — In selecting wines it is important to know how to read the label, as it contains information on taste characteristics and tells you what region the wine is from, and its age.

French Wines

are first of all identified by the area in which the wine was made (Bordeaux, Burgundy, Alsace, Loire, etc.). Then they are classified by the region within the area (Médoc, St. Emilion, Graves, Sauternes, etc.). Next, if the wines were made and bottled on one particular estate or Château, the name will appear, such as Château Grand Pontet. Finally, the year the wine was made (vintage year) will often be shown. Many French wines (the less expensives ones) are blends of several wines from one region and the vintage year only will be shown. (See also A.O.C.)

Other Wines

Wines from other countries do not have the same intricate labelling system. Often the name of the grape used will be the prime identifying mark on the label (such as Tokay, Sylvaner, Pinot Blanc, Riesling, Gamay, etc.). With other wines, the "type" of wine it is, based on the French wine being imitated, will be shown — so that you might see "Bordeaux" or "Chablis" wines from many countries. Many others will only show a local brand name, and tasting it yourself is the only way you will discover these wines' special characteristics.

Pétillant — Means "a little sparkle."

Port — A fortified dessert wine, originally from the Oporto region of Portugal.

Proof of Spirits — A phrase that confuses many people, but basically it refers to the volume of alcohol in a distilled or fermented liquid. As with many things, Canada and the U.S. use different scales to show proofs. The chart on the next page makes it easy to compare the true alcohol content.

* In the case of distilled spirits, the most common alcohol content by volume is 40%. This is referred to in Canada as either 30 under proof, or 70 proof. It is equivalent to 80 proof in U.S. measure.

At first it appears that the U.S. system of 50% alcohol = 100 proof, is a more logical measurement system, and by today's standards it probably is. But the Canadian (British) method (57.1% = 100 proof) has its origin in history. Centuries ago when distilled spirits were being bought and sold, there were no such things as government standards or on-the-spot testing methods to prove exact alcohol content. But it was found that a mixture of gunpowder and alcohol would burn and that water could even be added to this mixture and still ignite — up to a certain point. (It was later established that this "certain point" was 57.1% alcohol by volume.)

The sellers of spirits therefore established "proof" of the alcohol in their product by demonstrating it would burn when mixed with gunpowder.

% Alcohol by Volume		Canadian Proof	Equivalent U.S. Proof
100	Over Proof	75	200
97	Over Proof	70	194
91	Over Proof	60	182
86	Over Proof	50	172
80	Over Proof	40	160
74	Over Proof	30	148
69	Over Proof	20	138
63	Over Proof	10	126
57.1	—×—	100 proof	114.2
51	Under Proof	10	102
50	Under Proof	12.5	100 proof
46	Under Proof	20	92
43	Under Proof	24.7	86
*40	Under Proof	*30	*80
34	Under Proof	40	68
29	Under Proof	50	58

Racking — Drawing off the fermenting wine from one cask to another to remove sediment.

Rickey — Comes from the Hindustani word "Rekhta" meaning poured out, scattered, or mixed. Today it is a tall drink.

Rosé — A still or sparkling, medium-dry, pink table wine.

Rum — A liquor made from the fermentation and distillation of sugar cane, molasses or sugar beet. The colour of rum has nothing to do with its alcohol content but the flavour of the darker rums is stronger than that of the light varieties, the result of additional flavourings and caramel.

Rye Whisky — In Canada, it is synonymous with Canadian whisky, or Canadian rye whisky. However, in the United States, rye whiskey is a straight whiskey made from a mash that is at least 51% rye. So if you want Canadian whisky in the U.S., be sure to ask for V.O. or Seagram's Crown Royal.

Sabra — An intriguing liqueur from Israel, made with a base of Jaffa oranges and just a hint of chocolate.

Sangaree — A tall drink served in southwestern U.S.A. It is the corruption of the Spanish word, "Sangria" — a similar drink in Spain and Spanish America.

Schnapps — A clear, white spirit made from grain or potatoes, popular in Northern Europe. Usually consumed neat. Often flavoured with fruit essences.
sumed neat. Often flavoured with fruit essences.

Scotch Whisky — A popular whisky from Scotland with a distinctive taste sometimes described as "smoky". Traditionally, peat fires are used to dry the malted barley which is used in the mash, and thus the smoky taste is developed. Known as "Uisge Beatha" (water of life) in Gaelic when it was first produced at the beginning of the 16th century, its name was later anglicized and shortened to "whisky". Most Scotch whiskies are blends of malt whiskies, produced in pot stills in the Highlands of Scotland, and grain whiskies, produced in the Lowlands. Seagram's 100 Pipers Scotch, for instance, a particularly fine blend, is produced partially from malt whiskies from the Strathisla distillery in Keith, considered the oldest operating malt distillery in the Scottish Highlands. These malt whiskies are then blended with grain whiskies in the Lowlands, at Paisley, near Glasgow. 100 Pipers is exported and enjoyed throughout the world.
Because of its distinctive flavour, Scotch is often not mixed. Most Scotch-lovers prefer it straight, with club soda or water, or over ice.

Sherry — A fortified wine originally from the Jerez area in Spain. Although it is often considered an apéritif wine, it is actually a dessert wine by classification.

Sloe Gin — Not a gin, but rather a liqueur made from sloe berries (blackthorn berry).

Sparkling Wine — A fully effervescent, bubbling wine. Red, rosé or white.

Spirit — As a general classification, it is a beverage of high alcohol content, obtained by the distillation of grains, fermented grapes or fruit, sugar cane, etc.

Still — Apparatus used in distilling spirits. Pot stills are the oldest and simplest, used for making full-bodied rums and whiskeys. An alembic still is a kind of pot still used for brandy. Patent stills are newer "continuous" stills, producing purer spirit at a faster rate and in greater quantity.

Still Wine — Wine without effervescence.

Table Wine — A white, rosé or red wine not exceeding 14% of alcohol by volume. Usually dry to medium.

Tequila — A distilled spirit from Mexico made with the juice of the agave or "century plant". Olmeca tequila is a particularly fine example which is growing quickly in popularity.

Tokay — An amber coloured dessert wine. Made from the Tokay grape, grown in Hungary.

Tom Collins — A simple, tall, cold drink.

Triple Sec — A clear, sweet, orange-flavoured liqueur. An excellent mixer. **(Leroux Triple Sec.)**

V.D.Q.S. — "Vin Délimité de Qualité Supérieure" Just a grade below the Appellation Contrôlée (A.O.C.) wines.

Van Der Mint (T.M.) — A chocolate-mint-flavoured liqueur.

Vermouth — An apéritif wine, but one that today is most often used in the mixing of cocktails. French vermouth is a pale yellow, dry wine and few people drink it by itself. Italian Vermouth is a dark red, sweet wine which is often used as a mixer, consumed by itself, or poured over ice with a twist of lemon added. Vermouth is flavoured with herbs or other aromatics. (See Wine Selection Chart.)

Vintage Wine — The vintage is the annual gathering of the grapes and making of the wine. Thus, vintage wine is made from a single year's production, and the crop or vintage year is often indicated on the label. This is a common practice among French vintners, but as grapes, like all growing things, have good and bad years, a specific vintage year does not necessarily indicate a superior wine. Many fine wines are a blend of the products of many years and many vineyards. If you have enjoyed the wines from a specific firm or producer, you can usually depend on them for consistent quality from bottle to bottle and year to year.

Vintner — A person engaged in winegrowing or producing.

Vodka — Whether vodka originated in Russia or Poland is now somewhat academic. Today it is distilled in Canada from quality Canadian grains and is enjoying great popularity. In fact, it is ordered almost as frequently as gin for mixed drinks and cocktails. It is a clear colourless spirit with no distinguishing aroma or flavour to mask the taste of fruit juice or mixers. Bolshoi Vodka is exceptionally smooth and mellow, because it is the only Canadian vodka that is matured for two years before bottling.

Whisky — Whisky, by precise definition, is a single or straight liquor obtained from a particular grain mash through a specific process of fermentation, distillation and ageing. Each single whisky develops its own characteristic flavour, which is then blended with others to produce the final product known as a blended whisky (see Blending). This spelling (whisky) is reserved for Canadian and Scotch whiskies, whereas "whiskey" is used for other whiskeys such as Irish and Bourbon.